T0372735

Rebels and Conflict Escalation

Violence during war often involves upswings and downturns that have, to date, been insufficiently explained. Why does violence at a particular point in time increase in intensity and why do actors in war decrease the level of violence at other points? Duyvesteyn discusses the potential explanatory variables for escalation and de-escalation in conflicts involving states and non-state actors, such as terrorists and insurgents. Using theoretical arguments and examples from modern history, this book presents the most notable causal mechanisms or shifts in the shape of propositions that could explain the rise and decline of non-state actor violence after the start and before the termination of conflict. This study critically reflects on the conceptualisation of escalation as linear, rational and wilful, and instead presents an image of rebel escalation as accidental, messy and within a very limited range of control.

Isabelle Duyvesteyn is Professor of International Studies/Global History at the Institute of History at Leiden University. She is a member of the Scientific Advisory Board of the Netherlands Defence Academy. She sits on several editorial boards for book series and journals, and has published widely on the topics of war, peace and security in contemporary history and strategic studies.

Rebels and Conflict Escalation

Explaining the Rise and Decline of Rebel Violence

ISABELLE DUYVESTEYN

Shaftesbury Road, Cambridge CB2 8EA, United Kingdom

One Liberty Plaza, 20th Floor, New York, NY 10006, USA

477 Williamstown Road, Port Melbourne, VIC 3207, Australia

314–321, 3rd Floor, Plot 3, Splendor Forum, Jasola District Centre, New Delhi – 110025, India

103 Penang Road, #05–06/07, Visioncrest Commercial, Singapore 238467

Cambridge University Press is part of Cambridge University Press & Assessment, a department of the University of Cambridge.

We share the University's mission to contribute to society through the pursuit of education, learning and research at the highest international levels of excellence.

www.cambridge.org
Information on this title: www.cambridge.org/9781009009256

DOI: 10.1017/9781009008952

First published 2021
First paperback edition 2024

A catalogue record for this publication is available from the British Library

Library of Congress Cataloging-in-Publication data
NAMES: Duyvesteyn, Isabelle, 1972– author.
TITLE: Rebels and conflict escalation : explaining the rise and decline in violence / Isabelle Duyvesteyn.
DESCRIPTION: [New York] : Cambridge University Press, [2021] | Includes index.
IDENTIFIERS: LCCN 2020057994 (print) | LCCN 2020057995 (ebook) | ISBN 9781316518472 (hardback) | ISBN 9781009009256 (paperback) | ISBN 9781009008952 (ebook)
SUBJECTS: LCSH: Insurgency. | Escalation (Military science) | Political violence. | Terrorism – Prevention. | Guerrilla warfare. | Counterinsurgency.
CLASSIFICATION: LCC U241 .D89 2021 (print) | LCC U241 (ebook) | DDC 355.02/18–dc23
LC record available at https://lccn.loc.gov/2020057994
LC ebook record available at https://lccn.loc.gov/2020057995

ISBN   978-1-316-51847-2   Hardback
ISBN   978-1-009-00925-6   Paperback

Cambridge University Press & Assessment has no responsibility for the persistence or accuracy of URLs for external or third-party internet websites referred to in this publication and does not guarantee that any content on such websites is, or will remain, accurate or appropriate.

This book is dedicated to the loving memory of Jan Geert Siccama (1944–2012), great mentor and friend.

Contents

Tables

Vignettes

Preface and Acknowledgements

Rebels, such as terrorists, insurgents, guerrillas and warlords, pose prominent security challenges. These rebels are often perceived as subscribing to obscure political agendas and in possession of limited capabilities. How do their confrontations with the state escalate? This is the central puzzle this book aims to address. We find that there are several common escalatory trajectories that are observable across time and place. Knowledge about these routes could – we hope – make decision-makers more sensitive to the often unwanted and unexpected consequences of actions that seemed wise in the short term but turn out disastrous in the long run.

Many studies have been conducted, mainly since the early 1990s, to understand and explain the behaviour of rebels. Ideas originally developed to explain state behaviour, such as anarchy and rational actor models, have been used and extrapolated to explain the behaviour of rebels. Much of this work has found fault with the applicability of concepts such as the security dilemma and balance of power theories. Recent approaches have focused more on rebels as social movements with violent nuclei. Investigations have looked at the underlying and proximate causes of violence –opportunity and greed. Researchers have focused time and attention on the specifics of the indiscriminate and discriminate violence these rebels use. Furthermore, the possibilities and impossibilities for intervention and resolution – peacekeeping, counterterrorism and counter-insurgency – have been dissected.

This study builds on all the ideas that have been offered in the literature and that are relevant to understand rebel escalation. Therefore, I am foremost indebted to the excellent work conducted by peers and colleagues. This study should also be read as a further invitation and as encouragement to those grappling with the same and similar questions to bring our knowledge and insights further. The findings of this study can only give rise to humility. Even though the study of rebel violence has made tremendous progress over the past years, there is still a lot we do not know and properly understand. Humility is also the overriding feeling when looking at the often, limited possibilities of controlling escalation.

This book has a very long history. Some of the research was conducted as part of a research project entitled 'A History of Counter-terrorism 1945–2005', funded by the Netherlands Organization for Scientific Research and Utrecht University. In particular, the case study material used in this study came out of the investigations of a team of four researchers looking at the workings of state countermeasures in cases of violence by political non-state opponents.

The input of the members of the initial project team deserve a mention. The energy and enthusiasm of Jörg LeBlanc, Alastair Reed and Bart Schuurman was unrivalled. Without their input this study could not have been completed. All three joined the project fresh from the lecture benches, and it has been a very rewarding experience to coach them and see them grow in their research to the maturity they have attained today. All three have now obtained their PhDs. It has been a great experience working together.

We started out with the question how to measure effectiveness of counterterrorism, a pressing question in light of the huge expenditure to deal with the terrorist threat. Evaluations of counterterrorism measures instituted remained inconclusive. States were in a rush to institute one stringent measure after another in order to appear to be on top of the threat; wars have been fought against terrorists, among others in Afghanistan. Security and surveillance operations have been stepped up. New anti-terrorism legislation has been implemented and financial flows have been curbed. Also, better integration of cultural minorities into Western societies has been stressed. We still do not really know which of these measures has any positive effect on curbing violent activity.

In our initial investigations, we very quickly came to the conclusion that the question of effectiveness could not be answered because our state-based framework of analysis hampered investigation. The state is clearly part of the dynamic rather than outside of it. Instead, we opted for a more holistic approach and a focus on the armed interactions themselves and tried to process trace the development over time and explain the rises in the levels of violence before the conflict between the state and rebels terminated. By focusing our attention on a series of case studies, we found that indeed state action was an important dependent, rather than an independent, variable.

I had written a first full version of this book based on the case study material. When I showed my colleagues the results of the main thinking process, Jörg asked me why there was not more theory in the manuscript. His comment, although quite uncomfortable at the time, turned out to be that proverbial grain of sand in the oyster shell. A second part of the research contained in this monograph emerged from a subsequent thinking process regarding the theoretical implications of the causal processes we had uncovered. I would like to thank the Institute for History of Leiden University for awarding me a sabbatical in which these ideas could come to fruition. Jörg's comment led me to a complete re-write of all the material. I am far happier with this new version. Whether that grain of sand has actually acquired the shiny gloss of a pearl, I leave up to the reader to decide. Apart from Jörg, I would like to thank Ivan Toft, who suggested the hypothesis approach, which has turned out to be very productive in bringing my arguments across. Also, the advice of Mike Rainsborough all those years to 'keep it simple' has been most valuable. I am not sure if I have managed to heed it.

Furthermore, my colleagues both near and far, whom I have bothered with half-finished (if not half-baked) ideas and thoughts, drafts and elaborate manuscripts while they had other and more pressing things to do, deserve my gratitude. Nelson Kasfir, Bart Schuurman, Alies Jansen and Samuel Zilincik deserve a special mention because they offered to plough through the manuscript, serving me with detailed suggestions on how to better present and phrase my message. Their time and feedback have been much appreciated, and any errors remaining, of course, are my own.

I would like to thank my academic brothers in arms Jan Angstrom and Jeff Michaels for being a continual source of inspiration. Thanks also go to my colleagues near and far, whom I have consulted directly and indirectly about my work: Lawrence Freedman, Jan Willem Honig, John Horgan, Magnus Ranstorp, Paul B. Rich, Alex Schmid, Lee Seymour, John Stone, Hew Strachan, Ivan and Monica Toft, Pascal Vennesson and James Worrall. Also thanks go to my colleagues very close to home: Thijs Brocades Zaalberg, Mario Fumerton, Mirjam Grandia, Corinna Jentzsch, Christ Klep, Martijn Kitzen, Giliam de Valk and Allard Wagemaker. They have all been indispensable sources of both encouragement and harsh criticism, when required, in the process of completing this manuscript. I also would like to thank John Haslam and Toby Ginsberg at Cambridge University Press and Anitha Nadarajan and Priyanka Durai at Integra for their professional and skilful treatment of the manuscript.

This book is dedicated to my mentor and friend Jan Geert Siccama, who passed away suddenly in June 2012 at far too early an age and before the full gestation of all the ideas contained in this manuscript. He was always the voice of calm and reason when my arguments ran off in 1,001 directions. The reservations he had about the focus on changeable agendas in war I found myself tackling head on in the chapters that follow. This work could not have been completed without the unrelenting support of my family and friends. I thank my loving parents and particularly my late mother for teaching me the value of self-discipline and perseverance, which were very valuable in the creative process of writing this book. And last but certainly not least, I thank my husband and the rest of our six-member tribe who formed the necessary counterbalance when the book was in danger of outgrowing the confines of my desk.

Abbreviations

AAA	Alianza Anticomunista Argentina, Anti-Communist Association
APO	Außerparlementarischen Opposition or extra-parliamentary opposition
ANC	African National Congress, South Africa
BR	Brigate Rosse, Red Brigades, Italy
CDU	Christian Democrats
ELN	National Liberation Army, Colombia
EPL	Popular Liberation Army, Colombia
EO	Executive Outcomes
EPRLF	Eelam People's Revolutionary Liberation Front, Sri Lanka
EROS	Eelam Revolutionary Organisation of Students, Sri Lanka
ETA	Euskadi Ta Askatasuna, Basque Country and Freedom, Spain
FARC	Fuerzas Armadas Revolucionarias de Colombia Revolutionary Armed Forces of Colombia
FLN	Front de Libération Nationale in Algeria
FLQ	Front de Libération de Québec, Canada
FSLN	Sandinist National Liberation Front, Nicaragua
GN	Guardia National, National Guard, Nicaragua
IED	Improvised Explosive Device
IPKF	Indian Peacekeeping Force, Sri Lanka
IRA	Irish Republican Army, Northern Ireland
LTTE	Liberation Tigers of Tamil Eelam, Sri Lanka
M-19	El Movimiento 19 de abril April 19 Movement, Colombia
MNLF	Moro National Liberation Front, Philippines

NPFL	National Patriotic Front of Liberia
NPRC	National Provisional Ruling Council, Sierra Leone
PAIGC	African Party for the Independence of Guinea and Cape Verde
PKK	Partiya Karkerên Kurdistan, Kurdistan Workers Party, Turkey
PLO	Palestinian Liberation Organisation
PLOTE	People's Liberation Organisation for Tamil Eelam, Sri Lanka
PRN	Process of National Reorganisation, Argentina
RAF	Rote Armee Fraktion, Red Army Faction, Germany
RUC	Royal Ulster Constabulary, Northern Ireland
RUF	Rebel United Front Sierra Leone
SPD	Social-Democratic Party
TELO	Tamil Eelam Liberation Organisation, Sri Lanka
TULF	Tamil United Liberation Front, Sri Lanka
UP	Patriotic Union Party, Colombia

Rebels and Escalation

Controlling escalation is an illusion. It was an illusion during the period of the Cold War, when, fortunately, the reality of controlling nuclear escalation between the superpowers never presented itself. Unfortunately, today the reality of attempting to control escalation regularly presents itself. Many contemporary belligerents are either insufficiently aware of the escalatory potential of their actions or tend to be preoccupied by short-term considerations. This book details the variety in the processes of escalation and challenges the idea of seeing escalation as an entirely rational and linear phenomenon over which control can be exercised.

In the past few years, significant scholarly attention has been devoted to the changing character of war. Experts have noted shifts in the participants in war, its driving forces, its political utility and its practices. Far less attention has been given to the changes within individual wars over time. This book aims to address those changes that occur within wars, once hostilities have started and before they terminate. It operates from the premise that, as Carl von Clausewitz, the founding father of the scientific study of war has formulated: 'the original political objects [of war] can greatly alter during the course of war and may finally change entirely *since they are influenced by events and their probable consequences*' (Clausewitz 1993, 104, italics in original). How can confrontations that appear at first sight to start small-scale and inconspicuous – a bomb attack or skirmishes by a band of rebels in the countryside – end in large-scale conflicts with huge investments in human lives and material, dragging on for years, if not decades? How does this process of escalation occur?

Clausewitz stipulated that war, in fact, possesses a natural propensity to escalate (Clausewitz 1993; Cimbala 2012). War is a duel on a large scale, and the opponents seek out each other's weak points to gain the upper hand. This process, in principle, does not possess any boundaries. War has a natural tendency to escalate into infinity. This is absolute war. The main limits to escalation, in a Clausewitzean sense, are politics and friction. The first can be related to factors affecting the will of the actor to persevere and the second mainly to the capabilities to do so. Both form the parameters along which war escalates, constituting war in practice. Political will refers to the idea and use of power in a specific context. Capabilities, in contrast to will, are often but, not exclusively, material and revolve around those instruments and resources that can be used to press the willpower.

This book starts from the premise that Clausewitzean thinking applies to rebels just as much as it applies to states: 'Clausewitz theory of war will remain valid as long as warlords, drug barons, international terrorists, racial or religious communities will wage war' (Echevarria 1996, 80; Duyvesteyn 2005; Schuurman 2010).

Clausewitz used an analogy of war as a chameleon, which is very illustrative for the central problem this book aims to address.

War is more than a true chameleon that slightly adapts in characteristics to the given case. As a total phenomenon its dominant tendencies always make war a paradoxical trinity – composed of primordial violence, hatred and enmity, which are to be regarded as a blind natural force, of the play of chance and probability within which the creative spirit is free to roam; and of its elements of subordination, as an instrument of policy, which makes it subject to reason alone. (Clausewitz 1993, 101)

The analogy of the chameleon has been subject to a series of interpretations, because it touches the heart of what Clausewitz sees as the nature of war (Bassford 2007). According to Hew Strachan, 'war may indeed be a chameleon in that it changes its nature slightly in each individual case (its "character") but not its nature in general, which is made up of the trinity' (Strachan and Herberg-Rothe 2007, 3). While the political logic presses war into a constraining framework, the production of violence, including the ebb and flow of the levels of violence, derives from its three immutable elements: passion, reason and chance linked to people, government and armed force, respectively, which make up the trinity of war (Clausewitz 1993). Indeed, 'it is the interactive character of war – Clausewitz's famous chameleon "that adapts its characteristic to a give case" – that has proven the most original avenue for analysis' of war (Evans 2003, 141; Duyvesteyn 2012). These ideas will act as a guide in the investigations that follow. How does the trinity of people, government and armed forces contribute to, and shape, the production of violence?

The aim of this study is to think through the processes of escalation and de-escalation. The focus will be in particular on non-state actors or rebel violence, as this particular violent agent dominates in our contemporary experience of violence.[1] In fact, violent non-state actors have been a predominant actor in war for the past two centuries (Holsti 1996). Furthermore, in contrast to a large part of the literature in war studies, this book will not devote much attention to the causes of war but will focus in particular on the dynamics after its initial outbreak and before its termination. There is a need to carefully think through violence in war, and its escalatory and de-escalatory workings.

The main argument of this book is that escalation in the case of rebel conflict, rather than a clearly conceptualised ladder with ever-increasing thresholds of pain, is a messy process marked by unexpected consequences of choices that were rushed into or given little prior strategic thought. The study, exploratory in nature, uses existing material to piece together the potential pathways of escalation. These will be presented in the shape of propositions, which will await further testing and refinement. Important generic thresholds can be observed, mainly with hindsight, in which situations of war gain unprecedented characteristics denoting an aggravation of conflict. Escalation ensued, for example, when the saliency of the perceived issues at stake was raised, either as a result of violence or concessions. Escalation materialised when countermeasures were enacted, new actors became involved or new weaponry was introduced. Escalation also took shape when an extremity shift occurred within the rebel group, largely unrelated to external factors or pressure. De-escalation resulted in the past when groups de-legitimised themselves through strategic mistakes, lost the support of external sponsors or a convergence of norms between belligerents took place.

The case for explaining rebel escalation and de-escalation will be set out in this chapter. We will unpack the idea of the rebel and introduce the concepts of escalation and de-escalation. In subsequent chapters, the existing literature on the rise and decline of rebel violence will be discussed and a method for measuring escalation and de-escalation will be proposed. The rest of the study is set up along thematic lines. The three key elements in war, as identified by Carl von Clausewitz – politics, military

---

[1] Please note that the terms 'war' and 'armed conflict' will be used interchangeably denoting the same phenomenon.

and people – will be used as a starting point for discussion. These essential elements can in some senses be seen to overlap with an imaginary trajectory of conflict from incipient, aggravated, extremely violent to a winding down, lessening of aggression and eventual resolution. The ideas about the main thresholds of escalation will be illustrated by short vignettes or brief case examples to show how these different processes have played out in the past. The vignettes will be based on experiences of armed conflict since 1945. Firstly, the idea of rebels as strategic actors, embracing a political agenda linked to means and methods to carry this out, will be presented.

REBELS

The Rebel Actor

Looking at rebels, among which we count guerrillas, terrorist and insurgents, we are confronted with the fact that they form a very diverse, and according to some, even largely unstable analytical, category.[2]

Not only do underground organizations differ according to their goals, they also have varying organizational models and favor different forms of action. Any attempt to develop interpretative hypotheses about "terrorism" is therefore destined to fail without a typology that can identify their range of application. (Della Porta 1992, 4–5)

The rich material that scholars in the field of civil war studies have presented over the past years has, indeed, questioned practically every aspect of rebel violence. Rebels cannot be seen as unitary actors; their political agendas are highly changeable, as are their means and methods. Distinguishing them even from the state, that is seeing them as non-state actors is difficult in light of examples of state–rebel collusion (e.g. the discussion about militias: Staniland 2012c; Jentzsch 2014; Schneckener 2017; see also Idler and Forest 2015). Nevertheless, there continues to exist a pressing research agenda, also recognised by the many scholars involved in this enterprise. There is a need to explain the varied empirical reality of political violence in the international system today. Actors distinct from the state play a major role here. The aim of this paragraph is to unpack the concept of the rebel group and come to a workable delimitation of the phenomenon.

---

[2] These concepts will be further analytically separated later.

Rebels come in many shapes and guises. Some are well organised, hierarchical and centralised. Others are loose, flat networks or even systems, without a clear centre or leadership. Furthermore, there are several ways of looking at the development of rebels over time. Firstly, rebels can be the product of social movements, in particular social mobilisation. There is a large literature available on the establishment and growth of social movements (e.g. Goodwin and Jasper 2009). Social movements can be accompanied by a radical fringe from which violent rebel groups can spring (Marsden 2016). Examples are those groups originating from left-wing activism in the 1960s and 1970s, such as the Rote Armee Fraktion (RAF) in Germany and the Brigate Rosse in Italy but also the groups fighting independence struggles in the decolonisation period, such as in Algeria and Indochina.

Secondly, rebels can be the product of small-scale conspiracies or even individual enterprises. This is where terrorist strategies are historically derived from (Miller 1995). A small group of individuals, who adhere to a radical agenda, can decide to band together to trigger change. An example of an individual terrorist campaign is the so-called UNA bomber, Ted Kaczynski, who single-handedly terrorised the United States between 1975 until 1998 with a bombing campaign aimed at symbols of technological progress which he opposed, universities and airports (Chase 2003). The idea of leaderless resistance originates within right-wing extremist circles (Kaplan 1997; Michael 2012). Also, the Focoist idea of a small dedicated cadre igniting a people's revolution can be included here (Debray 1973).

Thirdly, rebels can also be a construct from the outside with little relation to any form of an organised unit (Simpson 2012). An interesting recent example is the conflict in Afghanistan, where it has been argued that 'the generic insurgency ... is a rhetorical rather than operational construct'. More than 'one-third of all violent attacks nationwide (and more than half in the South [of Afghanistan]) attributed to the insurgency involve local power tussles between communities and tribes – not Taliban members or insurgents – which perceive themselves as marginalized in the distribution of political power, land, water, and other government-controlled resources' (Barakat and Zyck 2010, 197). The insurgency is thus argued to be a perception, construct or even a convenient label.

Of course, rebels can move from a small group conspiracy into a social movement and vice versa and both can be perspectives constructed by the outside rather than a factual reality. The discussion about Al Qaeda as an

ideology or idea rather than an organisation is one such example
(Sageman 2011).

Scholarship focused on civil war has in recent years moved beyond the
conceptualisation of rebel groups as unitary actors. Attempts have been
made to model rebels according to their level of organisation. Using the
ideas of network, scholars have developed different perspectives on actor
coherence (Sanín and Giustozzi 2010; Bakke, Cunningham and Seymour
2012; Pearlman and Cunningham 2012; Krause 2014; Staniland 2014:
Bultmann 2018). By looking at the number of organisations in a social
movement, the degree of institutionalisation across these organisations
and the distribution of power among them, actor cohesion can be measured (Bakke, Cunningham and Seymour 2012). The main idea is that the
larger the number of organisations in the movement, combined with
a weak degree of institutionalisation and a large power disparity, the
greater the chances of violence. Conversely, one dominant, institutionalised and powerful actor will decrease the chances of fragmentation in the
conflict. To what extent this actor will be able to escalate and act wilfully
remains to be seen.

What is important at this stage is that the structure of rebel groups has
been found to have important consequences for the engagement in violence (Staniland 2012b; Cunningham 2013). Movement structures which
carry the favour of the members are more likely to withstand external
pressure and violence compared to groups with contentious structures.
The latter are more likely to disintegrate when outside pressure is applied
(McLauchlin and Pearlman 2012).

We have seen in recent years that violence among rebels themselves and
against unarmed civilians rather than the state has increased (DeRouen
and Bercovitch 2008; Cunningham, Gleditsch and Salehyan 2009). Some
scholars have gone as far as doubting whether the state as an object of
struggle is of any significance at all in contemporary armed conflict
(Kilcullen 2006). It cannot be denied, however, that the state often
remains the referent object. Issues of contention often relate to imperfect
state formation and consolidation: territorial contestation or power divisions in political systems (Weinstein 2007; Uppsala Conflict Data
Program 2020; Newman and DeRouen Jr. 2014). The warlords in
Afghanistan fought for access to the state. The militias in Sudan claim
that the government in Khartoum had forfeited its right to legitimate rule
in Darfur. The Fuerzas Armadas Revolucionarias de Colombia, or FARC
(Revolutionary Armed Forces of Colombia), apart from being involved in
the drugs trade, envisioned an overhaul of the perceived unjust political

and social order in the country. The Kurdistan Workers Party (PKK) fighting in Turkey aimed for the recognition of Kurdish minority rights and an independent Kurdish state. Therefore, this study has opted to predominantly focus on rebel–state interaction in particular, rather than intra-rebel conflict.

However, in a large part of the academic literature, there appears to be a disconnect between the activities of the rebel group and the state. As noted by some critical security scholars, rebel violence can only be understood in conjunction with the role of the state (Blakeley 2007; Jackson 2007). Most of the theories attempting to understand rebel violence are 'ultimately socially constructed in opposition to state authority and so there is an inescapable sense in which the state itself must play a role in their creation' (Parker 2007, 156–157). Overall, existing theories award '*some* regular importance to the actions of governments. In particular, official "coercion" –sometimes designated "repression" or "retribution" – is generally considered to affect the frequency, magnitude and intensity of violent action' (Snyder 1976, 278, emphasis in original). The state is, therefore, logically part of the phenomenon of rebel violence rather than outside of it. Still, many studies into terrorist or insurgent campaigns accept the role of the state uncritically; the 'conflict management approach conceptually mistreats violence by ignoring the state's role in it' (Snyder 1976, 283).

This state-centred perspective leads to a very fundamental disconnect between rebel violence in the shape of terrorism and insurgency and the countermeasures taken against these strategies. Few of the existing studies, perhaps with the exception of specific case studies, treat the strategy in conjunction with countermeasures. Countermeasures are highly dependent on the policy perspective the state maintains. In the case of the United States, 'counterterrorism policy is not just a response to the threat of terrorism, whether at home or abroad, but a reflection of the domestic political process' (Crenshaw 2001, 329). When terrorism is seen as a criminal act, counterterrorism is a law enforcement problem. When terrorism is seen as a security problem, counterterrorism becomes a police and security services problem. Counterterrorism and counterinsurgency are often taken unjustifiably, as distinct and separate from terrorism and insurgency.

Despite the challenges to the rebel concept highlighted in this paragraph, the rebel group in all its different guises remains an important subject for investigation. For the purposes of this study, a rebel group will be defined as a sub- or non-state actor which has mounted a violent challenge against state power. It is identifiable as an actor through its threats and acts of violence. Furthermore, the rebel group is a political actor. The reasons for ascribing political agency to the rebel group will now be outlined.

Rebel Ends

According to some notable recent assessments, rebels are non-strategic and non-political actors. Scholars putting forward this point of view have questioned the validity of an instrumental approach to rebel violence, and they have doubted the existence of a means–ends relationship in rebel conflict. These claims have been based both on theoretical and empirical arguments. These ideas are part of a wider discussion about what war is about, which started in the early 1990s with the publication of Martin van Creveld's book *Transformation of War* (Van Creveld 1991). Van Creveld argued that war is not a product of politically guided actors seeking the attainment of goals. Rather, war is pursued for its own sake, for personal recognition, prowess and honour. Subsequently, others pointed at the wilful targeting of civilians, barbarity, ethnic factors, culture and greed to argue that war was beyond the political reins that Clausewitz had argued, kept it in check (Keegan 1993; Kaplan 1994; Kaldor 2001; Collier and Hoeffler 2004; Abrahms 2008, 2011, 2018). Several scholars have in fact argued that rebel violence should not be seen as possessing any kind of strategic attributes at all but as primarily geared towards communication, theatre and performance (Crelinsten 1987, 2002).

Nevertheless, there is plentiful evidence in social science investigations that rebel violence does bear witness to larger means–ends logics. For the case of terrorist groups, for example, Ted Robert Gurr has concluded that violence is a conscious choice made by groups in conflict (Gurr 2006). To illustrate this point, on more than one occasion, substitution behaviour by groups using terrorism has been witnessed, which will be further elaborated in Chapter 6 (Sandler, Tschirhart, and Cauley 1983; Cauley and Im 1988; Enders 2004; Arce and Sandler 2005). Substitution, or the waterbed effect, points to a shift or refocus of activities. If an attack is made more difficult in one area or with one particular means, a shift can be observed to other targets or instruments. This can be interpreted as a sign of collective rationality. Some have described these activities as a 'collectively rational strategic choice' (Crenshaw 1990, 9; Kydd and Walter 2006). Other studies have also hinted at the strategic rationale behind ostensibly a-strategic phenomena, such as suicide terrorism, which fits into a pattern of nationalist campaigns (Pape 2005) or barbarous warfare, which possesses a measure of strategic logic in poverty-stricken areas such as West Africa (Richards 1996). Yet others have described rebels as strategic calculators when it comes to alliance behaviour in often highly complex conflicts (Christia 2012) or compliant with international law and regulations in warfare (Jo 2015). Also based on interviews with rebel group leaders and cadres, the evidence points to rational and deliberate policy development (Dudouet 2012, 96). All these studies indicate and demonstrate that rebel groups are political and strategic operators.

A potentially more significant challenge than proving that rebels are strategic and political actors comes from investigations of micro-level conflict. On the individual level, interviews with individual combatants and polls among populations involved in political violence have shown a diverse set of reasons why people engage in violence. Self-preservation, peer pressure, social bonds and self-betterment are often referred to issues in these studies (Peters and Richards 1998; Argo 2009; Ladbury 2009; Alexander 2012). Remarkable is that categories are similar for very different conflict locales with different rebel groups espousing different political agendas. Furthermore, some scholars have claimed that 'people participate in terrorist organizations for the social solidarity, not for their political return' (Abrahms 2008, 94).[3] This series of explanations is notable for the absence of politics or ideology as a motivating factor.

These insights are part of a challenge, which social science has tried to grapple with for many decades; explanations on the individual level about engagement in violence are often difficult to translate into explanations about group behaviour and strategic effect, especially in an interactive fashion with the state. While valuable in terms of dissecting the development and logic of war, explanations focusing on individual worth, social meaning and honour possess little all-encompassing explanatory value for either the empirical phenomenon that is the focus of this study or the escalation of rebel violence. When individuals continue to engage in violence out of peer pressure, a quest for self-worth or social solidarity, this does explain primarily individual motivation but says little about the behaviour of the larger group, its leadership and the actual employment of force, let alone explain sudden spikes in the level or spread of violence, that is escalation. Still, we will return to the topic of individual engagement in Chapter 7.

A subsequent question is whether there is indeed a link between group behaviour and strategic effect:

---

[3] This obviously also applies to war in a wider sense (Keegan 2011).

[g]roups may use violence to pursue both organizational and strategic ends, but the link between the two is not well understood. Is the achievement of one necessary for the achievement of the other? Are organizational and strategic goals complementary or contradictory, and under what conditions? (Krause 2013, 292)

There are a few studies that have been successful in explaining the interaction between individual disposition towards continued engagement in political violence in conjunction with the interests and agenda of the rebel group leadership and specifically strategic output (Della Porta 1995b; McCormick 2003). One suggestion has been that organisational considerations take centre stage when rivalries exist among the social movement family from which the rebel derives (Krause 2014). When there is a strong and hegemonic organisation representing the specific agenda, strategic considerations have free reign. When there is rivalry, organisational survival and infighting play out, which preclude a concentration of generating strategic effect. While insightful, it does not solve the puzzle of the generation of strategic effect as a result of diverse individual participation in rebel groups.

Other avenues to link the distinct sets of explanations are as follows: firstly, the war systems ideas, which stress economic self-betterment as an important force overlapping with the interest of a continuing existence of a war economy (Reno 2000; Weinstein 2007; Keen 2012). Secondly, socialisation and rebel culture could also act as a transmission mechanism among the leadership, group and individual levels (Wood 2003; Sageman 2004; Mitton 2012; Beevor 2017). Rebel culture, for example, in the case of Sierra Leone, benefited the strategic necessities of the rebel leadership, in this case the Rebel United Front (RUF), which also links the two sets of explanations (Mitton 2012).[4]

This investigation will not solve the fundamental research problem. We deem it justifiable to continue based on the means–ends presumption, awaiting further investigation. In cases where ideas about group dynamics do offer causal explanations for escalation, this will be addressed separately (see again Chapter 7 in particular).

While this study takes as a starting point the nature of war as essentially political, following Clausewitzean thought, the black box of politics can and should be pried open more. Some scholars have argued that politics can only be time and place specific; therefore, any endeavour to investigate the specifics of politics will end up demonstrating the limits of the social

---

[4] The Sierra Leonean case will be further investigated in Chapter 3.

science investigator's toolkit (Smith 2012). The question *why* violence is used to further political goals might indeed demonstrate these limitations and be highly context dependent and indeed unique in every case. However, the question *how* politics, in its different shapes and guises, is instrumental in the process of violence and where the use of violence runs into limitations is scientifically productive and very pressing.

Previous explanations of political violence have importantly focused on the causes and the termination of conflict. We know, through elaborate studies, that both grievance and opportunity can lead to conflict (Berdal and Malone 2000; Fearon and Laitin 2003; Collier and Hoeffler 2004; Collier and Sambanis 2005). The literature about grievance places emphasis on psychological processes among a disaffected or disadvantaged population. Deprivation, injustice or resentment plays a role as conflict-generating factors (Gurr 1970). Despite a long pedigree in conflict studies, there is little solid evidence that grievance in and of itself causes armed conflict. How do groups organise to express grievances violently, and at what point in time does mobilisation occur? This literature emphasises cost–benefit calculations within a particular opportunity structure (Fearon and Laitin 2003; Weinstein 2007). The political opportunity structure sees the personal calculation of expected benefits and rewards with an organisational capacity and political opportunity as the combination of factors that holds explanatory value for non-state actor violence. While there is evidence to support this point of view, the question why some groups with the same opportunities take up arms and others do not remains an important puzzle.

These grievance theories face several obstacles at present; significant for this study are the following issues: firstly, the existing dichotomy of grievance versus opportunity cannot account for overlapping and/or changeable motivations; secondly, the explanations do not possess the ability to explain the dynamic nature and strategic interaction between the state and the non-state actor, which is the essence of conflict; thirdly, these explanations focus on the causes of non-state actor violence, they are often based on large-n studies, and it is generally expected that by extrapolation these ideas will be illuminating to understand the continuation of conflict. This can and should be questioned. This study is specifically aimed at moving away from the preoccupation in the study of war from its causes and labelling and explaining motivation of warring parties with often ex ante claims. Rather, it asks attention for the dynamics after the outbreak of violence and the highly changeable character of conflict during its course.

These existing ideas explaining organised political violence, such as opportunity and grievance explanations, rely heavily on bargaining theory and utilitarian explanations, which inform the core of this field of research (Powell 2002; Reiter 2003; see also discussion in: Abrahms 2011). Bargaining theory originates from scholarship into economics. In essence there is a bargaining process going on in war where one actor desires something and another fails to deliver it. It is presumed that both are subject to rational calculations, weighing costs and benefits of particular behaviour in the course of their exchanges. The necessary prerequisites in this interaction process are political will and capability. By exercising power and reducing the courses of action open to an opponent, compliant behaviour can be elicited. We know from previous studies that force is an instrument that is often and quite easily referred to in international affairs (Hironaka 2005; Regan and Aydin 2006). When the expected utility of resistance of the actor subject to coercion exceeds the worth of the prize, the latter actor will start to show compliance with the demands of the coercer.

Framing this political will via ideological categories is a very common approach. A large number of academic studies place centre stage the ideological agendas of rebels. Ideologies, such as nationalism, anarchism, Marxism, political Islam and ethnicity, have individually, or in combination, been used as labels for many conflicts throughout modern history. Different opportunity structures but also issues of contention can produce different conflict dynamics. David Rapoport, for example, has identified four waves of modern terrorism since the late nineteenth century, which have been distinguished according to their ideological content (Rapoport 2001b). The first wave from 1880 until roughly 1920 was concerned with social reform movements, which used violent means, and anarchism, which had adopted the 'propaganda by deed' philosophy in the 1880s. The second wave from 1920 until 1960 was focused on national self-determination and nationalism, exemplified by violent decolonisation struggles in Asia and Africa. From 1960 until 1979, Rapoport identified a left-wing revolutionary wave. The fourth and last wave started in 1979 after the Iranian revolution and lasts till today. It is defined by political ideologies based on religion.

The approach of placing centre stage ideological aims or goals is a prevalent one in the investigation of rebel activities. Ideology can be understood as a more or less systematic set of ideas that includes the identification of a referent group (a class, ethnic, or other social group), an enunciation of the grievances or challenges that the group confronts, the identification of objectives on behalf of that group (political change – or defense against its threat), and a (perhaps vaguely defined) program of action. (Sanín and Wood 2014, 215)

The focus on ideology has given rise to a large body of scholarship. For example, political Islam, as a defining feature of many contemporary conflicts, has been offered as an explanation for conflicts as diverse as Afghanistan, Algeria, the Central African Republic, Iraq, Nigeria, Somalia, Sudan and Yemen. Arguments in the debate have focused on the local/national and global level interconnecting in these conflicts (Clifford 2005; Kilcullen 2009; Mackinlay 2009) and the idea of political Islam as a franchise with a label that can easily be adopted to attract support, fighters and capital.

Ethnicity, another motivational label, has also gained a large body of scholarship (Brown 1993; Sambanis 2001; Duyvesteyn 2005). Ethnicity can be seen as an ideology and can define the agenda of rebels (Kaufmann 1996a, 1996b). For African civil wars, for example, '[t]he ethnic group is the natural component of a rebellion against the state, as the many links that exist among its members provide an efficient way of overcoming the free-rider problems involved in mobilizing a rebellion or insurgency' (Azam 2001; Posen 1993; Kaufmann 1996b, 430). Within certain political structures, ethnicity can play a constitutive role and define the boundaries of networks.

Ideology can motivate individuals and collectives; act as an instrument of socialisation; provide an organisational template and a doctrine for strategy and tactics, for weapon and target selection; provide justification and legitimation of the use of violence, as well as inform the timing of violence. These aspects have mostly come to light in the debate about jihadist violence and the attempts to explain it. The jihadist political agenda informs a specific way of fighting. The types of weapons that are selected are linked to the acceptance of (in)discriminate violence in the rebel ideology. Jihadist attacks have, for example, been linked to high and increasing casualty rates per attack compared to other ideologically motivated fighters (Hoffman 1998; Asal and Rethemeyer 2008; Jäckle and Baumann 2017). Suicide terrorism has been both prevalent among nationalist groups (Sri Lanka) and adopted by jihadist groups (Pape 2005). In the case of Chechnya, the occurrence of indiscriminate violence has been explained based on the lack of reliance on local support bases (Toft and Zhukov 2015). Not only was their agenda defined by jihadist ideology, their way of organising themselves as well as the selection and justification of targets, that is, (in)discriminate killings, were all connected (Moghadam 2008; Sanín and Wood 2014). Moreover, ideology also informed the organisational fissures and factionalisation within rebel movements (Hafez 2020). All these factors related to the ideological focus create a certain measure of path dependency.

However, ideological labels are not without problems (Lyall 2010). While very prevalent, they run the risk of obfuscating many important conflict dynamics. Firstly, ideological issues that are claimed to inform and drive conflict are highly changeable. Shifts in ideological content can occur. For example, both the IRA and ETA not only espoused nationalism but also adopted social revolution and Marxism in the course of their existence (Zirakzadeh 2002; Duyvesteyn 2004; Parker and Sitter 2015). Also, ideological interpretations can change over time: 'it is difficult to use ideology as the critical variable that explains the resort to or continuation of terrorism. The group, as selector and interpreter of ideology, is central' (Crenshaw 1985, 471). Ideology is therefore flexible rather than static.

Secondly, the existence of political entrepreneurs who capitalise on the political opportunity structure and opportunistically adopt ideological cloaks as rallying mechanism put into question the motivational claims of conflict (Tilly 2003). Political entrepreneurs are individuals who try to affect the course of politics (Schneider and Teske 1992). They attempt to engage with the issues in the political opportunity structure and press a specific agenda. In the conflict in Afghanistan, for example, political entrepreneurs have played a central role (Thruelsen 2010). The conflict in Liberia in the 1990s can also be seen through the lens of political entrepreneurship (Duyvesteyn 2005) as well as the many conflicts in the Caucasus after the demise of the Soviet Union (Zurcher 2007, 6). Political entrepreneurs will attempt to overcome the so-called free rider problem, trying to actively enlist the engagement of those hoping to benefit from the positive effects of collective action without wanting to make the effort. Political entrepreneurs dealing with free riders can offer selective incentives to these potential supporters. Rebel groups, in order to function, need to provide selective incentives to group members. Selective incentives can include status incentives but also material incentives. Some scholars have pointed out that it is 'the on-going provision of such collective and selective goods, not ideological conversion in the abstract that has played the principal role in solidifying social support for guerrilla armies' (Goodwin and Skocpol 1989, 494).

Third, apart from changeability of ideological content, and the role of opportunistic political entrepreneurs, rebels have a tendency to pragmatically incorporate local grievances and discontent. They have been known to incorporate local grievances to propel their struggle forwards (Kriger 1992; Kalyvas 2003, 2006; Duyvesteyn 2005; Weinstein 2007; Kilcullen 2009). Competition, control and local considerations offer explanatory value when it comes to witnessing more or less violence in insurgencies. Among others, Charles Tilly has suggested that there are repertoires of contention and violence and pre-existing histories of violent exchange that can shape and define a struggle (Tilly 2003). Culture has also been found to influence rebel violence; collectivist, as opposed to individualist, cultures have been alleged to stand out for attacks on out-groups, foreigners and indiscriminate violence (Weinberg and Eubank 1994). This interesting debate about the precise role of ideology notwithstanding, these findings overall confirm the rebel group as a political actor, pursuing explicit political ends.

Rebel Means and Methods

In order to fight, a rebel group has several approaches available to conduct its armed engagements, among which terrorism and insurgency predominate (Kalyvas 2011). There is a limited number of cases where non-state actors have used direct or conventional strategies to conduct a war, such as the Spanish civil war, the Sri Lankan and Chechen wars (Kalyvas 2011). In recent years, conventional confrontations were also visible in the conflicts in Syria, South Sudan and Ukraine.

A strategic approach can be investigated based on the presence or absence of the levels of strategy (Luttwak 2001; Freedman 2013). Several levels can be distinguished: tactics or tactical attacks serve as a conduit to provoke the opponent, for rebel groups usually the state. The tactical use of force relates to the operational plan of drawing out the opponent or provoking him or her into overreacting. The provocation and confrontation, on the operational level, comes together with a form of coercion, with recruitment and propaganda aims. As with all strategic approaches, the levels work both up and down: the tactical level attacks bring closer the operational level coercion in order to effect political change. Conversely, the political program infuses the operational level coercion and intimidation campaigns and dictates the shape of the tactical level attacks.

Before discussing the tenability of this strategic framework to understand rebel groups, it should be noted, first, that there is large-scale conceptual and definitional confusion in the debate about rebel approaches. In particular, the use of the terms terrorism and insurgency often create misunderstandings. At some point in the past, in fact, the terms were used interchangeably denoting the same phenomenon (Kilcullen 2005, 604). This problem still persists in some treatments in which categories are conflated, resulting in a conceptual muddle (e.g. Abrahms 2008; Della Porta 2018; see for a critical discussion: Chenoweth et al. 2009). Moreover, historically there has also been a tendency to emphasise insurgency at the cost of terrorism, as the less significant social phenomenon, in particular until the 1970s (Beckett 2005, 24). Finally, guerrilla is also an important term often used interchangeably with insurgency, and conceptualised as a tactic of warfare.

Analytically, terrorism and insurgency are not the same and need to be separated (Fumerton and Duyvesteyn 2009; Cronin 2015, 87). While modern terrorism has roots in the nineteenth century and important predecessors in the shape of regicide and tyrannicide (Rapoport 2001a), insurgency has more recent foundations. Originally, small-scale ambushes and hit-and-run attacks were called guerrilla or small war, deriving from the Spanish resistance against Napoleonic occupation of the Iberian peninsula. These activities were warfare or tactical activities and part of the larger conventional war effort, as also conceptualised by Clausewitz (Daase 2007, 182; Heuser 2011).[5]

The linking of the guerrilla tactics with political ideology and a strategic agenda at the time of Mao's Great March gave rise to the idea of revolutionary war or insurgency (Rich and Duyvesteyn 2012). Revolutionary war, or insurgency, was first conceptualised by Mao Zedong as an independent strategic approach (Tse-Tung and Guevara 1961; Rich and Duyvesteyn 2012). Mao identified three phases of revolutionary war: the first phase consisted of hit-and-run attacks to liberate territory in the countryside and contest government control. This is in essence defensive. The second phase aimed at extending the liberated areas into liberated zones. The third phase consisted of a conventional confrontation against weakened government forces. This is in essence offensive.

Important arguments have been raised against the claim that rebels use carefully considered means and methods to realise their political aims (Eppright 1997; Hoyt 2004; Abrahms 2006; Simpson 2012). Rebel activities are argued to be limited to tactical skirmishes with a preference for

---

[5] Obviously before the emergence of the specific terminology, the empirical phenomenon has a larger pedigree (see Rapoport 1984).

the spectacular, and devoid of any strategic logic giving witness to a process of aligning ends, ways and means (Crelinsten 1987, 2002; Post 1990).

However, others have put forward that rebel violence tends to be mainly tactical (Ucko 2012). When rebels are lucky, their activities can translate directly into political effect. A useful distinction can be made between intended and actual strategic effect (Roberts 2005). The effect might be accidental. Some speak of collapsing levels of strategy (Eppright 1997). An example of tactical attacks possessing political strategic effect are of course the 9/11 attacks. Even though intended strategic effect might be hard to realise when applying rebel strategies, it cannot be denied that actual effect is present.

As for operational effect, it is true that insurgents often find it hard to generate operational output with the limited means they have available (Simpson 2012). According to some analyses, the global jihad possesses a clear operational level: 'the essence of jihadist "operational art" is the ability to aggregate numerous tactical actions, dispersed across time and space, to achieve an overall strategic effect' (Kilcullen 2005, 609). Even highly fragmented insurgencies have the potential to produce strategic effect (Jardine 2012).

This study departs from the more mainstream view that terrorism and insurgency cannot be seen as strategies. While some experts have claimed that insurgency is not a strategy, and has never been one (Hammes 2012), others have argued: '[i]t may be that the single most important similarity between terrorism and traditional warfare is in its inherently strategic nature' (Arquilla 2007, 377; Thompson 2014). Indeed, terrorism and insurgency constitute two strategies that can be employed by non-state groups –but also states for that matter – guided by a variety of political agendas. An advantage of such an instrumental approach is that it shifts attention away from the actor and its motivation, towards the act of force itself, avoiding among others the terrorist versus freedom fighter discussion. Terrorism and insurgency are acts of coercion to change the behaviour of an opponent.

Terrorism can be conceptualised as a strategy with the ambition of realising political aims with the use of violent means. The strategies of terrorism and insurgency can be distinguished in three respects: their political-strategic logic, organisational and relational characteristics (Fumerton and Duyvesteyn 2009; Cf. Khalil 2013). As a strategy, insurgency aims for political power. All insurgent actions are geared towards the ultimate take-over of power, whereas terrorism's goal is to merely provoke political change, which has to materialise through other means, either through a full-blown insurgency or through the de-legitimising acts of the state itself. In organisational terms, insurgents systematically organise and prepare as an alternative centre of power. Terrorists, in general, make few, if any, preparations in this direction. The relationship with the population is therefore also different. The terrorists remain highly secretive in order to increase the effectiveness of their strategy. Insurgents aim to mobilise and organise the population in order to establish an alternative form of social order. We should be aware that a strategy of terrorism can develop into an insurgency strategy. Furthermore, insurgency struggles can turn to the strategy of terrorism to further their cause (Dixon 2020). On top of that, the insurgency strategy also tends to use terrorism on a tactical level (Arreguín-Toft 2012).

As for the levels of strategy and their application to insurgency, the strategy relies on the tactical level similarly, on hit-and-run attacks using a variety of weaponry and material against unwitting but symbolic targets. On the operational level, insurgents also aim to provoke and coerce the opponent into changing its course of action. Furthermore, the highly visible acts are also geared towards recruitment and building a supportive environment. The operational plan includes the establishment of an organisation that can act as a shadow state or alternative political order. This base organisation needs to propel the struggle towards strategic political success. This comes in the shape of political control over population and territory as ultimate victory of an insurgent strategy.

As already noted, recent departures in the debate have questioned the central role of the state in insurgencies (Kilcullen 2006, 112) and the role of territory (Salehyan 2007; Smith and Jones 2015; Toft 2014). The state is argued to have lost its relevance because of a lack of pre-occupation of rebels with obtaining state power. Rather, rebels have been claimed to now espouse a global perspective fighting against an unjust global order. These post-territorial arguments are closely linked to researchers posing the fundamental question: "To what extent is territory still a factor in a conflict over values?" We contend that even warlords and insurgent leaders prefer to exert power through less costly means such as legitimacy and authority, which can come in the shape of some form of social contract, rather than through costly means, such as continued coercion and repression, which require substantial and consistent enforcement power. Therefore, the role of the population and territory remain important. We saw, for example, how the Islamic State in Iraq and Syria clearly identified a need to focus both on population and territorial control to build a Caliphate (Whiteside 2016).

The choice for a terrorist or insurgent strategy is not set in stone. Rebels can and do change between strategies. When circumstances allow and means become available, rebels have been known to shift from terrorism to insurgency strategies. Insurgents, when repression is fierce and life in the open becomes dangerous, have in the past reverted to terrorism. Furthermore, within an insurgency struggle, terrorism can be used as a complimentary tactic to achieve desired ends. Both terrorist and insurgency strategies exhibit the inherent feature of strategy, raising the price of further resistance by the opponent via the crossing of thresholds, that is escalating the confrontation.

Summarising, the rebel group is a viable analytical category representing an important empirical phenomenon that begs for further explanation. The rebel group is a political actor capable of using means and methods to further its political goals. Their armed conflicts tend to display recurrent rising and declining levels of violence. How can we explain these?

ESCALATION

Escalation is a surprisingly under-investigated concept in social science.[6] At the same time, the word is heavily used in the study of international affairs, often with a very imprecise meaning. The term originally emerged in the field of strategic studies in the 1960s in the context of the superpower confrontation and the risk of nuclear escalation (Smoke 1977, 35; Schelling 2008; Kahn 2012). The use of the term has been strongly linked to the Cold War, state actors and international confrontations (Carlson 1995). Escalation has been defined, in the Cold War context, as 'an increase in the level of conflict' (Kahn 2012, 3). The basic idea of escalation is that an actor deliberately steps up the level of conflict or seeks its spillover to demonstrate resolve. By using the credible threat of violence, it aims to bring his or her desired outcome closer.[7]

---

[6] This section is partly based on Duyvesteyn (2012).

[7] Jan Angstrom and Magnus Petersson have noted that the escalation literature has a second significant understanding of escalation as 'conflated with causes of war' (2019, 283). Since this present study is not focused on the causes of conflict, this discussion will be not be treated here. Another conceptual approach to escalation is to equate it with radicalisation (see for example Alimi 2011; Alimi et.al. 2012, 2015; Bosi et.al. 2014; Della Porta 2018). In this discussion, the word escalation is generally used to denote the transition from non-

In contrast to the wide-ranging debate about rebels, detailed earlier, the concept of escalation is relatively uncontested. Escalation is, according to Herman Kahn in his seminal work on the subject, a 'competition in risk taking or at least resolve' and stops when 'the fear that the other side may react, indeed overreact' manifests itself. This 'is most likely to deter escalation, and not the undesirability or costs of the escalation itself' (Kahn 2012, 3). Escalation has furthermore, been conceptualised as

> an action that crosses a saliency which defines the current limits of a war, and that occurs in a context where the actor cannot know the full consequences of his action, including particularly how his action and the opponent's potential reaction(s) may interact to generate a situation likely to induce new actions that will cross still more saliencies. (Smoke 1977, 35)

The essence of escalation, going back to the pioneering work of Thomas Schelling, is that it signals to a defender that a challenger is both capable and willing to inflict harm in case the defender does not comply with the challenger's wishes (Schelling 2008). In a process of coercive bargaining, there are deliberate steps that an actor can take to demonstrate resolve. This challenger has information that it shields from the defender about its measure of resolve to be victorious in the dispute. The measure of resolve reveals to what extent it is able and willing to pay the price in blood and treasure. These 'sunk costs' are fundamental in the process of escalation, as conceptualised by Schelling. The coercive bargaining process, moving from a crisis towards conflict, escalation steps can be used. It is a process of 'brinkmanship' with an uncertain outcome, and according to Schelling, importantly, 'leaves something to chance' (Schelling 1980).

These approaches to escalation are characterised by two main features. Firstly, escalation is conceptualised as largely linear and seen as a step-by-step process leading from peace to war (Holsti 1972; Kahn 2012). A very common way of conceptualising escalation is by using the analogy of a ladder. Herman Kahn's escalation ladder, developed in the 1960s, had forty-four rungs. The upper half of the ladder involved nuclear weapons, leading to a highest rung of 'insensate war' (Kahn 2012, 38).

Secondly, not only is the linear approach dominant, escalation is seen as a rational phenomenon with state actors making choices to either escalate or de-escalate. Both courses of action are based on cost–benefit calculations. The expectation is that the opponent acts based on a same or

---

violence to violence and de-escalation as vice versa (e.g. Della Porta 2013; Matesan 2018). Since this perspective also deviates from the main preoccupation of this book, the literature embracing this approach will only be referenced when directly relevant.

similar calculus. The ideal is to possess escalation dominance, a situation in which any action of the opponent can be matched or surpassed, making the exercise of further manoeuvring by the opponent futile. A second-best option would be to create escalation asymmetry, a situation in which the opponent becomes unable or unwilling to follow suit. Thresholds or rungs on the ladder focus preferably on weaknesses of the opponent that are not easily remedied or patched up.

The criticism that has been levelled against the Cold War scholarship on escalation has not only challenged the moral foundations of the ladder approach and the theorising of the 'unthinkable'. Other aspects, such as the overriding ideas of rationality and linearity of escalation, also received criticism. In a reflection on the Cuban missile crisis of 1962, Albert and Roberta Wohlstetter, for example, raised pressing questions regarding the supposed linearity of escalation:

> The aspect of 'escalators' that inspired its use in this connection, we suspect, is the fact that moving stairways carry a passenger on automatically without any effort of his will. However, as we have suggested there are down-escalators as well as up-escalators, and there are landings between escalators where one can decide to get off or to get on, to go up or down, or to stay there; or take the stairs. Just where automaticity or irreversibility takes over is an uncertain but vital matter, and that is one of the reasons a decision maker may want to take a breath at a landing to consider next steps. It is apparent from President Kennedy's own descriptions of the Cuban crisis ... that he gave enormous value to the cautious weighing of alternatives made possible by the interval of almost a week; to the five or six days mentioned for hammering out the first decision. And the decision made was precisely one that left open a variety of choices. (Wohlstetter and Wohlstetter 1965, 24)

They conclude that the variety of choice in case of Cuba was far larger than initially conceptualised. More recently, scholars have taken issue with the deliberate nature of escalation (Morgan et al. 2008). This present study will clearly echo these earlier reflections on escalation.

Few of these classical ideas about escalation have found their way into discussions about rebel violence. Still, a need has been recognised for more research into escalation in the case of civil unrest (Tarrow 2007, 595; see also Collier and Sambanis 2005, Volume I 318–319, Volume II 314–315; Davenport, Armstrong, and Lichbach 2008, 22–25). These calls have stayed very close to the Cold War conceptualisation of escalation as emphasising the development towards war in crisis situations, rather than the dynamics of violence after the outbreak (see also Della Porta 2013). For the period of the Cold War, this was of course understandable in light of the theoretical exercise to think through a confrontation involving nuclear weapons. In the post–Cold War world, this emphasis is more surprising because of prevailing conflict patterns.

Some authors have used the concept of escalation in the context of rebel violence without paying much attention to the concept itself (Daase 2007, 194). Other experts, omitting the use of the word 'escalation' altogether, have looked at its properties in practice. One example focusing on enduring conflicts notes that the longer a confrontation lasts, the more protracted it tends to become; 'protracted conflict keeps creating derivative issues, factionalizes opponents, destroys trust, invites outside intervention, and brings to power hard-liners and extremists' (Oberschall 1993, 104). Duration is linked here to the rising and falling levels of violence.

The contemporary prevalence of rebel violence in the international system makes it an important and necessary subject of investigation. What happens when state and non-state actors engage in violent confrontations? We know from previous research that non-state actor violence tends to show many recurrences of escalation and de-escalation. These confrontations usually end in an indeterminate fashion, rather than in a clear-cut victory, defeat or ceasefire (Kreutz 2010). Furthermore, there is an important 'spectrum between phases of escalation and de-escalation of violence . . . [which] accounts for the many situations of "neither peace nor war," which nowadays constitute a specific form of social order in many areas and regions' (Bakonyi and Bliesemann de Guevara 2009, 407). There is much room for furthering the explanations of the occurrence and re-occurrence of violence between a state and non-state actor since a systematic investigation or 'empirically based explanation of the escalation and de-escalation of political conflict' to date is lacking (Della Porta 1995b, xvi; Oberschall 1993, 104). Furthermore, the dynamic interaction between rebels and the state deserves further investigation; the role of the state, rather than the rebel, has received scant attention in recent studies into the logic of violence (Pierskalla 2010). This is the challenge the present study takes up.

Before we proceed, it needs to be noted that escalation should not be interpreted a priori as a phenomenon that is always preferably avoided. Lewis Coser argued in the 1950s that '[c]ommitment to the view that social conflict is necessarily destructive of the relationship within which it occurs leads ... to highly deficient interpretations' (Coser 1956, 8). Conflict can act '[a]s a stimulus for the creation and modification of norms, conflict makes the readjustment of relationships to changed conditions possible' (Coser 1956, 128). Furthermore,

[i]n the short term, a polarization in the political spectrum follows; in the long term, new forms of collective action become part of the accepted repertoires. This means that, from a historical perspective, social movements do influence even the more stable institutions and deep-rooted political cultures. These changes are, however, not produced by the social movements alone, but by their interactions with other actors both allies and opponents. (Della Porta 1995b, 74; Tarrow 1994)

Radicals, conflicts and escalations perform functions in shaping political power and social relations; 'one of the creative functions of conflict resides in its ability to arouse motivation to solve a problem that might otherwise go unattended' (Deutsch 1973, 360); moreover, 'the creation of essentially disciplined forces from bands of people who are, or act like, criminals and thugs has been at the center of much state building' (Mueller 2004, 23).

This caveat should not be read as a categorical endorsement of rebel agendas. However, it is important to stress that recent research has put forward the unrecognised positive role of rebel groups as successful in democratic transformation and economic development (Toft 2010). Furthermore, the capacity of violent groups to provide rebel government (Mampilly 2011; Arjona, Kasfir and Mampilly 2015) and legitimacy (Duyvesteyn 2017) has been notable. There is a clear and urgent need to further these understandings.

This study will aim to explore in more detail the rebel collective utilitarian model of strategy in conjunction with group and individual level explanations. It will, by looking at the available material, try to think through some of the processes that can be witnessed. There is substantial evidence that the rebel collective utilitarian model of strategy is relevant, exists and operates, and there are indications that this can be linked to escalation and de-escalation processes (Duyvesteyn 2005). The focus will be on *how* the process of escalation occurs. The rest of this study will proceed as follows. In Chapter 2, the concepts of escalation and de-escalation will be discussed based on the existing literature on the subject. The aim of the chapter is to dissect the existing approaches and to develop a methodology for assessing escalation and de-escalation. Chapter 3 and subsequent chapters will discuss the more detailed propositions relating to processes of escalation and de-escalation.

2

Escalation and De-Escalation

In light of the rising tension between the United States, the Russian Federation and China in recent years, the topic of escalation is experiencing something of a rebirth. The current modernisation of the nuclear arsenals has led some to the dusting off of handbooks from the period of the Cold War to gain a renewed understanding of the concept of escalation. This recent resurgence of interest in the topic continues along the lines of escalation as a rational and linear phenomenon (Colby and Solomon 2015). Moreover, in an analysis of the global jihad, Osama bin Laden is credited with using escalation in a very linear and calculated manner. Allegedly, bin Laden was aware of the concept's features and used a deliberate and rationally calculated stepping up of escalation against Western states (Morgan et al. 2008). The overriding characteristics of escalation as something that is of a linear nature and which can be rationally controlled are very prevalent. The aim of this chapter is to take a closer look at these existing ideas about escalation and de-escalation and to develop a measurement for observing and assessing their occurrence.

The discussion will highlight that there are two main approaches to gauging escalation. The first has predominantly been inspired by conceptualisation of escalation during the Cold War, which revolves around thresholds of atrocity. The second approach has been informed by other more qualitative features of thresholds, based on investments, commitment, perceptions and sensitivities. It is in particular this second approach that deserves more attention to assess the process of rebel-state conflict escalation on which this study will build.

ESCALATION: THE THRESHOLD OF ATROCITY

Thomas Schelling in his book *Arms and Influence* talks about escalation as crossing thresholds. These thresholds possess a 'quality that when they are crossed there is unavoidably a dramatic challenge'. In particular, '[g]as and nuclear weapons have this character' (Schelling 2008, 154). This description implies that escalation in essence is an increase in atrocity. This constitutes one, and at present, the dominant approach to conceptualising escalation.

In one of the few studies in which escalation is specifically linked to sub-state political violence, M. L. R. Smith and Peter Neumann argue that the ability of terrorist groups to escalate or to cross thresholds is limited. The only logical extension of the struggle, they identify, is to raise the level of indiscrimination (Neumann and Smith 2007; Smith and Jones 2015). The one main source of escalation, it is argued, both for the terrorist and the insurgent, is crossing the threshold of atrocity (Stone 2012).

One of the ways in which rebels can raise, and have raised, the level of atrocity has been by the targeting of civilians (Stone 2012; Dixon 2020). Significant scholarship, without directly referring to the issue of escalation, has proposed that the targeting of civilians possesses a strategic rationale directly linked to interactions between belligerents (Abrahms 2018). A coercion-control mechanism has been found that could explain the occurrence of indiscriminate violence against civilians in civil wars (Kalyvas 2006). This importantly denotes a transgression of the non-combatant threshold in war and leads to an increase in the measure of atrocity. The use of this indiscriminate violence can be seen as a significant threshold in conflict. Looking, for example, into the non-state actor violence in Algeria in the 1990s, the interaction between the participants in this conflict produced significant escalation (Kalyvas 1999). In those areas where government control was strong, violence was measured and discriminated. Where control was contested, violence tended to be indiscriminate and massacres occurred. The underlying reason of this indiscriminate violence is to deter defection. Violence is used against civilians to deter defection to the opponent (Kalyvas 1999).

There are indications that the occurrence of indiscriminate violence is not only a deterrence measure, but it can be a product of agency problems within the rebel group. Strategically operating rebel leaders have tended to be far less supportive of targeting civilians in their public statements, compared to the actual patterns of violence their groups carried out (Abrahms et al. 2017; Abrahms 2018; Holtermann 2019). Furthermore, effecting political change through civilian targeting has been assessed as largely unsuccessful (Wood and Kathman 2014; Abrahms et al. 2017).

A rise in violence via the changing behaviour of insurgents towards the population can not only be explained from the perspective of control but also through the presence or absence of active rivalries between rebels (Metelits 2009; Wood and Kathman 2015). This theory seems close to the theories of the balance of power and the security dilemma among states. In the state system, power transitions tend to be violent when there is an active threat from an upcoming competitor.[1] When insurgents have to fight for survival against competitors aiming for similar goals, coercion and indiscriminate violence can be expected to occur. When such rivalry is absent, the insurgent can invest in establishing contractual obligations towards the population, which make the exercise of authority less costly and the necessity of coercion dissipates (Schlichte 2009; Arjona, Kasfir, and Mampilly 2015; Arjona 2016). In many cases of so-called barbaric violence, such as in Sierra Leone and Mozambique (Young 1990; Richards 1996), indiscriminate violence has also been used to intimidate the population, when other instruments of power to entice the population were lacking, that is the ability to provide social goods.

A variation on this theme of the indiscriminate targeting of civilians and the raising of the level of atrocity is the moral hazard thesis introduced to explain the advent of external military intervention. Alan Kuperman has argued, based on investigations of the Balkan interventions in the 1990s, that the expectation of a foreign intervention in the ongoing conflict triggered extreme violence, even genocide (Kuperman 2008; Kuperman and Crawford 2014). This argument of moral hazard, provoking risky behaviour in the expectation that intervention to protect the victims would politically benefit the leadership, deals with a form of escalation. While the concept was not used as such in the original article, the idea of raising the level of atrocity conforms with the suggestion of an atrocity threshold in the literature.

The strength of these explanations is that they can account for some of the changes in behaviour and violent outbursts of the rebel group over time. The shortcomings are that they are heavily actor-centred rather than process-oriented and the state as actor in explaining violence remains in many cases underplayed or implicit. There is some recognition that the state can feature: 'The state *can* enter the dynamic as a competitor, and it does so if it is reforming and has the potential to offer something better

---

[1] This is also called the Thucydides trap (Allison 2017).

than what the insurgents are offering' (Metelits 2009, 167 emphasis in original). It is not seen as an endogenous factor in the production of violence. For some conflicts in failed states this is logical. We will return to this problem later.

A third observation on this literature is that, according to the scholarship, the threshold of atrocity, when identified, possesses an important limitation. When thresholds are crossed, they possess a culminating point, according to Peter Neumann and M. L. R. Smith. This they call the 'escalation trap' (Neumann and Smith 2007). There is a point beyond which force becomes counterproductive. Rebels often fall victim to this escalation trap. They show limited ability to control escalation beyond its point of utility, that is, the state responds with actions that hamper the progress of the rebel. Neumann and Smith conclude that 'the onus for calculating the potential effects of escalatory action is particularly severe for the weaker combatant in irregular war. The efficacy of a violent campaign is likely to be premised upon the quality of its analysis as to the effects of its violence on a stronger actor' (Smith 2012, 633; see also Busher et al. 2019, 6, 8, and passim). Weaker actors are prone to overestimate their own capabilities, leading to rash acts of escalation that provoke counter-actions which lead to their ultimate demise. Force has thereby stopped being a useful instrument to bring goals closer. The impact of each successive attack is subject to a law of diminishing returns, where each new attack has to hit harder to reach the same effect, which tends to lead to a steep curve of atrocity (Neumann and Smith 2007).

So far, the discussion has highlighted that escalation possesses a certain number of key features. Escalation is all about the crossing of thresholds, where the resolve of the actors is translated in deliberately crossing thresholds of atrocity. This literature largely follows the premises identified already that escalation is conceived of as linear, with consecutive steps being logically in line with previous actions. The most important shape of escalation in these state-rebel confrontations is the crossing of ethical boundaries (Smith and Jones 2015). This type of threshold is constituted by the use of controversial weapons (gas, nuclear, suicide terrorism) or controversial targets (indiscriminate killing and genocide). By crossing this type of threshold, it is expected that the opponent, and in some cases its supporters, will be coerced and start to show compliance. The limitation in raising the level of atrocity is the escalation trap. The trap shows itself when the atrocities committed surpass the level of political utility, when they provoke countermeasures that lead to the end of the rebel group.

However, it is likely that, apart from the threshold of atrocity and outrage, rebels have a modus operandi that might yield insights into how thresholds are crossed and violence reaches new heights and develops new shapes during the course of conflict. The next paragraph will explore these possible other avenues of escalation.

ESCALATION: THE THRESHOLD OF COMMITMENT[2]

Apart from escalation as crossing the threshold of atrocity, there is a second, far less emphasised approach to escalation. This is based on other qualitative assessments of observable thresholds. During the period of the Cold War, scholarship brought forward several alternative causal factors linked to the phenomenon of escalation. These consist of escalation as caused by political resolve, previous commitment, power perceptions, the need for cognitive consistency and tapping into unwitting sensitivities of the opponent.

First are those factors that are related to political will and resolve. Once a state has decided to commit itself, a competition process ensues and the desire to win is natural (Deutsch 1973). Escalation is a sign of political resolve: 'Many ... escalations were also executed as demonstrations of will and commitment' (Smoke 1977, 242). This escalatory potential is closely linked to what is called 'low perceived integrative potential'. When norms and values that are at stake in the competition continue to diverge rather than converge, escalation is a natural outcome (Pruitt and Rubin 1986, 86; Pruitt, Rubin, and Kim 2004).

Previous commitment is a second route towards escalation (Deutsch 1973, 352). When a course of action has been adopted, it starts to possess its own logic and past investments need to pay off. When more investments are made, de-escalation becomes increasingly more difficult: 'the higher the level of violence, the greater the casualties and other costs, the greater the risk of more escalation' (Smoke 1977, 242). Previous commitment can develop into 'over-commitment' and de-escalation becomes less and less likely. This is a form of path dependency.

Apart from political will and commitment, perceptions can play a role. There are several versions of differing perceptions driving escalation. Perception biases and self-fulfilling prophecies can emerge in crisis situations in which information is either scarce and/or misinterpreted (Deutsch 1973). Actions of an opponent are interpreted as hostile even

---

[2] This paragraph is based on Duyvesteyn (2012).

when they do not have a hostile intention (Smoke 1977, 289). Also, when actors perceive their own power to be superior to that of their opponent, escalation is likely, and again a certain path dependency is created (Pruitt and Rubin 1986, 86). Another version of the perception argument is the idea of cognitive consistency. Cognitive consistency forms another avenue towards escalation and also promotes its continuation: '*escalation sequences cumulatively activate cognitive consistency and thereby narrow policy-makers' fields of expectation*' (Smoke 1977, 286 italics in original). Even when alternative information is offered, it is often discounted because it does not fit into preconceived information patterns explaining the opponents of his/her behaviour: 'warfare often creates a peculiarly nonsupportive environment for effective decision-making' (Smoke 1977, 260). Morton Deutsch uses the term 'situational entrapment', denoting that '[w]ell-intentioned actions sometimes produce effects opposite to those intended because the actions do not take into account the characteristics of the setting in which they take place' (Deutsch 1973, 358). Furthermore, maintaining cognitive consistency is of paramount importance because the 'pressure for self-consistency may lead to unwitting involvement in and intensification of conflict because one's actions have to be justified to oneself and to others' (Deutsch 1973, 358).

Fourth, not understanding the opponent can also lead to escalation. These are 'failures of analysis', which express themselves in 'inattentiveness to, or outright unawareness of, the basic assumptions and presuppositions of decision-makers ... and their overall perspectives on the situation; their underlying goals (as opposed to immediate objectives)' (Smoke 1977, 253). This might overlap with the previous point of perceptions playing a role in assessments of the opponent but the lack of understanding might also be broader. The actors display here 'failures of imagination, failures of empathy, or failures of conceptualization and analysis' to understand the opponent (Smoke 1977, 253). These failures are prevalent at the highest echelons of power: 'Events can begin to get out of hand when one side does not adequately comprehend the other's basic *frame of reference*' (Smoke 1977, 256).

Lastly, apart from limitations related to a shortfall in self-awareness, the existence of sensitivities of the opponent that the actor is not aware of can lead to escalation; there might be 'latent objectives, which may be axiomatic, unconscious, or simply not yet operationalized', which 'may have decisive effects on the prospects of escalation when they are activated' (Smoke 1977, 248). These sensitivities could relate to culture or practices and create further animosity;

these might be 'adjacent combustible material, lines of connection, means for reinforcing limits, latencies, and asymmetries in capabilities, motivation and interest', which, 'in the framework of a particular conflict and that may have a triggering ... effect on escalation' (Smoke 1977, 251).

This set of thresholds of escalation has focused on the issues at stake in the shape of propositions relating to political resolve, power perceptions, previous commitment, cognitive consistency and unwitting sensitivities. These ideas, however, fail to explain how and when these thresholds are crossed. When is the issue of political resolve of such weight that it triggers a raising of the level or spread of violence? When is cognitive consistency so pressing that more or different violence is seen as necessary? It appears that not every case of a failure of analysis or previous commitment will result in escalation. Answering these questions is where the present study aims to break new ground.

ESCALATION DOMINANCE

Classical strategic thought has, on the one hand, focused on denying the enemy control over his or her capabilities, for example the central idea of the decisive battle with a concentration in time and place of overwhelming force against the capabilities or the armed forces of the enemy. On the other hand, strategic thinking focusing on the political will of the opponent has been strongly linked to all forms of irregular war, that is the application of terrorist and insurgent strategies to compromise the will to further resist. Thomas Schelling has written:

> War is always a bargaining process, one in which threats and proposals, coun-terproposals and counterthreats, offers and assurances, concessions and demon-strations, take the form of actions rather than words, or actions accompanied by words. It is in the wars that we have come to call "limited wars" that the bargaining appears most vividly and is conducted most consciously. The critical targets in such a war are the mind of the enemy as much as on the battlefield; the state of the enemy's expectations is as important as the state of his troops; the threat of violence in reserve is more important than the commitment of force in the field. (Schelling 2008, 142–143)

War as a bargaining process is ultimately geared towards delivering the will of the opponent. By diminishing his will to resist, strategic ends would be obtained. Irregular war strategies, the dominant choice for rebels, are more directly targeted at delivering that will, instead of using the opposing forces' capability as an intermediate to delivering the will.

In the original conceptualisation of escalation, as discussed earlier, the issue of escalation dominance played a large role. Escalation dominance, as defined by Kahn and Schelling, has been very much focused on capabilities. Kahn described escalation dominance as 'a capacity, other things being equal, to enable the side possessing it to enjoy marked advantages in a given region of the escalation ladder .... That side which has least to lose by eruption, or fears eruption least, will automatically have an element of escalation dominance' (Kahn 2012, 290). The most important way to reduce the fear of further eruption is to outmatch the opponent in material capability, more, heavier weapons and better defences to continue to safeguard their operation. Political will is mostly taken as a given.

A discussion of escalation dominance, as a topic for investigating rebel groups, is practically non-existent. One of the few statements relating to rebels and escalation dominance, unfortunately, has not elicited much attention. It has been claimed that '[i]n small wars, the escalation dominance lies with the insurgent since the state will be the first to quit the "competition of outrage"' (Daase 2007, 194). While an elaboration of the conceptualisation or the exact workings of this mechanism is absent, the continuation of seeing dominance purely via the atrocity threshold is striking. However, there is reason to reconsider the tenability of the claim, in light of the strategic logic of many rebel struggles, focusing on political will. When a stronger will to resist is present, other mechanisms than simply raising atrocity must be present to signify escalation.

We will take these existing ideas about escalation as a starting point for informing the propositions that will be generated later. In particular, we will build on the dimensions of escalation with a focus on actors, issues of contention and means and methods. Escalation will be conceptualised as the crossing of a threshold in war that is empirically observable. It does not only rely on perceptions of the participants, as some other scholars have argued (Morgan et al. 2008). Thresholds, as we will detail later, can be found in regard to political will and capabilities. In other words, civil wars can aggravate when a threshold in political will is crossed, for example, in light of commitment to the issue(s) at stake or by crossing a threshold in regard to capabilities, such as calibre and type of weaponry. We will find in the rest of the study that there are several other and very significant thresholds that can be crossed by rebel groups, constituting escalation, other than the atrocity threshold, emphasised so far in the literature. Before discussing the methods and further set-up of this study, the topic of de-escalation deserves attention.

DE-ESCALATION

De-escalation is not necessarily the exact opposite of escalation and is not necessarily 'escalation in reverse'; 'there are typical de-escalation gestures that do not have the simple character of a reversal of a previous escalation' (Kahn 2012, 231). In other words, the steps going down the escalation ladder are not the same ones as going up. Refraining from crossing the threshold of indiscriminate killing does not automatically lead to de-escalation. Moreover, de-escalation is not the same as conflict termination. Conflicts can terminate based on overwhelming escalation. Furthermore, de-escalation is neither synonymous with the concepts of concessions or negotiation, as both can also serve as triggers for more violence. It is not necessary that escalation reaches a climax before de-escalation can take place. Conflict can escalate and de-escalate multiple times before it terminates.

Contrary to the concept of escalation, de-escalation seems to have been far less theoretically developed. While there are a host of studies that investigate the ending of terrorist and insurgency campaigns, suggestions about how to de-escalate specifically are far more scarce. There is quite a substantial literature and lively debate on the issue of how violence ends. Investigations into the termination of conflict, including the role of resolution, negotiation and settlement, have shed light on the causal mechanisms at play here. Stalemate, war weariness and alternative routes for political expression have been found of importance, as have intermediaries and intervention forces. Multiple factors are usually at play (Walter 2002; Cronin 2009). One of the main challenges at present for our research agenda is to find out more about the intermediate phase, after the outbreak and before the termination of conflict. We need to find out more about how the confrontations between violent political opposition groups and the state escalate, and how the process develops towards a termination of hostilities (Duyvesteyn 2012; Becker 2015, 4).

In the 'declinist' literature about how violence ends, several factors have surfaced that are relevant for our discussion (Crenshaw 1999; Cronin 2009; Connable and Libicki 2010; Matesan 2018). As with processes of escalation, these can be deliberate, for example the transition and formation of a main-stream political party can be a conscious choice. Or these processes can be accidental, for example group demise can be beyond any individual control. Several routes out of violence can be identified. We know that rebels can be victorious, can simply be defeated, can end up in a stalemate, can opt for mainstream politics, turn to a life of crime or can wither away without ever formally renouncing violence. Violence can abate when the goals of the group have been reached (Cronin 2009). As has been pointed out in several statistical analyses, this is not a very common occurrence for rebels (Arreguín-Toft 2005; Abrahms 2006, 2011; Chenoweth and Stephan 2011).

Very direct suggestions for the process of de-escalation seem to be absent in this literature. Indeed, there is a serious neglect in the literature of 'an analysis of the differences between temporary declines in violence', which we know very little about, compared to 'the "end" of an organisation', on which most of the debate has focused (Becker 2015, 4).

Three main suggestions can be identified in the literature, which are of potential relevance to further our understanding of de-escalation. Based on Cold War scholarship, de-escalation emerges as a result of deterrence. The prospect or threat of further pain and punishment can lead to backing down, and a lessening of the level or spread of violence. Second, de-escalation can be a consequence of a norm convergence shift. When the expectations of the belligerents start to converge rather than diverge, an understanding can be created which has the potential to lessen the (threat of) violence. Finally, de-escalation can result when the belligerents have become war weary or have reached parity and a continuation of violence is recognised as beyond utility. These three sets of ideas will be discussed in turn.

DE-ESCALATION THROUGH DETERRENCE

De-escalation in the Cold War literature was primarily dealt with through deterrence. States could be deterred from going further up the ladder of escalation based on the threat of punishment or the prospect of further pain. Deterrence is a major route towards preventing escalation (Freedman 2004). Deterrence is aimed at affecting the cost–benefit calculations of states by mounting a credible threat, if an unwelcome course of action is adopted. This manipulation is either shaped by a prospect of punishment or by denial (Snyder 1961; Freedman 2004). The manipulation of the costs could involve the prospect of punishment via exacting pain of retaliation. Alternatively, it could raise the costs of investments to continue on the course of action, which at a certain point will outweigh the prize that could be gained. The manipulation of the benefits could involve a decrease in opportunities to carry out attacks, for example, by increases in security measures or robbing the actor of any benefits by lowering the expected pay-offs. At a certain point deterrence will work and de-escalation of a crisis or conflict will occur.

This discussion, while highly interesting, provides challenges when applied to rebel groups, which form the central focus of this study. Many authors have noted that interstate deterrence models run into problems when used in confrontations with rebels. The deterrence literature is focused very heavily on dyadic relations involving states. The similarity in state actors creates an interaction which has been studied extensively and has led to a specific understanding of this phenomenon. When one actor is able to fundamentally threaten something that the other one holds dear, deterrence can be made to work. This literature is based on certain presumptions about the characteristics of the adversaries, and importantly the ability to communicate. In the case of rebels, as has been noted earlier, specifically in the case of terrorism, there is often no return address and it is difficult, if not impossible, to directly threaten something they hold dear or raise the price to such an extent that the mechanism of deterrence can work (Freedman 2004, 3; Knopf 2010; Miller 2013). Furthermore, among the rebels that interest us here, there are those who actively seek to attract retaliation and are not deterred by its prospect, in order to trigger the provocation and action imperatives on which they thrive. A notable example is the prevalence of suicide terrorism in which the perpetrators actively seek to kill themselves.

Despite these challenges, there are several authors who continue to stress the relevance of the deterrence by denial option (Ross and Gurr 1989; Crenshaw 1991; Morral and Jackson 2014). By denying rebels access to targets, it is suggested that deterrence might work. However, rebels have a tendency to shift between targets when their access is compromised. This points to the fact that the state and rebel actions possess important second- and third-order effects that are not, or insufficiently, taken into account either in academic investigations or in political decision-making.

Deterrence by punishment can also be seen as having continued relevance according to some other scholars and they specifically point to targeted killing (Dugan and Chenoweth 2012; Morral and Jackson 2014). By punishing the rebel group by taking out its leadership, a deterrent effect is supposed to occur. The logic is that by weakening the rebel group, it will no longer be able to engage in violence due to the lack of a successor, an undermining of the organisation or the inability to reorganise.

Deterrence by punishment does seem to be a viable approach against those rebels who use an insurgency strategy and are in command of territory. Punishment in the shape of direct attacks against territorial strongholds of rebels could fall into this category. Rebels tend to defend themselves by, for example, using human shields to ward off attacks or force intervening states to violate international humanitarian law.

A last strand of thinking in favour of a continued relevance of deterrence is the idea of indirect deterrence (Harkavy 1998). Several experts have noted that one of the most important features of successful insurgencies is the foreign ties of the rebel group (Record 2007; Connable and Libicki 2010). Deterrence, it is argued, could be successful by targeting the rebel's state sponsors.

It is safe to conclude at this point that deterrence is a far less useful concept in the dyads that this study is interested in, compared to interstate constellations. Overall, in this discussion there does not seem to be any claim linking deterrence of rebels to de-escalation directly.

DE-ESCALATION: THE NORM CONVERGENCE THRESHOLD

The record of violent interaction between the state and the rebel group can create major impediments to conflict transformation. When violent exchange is the main channel of communication, the sides will suffer from a commitment problem when alternatives are sought. One main suggestion from the Cold War literature is the idea of norm convergence as a route to de-escalation. Thomas Schelling has suggested that de-escalation is linked to an emergence of common frames of reference. Referring to early work in experimental social psychology, Schelling notes that states can learn in an interactive fashion: 'when norms are created for two parties in the same process, each player's developing norm influences the other's; each side adapts its own system of values to the other's, in forming its own'. Direct communications are not necessary: '[i]n an almost unconsciously cooperative way, adversaries must reach a mutually recognized definition of what constitutes an innovation, a challenging or assertive move, or a cooperative gesture' (Schelling 1980, 168–169). However, when and how do these norms emerge? Other scholars have built on these ideas and formulated some suggestions: 'The likelihood of escalation is reduced (and hence the situation tends towards stability) in the presence of conflict-limiting norms and institutions' (Pruitt and Rubin 1986, 86). Not only institutions but also actors and identifications can play a role:

Other factors … may serve to limit and encapsulate conflict so that a spiralling intensification does not develop. Here, we refer to such factors as: the number and strength of the existing cooperative bonds, cross-cutting identifications, common allegiances and memberships among the conflicting parties; the existence of values, institutions, procedures, and groups that are organized to help limit and regulate conflict. (Deutsch 1973, 352)

A prerequisite for de-escalation is thus the existence and mutual recognition of common norms and practices (Webel and Fischer 2013).

These claims, however, are not without problems. The idea of norm convergence seems to imply that this process might be unique for each case as these descriptions do not directly refer to universal or the universalisation of norms (Finnemore and Sikkink 1998; Jo 2015). Furthermore, most of these processes of norm convergence can only be established with hindsight, which leaves policy makers rather empty-handed. Nevertheless, this suggestion for a causal relationship with de-escalation will be subject to further analysis next.

DE-ESCALATION: STALEMATE OR PARITY

When the belligerents become unable or unwilling to continue the contest on the same level of intensity, a stalemate can ensue. War weariness and stalemates are not very common occurrences in struggles involving rebel groups (Connable and Libicki 2010, 19). Indicators for war weariness are, for example, defection, desertion and infiltration (Connable and Libicki 2010).

The idea of a mutually hurting stalemate, introduced by William I. Zartman, has been latched upon by many scholars to identify factors that can contribute to successful conflict transformation, in particular openings for negotiation (Zartman 1989; see also Zartman and Aurik 1991; Zartman and Faure 2005; Pechenkina and Thomas 2020). A mutually hurting stalemate is a situation of deadlock in which the belligerents realise that more violence will not pay off. Moreover, a solution that carries the potential favour of all the parties can be identified. The idea is based on a cost–benefit calculation by the opponents.

The mutually hurting stalemate has been a heavily used concept and there is indeed evidence of its existence. It is by no means clear whether a mutually hurting stalemate is the same as, or similar to, de-escalation. A mutually hurting stalemate might precede de-escalation or be its consequence. This is illustrated by findings related to the conditions under which mediation is accepted; this is most likely when 'conflict intensity increases, but neither conflict party sees a particularly high probability of victory' (Ruhe 2015, 256).

The suggested link between the recognition of elusive chances of victory and de-escalation overlooks the many examples of conflict which carry on despite limited chances of any side coming out victorious (Abrahms 2008, 2011; Fortna 2015). Rebels have a tendency to continue the struggle despite the observation that indeed victory is distant or unobtainable. This paradox will be further dissected later in the conclusion.

As has been noted by the scholarship on the mutually hurting stalemate, there are problems with making the concept operational and with its measurement (O'Kane 2006; Tonge, Shirlow, and McAuley 2011). A mutually hurting stalemate is generally a perception rather than an objectively observable situation. Furthermore, it seems that only with hindsight such a stalemate could be ascertained. There is also a large discussion on so-called tipping points in war, which can mostly be established after termination and focus on the end of war rather than de-escalation (Connable and Libicki 2010). For the purposes of this study, there is a third problem. Parity and recognition of elusive victory cannot necessarily be equated with lowering of the level of violence or going down a threshold in war. Therefore, this body of scholarship does not offer too much to further conceptualise de-escalation.

De-escalation, similar to the concept of escalation, is treated as largely rational and linear. Linearity is particularly notable; 'a consensus has emerged that most terrorist organisations conform to a pattern of a) an initial embrace of violence b) an escalation period, and finally c) a period of decline' (Becker 2015, 2). A similar picture emerges in studies of insurgency.

Not only is there a problem with the linearity claims, also the idea of the deliberate nature of de-escalation is problematic. A 2008 Rand study claims that de-escalation is always a deliberate affair: 'accidental de-escalation is essentially unheard of' (Morgan et al. 2008, 34). Furthermore, it has been claimed that self-imposed de-escalation results from considerations of popular support or the need to recuperate after previous losses. According to one expert, these downward turns should mostly be read as signs of weakness on the part of the rebel (Becker 2015). This de-escalation, it is claimed, is far less likely to be of longer duration than de-escalation imposed from the outside. However, in this study, we find that there are several examples of what can be seen as unwanted and accidental de-escalation. These claims about de-escalation, with too little grounding in empirical or theoretical investigation, invite further reflection.

The problems we have identified earlier for escalation also seem to play a role for the concept of de-escalation. When and how does de-escalation occur? This study aims to investigate the rise and decline of violence in armed conflicts between rebel groups and the state. We have delimited rebel groups as identifiable entities with an observable degree of organisation that are engaged in political violence in which a means–ends relationship is present. This study has opted to take the rebel as generic category as a starting point. As with conflict, it is clear that the idea and the internal make-up of the rebel changes over time and is affected by countermeasures, interaction and changeable context. To do justice to these changes and processes, a variety of conflicts and actors, both strong and weak, and diverse contexts, that is democratic and non-democratic entities, will be addressed.

MEASURING ESCALATION AND DE-ESCALATION

Generally, five dimensions of escalation have been distinguished. Firstly, escalation can be witnessed in the number of actors involved in the dispute. Secondly, the issue of contention can also grow. As the conflict develops, the issues that gave rise to the dispute can start to become more comprehensive and start to include new and more issues. Also, the weight attached to the issues can increase. Thirdly, conflicts can escalate through the use of more and heavier instruments, with usually more casualties as a result. This is called vertical escalation. Fourthly, escalation can take place in time – this means a prolongation of the dispute. Fifthly, escalation can occur in terms of space – a larger geographical area becomes involved, spillover occurs and different combat domains can become involved (land/air/sea). This is also called horizontal escalation (Pruitt and Rubin 1986).

Herman Kahn, in his authoritative work on the subject, only emphasised the vertical and horizontal versions of escalation (Kahn 2012, 4–6). The other literature discussed earlier in the shape of the atrocity threshold and the commitment threshold emphasise vertical escalation and the issues of contention, respectively. This means, in fact that, so far, a comprehensive treatment of escalation in all its identifiable facets is missing.

Furthermore, apart from these suggestions taken from the existing escalation literature, there are two more dimensions of escalation that can be added to this list. It seems implicit in the category of instruments that these are used for certain purposes. However, the specific tactics used and the targets they are aimed at deserve further investigation. We have already seen that in the discussion of escalation as raising the level of atrocity, the indiscriminate killing of the population is significant. Rebel campaigns can thus theoretically move from discriminate to indiscriminate killing and vice versa. Moreover, the tactics used in rebel violence also deserve further consideration. Tactics, as already noted in the discussion about correlations between ideology and violence, can move from simple to sophisticated, using guns or bombs in single or multiple attacks. These require not only specific skills but are also potentially reflective of a step up or down in the conflict.

TABLE 2.1 *Dimensions of Escalation*

Number of actors	
(New) Issues of contention or weight attached to issue of contention	
More or heavier instruments	Vertical escalation
Targets	
Tactics	
Time	
Territory	Horizontal escalation

The problem with the identified list of dimensions of escalation is that they signify both deliberate acts and structural or environmental conditions, which can be much less influenced (Morgan et al. 2008). There are, in fact, two images of escalation: the 'actor image' and the 'phenomenal image' (Smoke 1977, 21). The actor image, heavily emphasised in the existing literature, sees escalation as a wilful act and as a product of conscious choice. The phenomenal image stresses the lack of control and sees it as a result of the process of interaction. Horizontal escalation is, for example, a course of action that can be pursued by the participants in the conflict. Expanding the territory affected by terrorism can aid in the creation of a surprise effect and might contribute to greater leverage for the groups. At the same time, existing geographical conditions might be physically inhibitive to spillover because of the presence of mountains or water. This study will use both actor and phenomenal images at the same time: '*both* perspectives are true and valuable, as long as they are accepted *together*' (Smoke 1977, 22 italics in original). Escalation can be a deliberate, an inadvertent or an accidental phenomenon.

An important claim in the existing literature is that escalation thresholds in confrontations involving rebel groups are extremely difficult, if not impossible, to identify: 'escalation thresholds are fluid and difficult to ascertain' (Morgan et al. 2008, 132). Herman Kahn in his study claimed that it was necessary to 'be deliberately vague and not usually specific [about] the criteria being used to determine the degree of escalation. However, in most situations the context (or correlation between the possible criteria) will be clear enough to avoid confusion' (Kahn 2012, 9). These are very debatable claims, which will be tackled in the rest of this study.

In order to prove that indeed thresholds can be identified, the concepts of escalation and de-escalation have, so far, been made operational via the seven dimensions detailed earlier. We will investigate whether escalation and de-escalation can be better understood by using these seven dimensions. Furthermore, the emphasis will be on investigating escalation as predominantly an aggravation of conflict and de-escalation as its opposite. Still, the list of dimensions of (de)-escalation points out that a more fine-grained analysis is both possible and necessary.

APPROACH

So far, we have defined in Chapter 1 rebel groups as political and strategic actors and presented an instrumental approach to the use of force. Moreover, we have discussed in Chapter 2 the different approaches to understanding escalation and de-escalation and highlighted the lacunae that invite further questioning and investigation. The rest of this study will use the two main parameters of war, as derived from the Clausewitzean interpretation of war, of political will and capability. Politics will be defined and delimited as involving power, and the distribution processes of power in a given society (Lasswell 1950; Dahl 1965; Bassford 2007). Capabilities will be delimited as material and immaterial resources that can be used to press the will power of the belligerent.

When we combine these, in theory, there will be four possible escalation scenarios (Table 2.2). Firstly, there is the scenario of increased political will coupled with existing capabilities. Obviously, there is always a base level of political will present otherwise we cannot speak of war. An asymmetry in political goals and commitment can, however, mark an armed engagement. When thresholds are crossed in regard to political will, this can be seen as escalation. A good example is the Vietnam war, where it is generally understood that increased political will on the part of the Vietcong substantially contributed to the escalation of violence, and also to the ultimate victory and a communist takeover in 1975 (Arreguín-Toft 2001, 2012). In this scenario, we can place the factors of increased resolve, perceptions, commitment, cognitive consistency, and unwitting sensitivities as dimensions of escalation derived from the Cold War literature, discussed earlier.

A second scenario is when no increase in political will nor a change in capabilities occurs. This approach precludes escalation and will not be discussed further.

Thirdly, a scenario is possible where political will remains constant but new capabilities are introduced. This occurs in cases where the issues at stake, or the weight attached to them, remain stable but where there is, for example, an influx of new recruits or material or a change of strategy that contributes to the raising of the level or spread of violent exchange. An example could be the ebb and flow of the conflict in Rwanda, where the Tutsi minority had tried in several wars to regain a foothold in what they considered their natural home in Rwanda. Support from the Ugandan regime after the accession of president Museveni in 1986 provided the opportunity for a successful advance in the early 1990s (Mamdani 2014).

Fourthly, there is a scenario of both increased political will and augmented capabilities. A dual threshold can be crossed when the stakes are raised and commensurately the capabilities are reinforced. A dominant example of this scenario is of course the Second World War, where the growing number of states involved over the course of time raised the political will to resist and brought with it an ever-larger pool of resources until a complete military defeat could be possible. The atrocity threshold, as the dominant existing approach to gauging escalation, could also fit into this scenario. Raising atrocity by engaging in indiscriminate killing both requires an augmented political will for ethical transgression and an increased capability to do so.

TABLE 2.2 *Four Scenarios of Escalation: Political Will and Capability*

Political will	Political will + Capabilities ~ (thresholds: resolve, perceptions, commitment, cognitive consistency, sensitivities)	Political will + Capabilities + (threshold: atrocity)
	Political will ~ Capabilities ~ no escalation	Political will ~ Capabilities +
Capabilities		

Table 2.2 provides an overview of these scenarios identified so far.

A similar quadrant can be filled based on the expectations related to de-escalation. For de-escalation, there are also four scenarios (Table 2.3). Looking at the quadrants in a counterclockwise order, firstly, in the top-left quadrant, there is a decrease in political will, while the capabilities remain unchanged. The idea introduced earlier about norm convergence would fit into this scenario. Norm convergence refers to a lessening of conflict based on a decrease in significance of political will or the availability of alternative courses of action for the attainment of political goals. The second scenario, in the bottom-left quadrant, with no change in political will nor in capabilities, will not lead to de-escalation and will therefore be excluded. Thirdly, in the bottom-right quadrant, capabilities witness a decrease but political will remains unchanged. This situation will resemble a militarily weakening of the actor, if not a military defeat. It is important to stress again that a military defeat of rebel group is not commensurate with a political defeat. This paradox will be addressed more fully in the concluding chapter. Fourthly, in the top-right quadrant, when there is both a lessening of will and capability, this forms the clearest case of de-escalation. When both the will to continue fighting and the capability to do so are lacking, this form of de-escalation will emerge. This will amount to defeat.

These scenarios can apply both to the rebel group and the state. For the purposes of this analysis, our main focus will be on the rebels.

TABLE 2.3 *Four Scenarios of De-Escalation: Political Will and Capability*

Political will	Political will – Capabilities ~ (threshold: norm convergence)	Political will – Capabilities –
	Political will ~ Capabilities ~ no de-escalation	Political will ~ Capabilities –
Capabilities		

As already noted, the main aim of this study is to think through theoretically and empirically the phenomena of escalation and de-escalation and arrive at informed hypotheses about the rise and decline of violence in state-rebel group confrontations. This investigation will talk specifically about mechanisms and processes. We are interested in explaining the phenomenon of (de-)escalation as the outcome of a process of interaction which displays causality or a causal chain which is observable. What common mechanisms are visible when we look at escalation? When and how does this emerge? What factors commonly occur and play out when we observe (de-)escalation? We conceptualise a mechanism as 'a precise, abstract and action-based explanation which shows how the occurring of triggering events regularly generate the type of outcome to be explained' (Hedström and Swedberg 1998, 6; also Della Porta 2013, 23).

We will formulate these causal mechanisms in the shape of hypotheses. These hypotheses will be derived from existing findings, both from the theoretical and empirical literature. They are intended as stepping stones for further study. This approach borrows heavily from Stephen van Evera's 'Hypotheses on Nationalism and War' and Robert Jervis's 'Hypotheses on Misperception' (Van Evera 1994; Jervis 1968). Both studies are based on the idea that a very interesting and worthwhile topic requires investigation but, as van Evera writes, it might be the case that 'the stock of hypotheses ... is meagre, hence our first order of business is to expand it' (Van Evera 1994, 7). There is indeed proof for some causal processes explaining escalation but the evidence for others is more limited. The series of hypotheses that this study presents later consist of those propositions that make sense both theoretically and empirically. These hypotheses will need to form not only starting points for further investigation, but might also provide some food for thought for policy makers.

We conceptualise a hypothesis as a proposed explanation for a causal relationship. Hypotheses are conjectural and need to be formulated in such a way that allows for testing and falsification. In our specific case of escalation, we would be looking for a causal chain that involves an action or activity A that is followed by a crossing of a threshold in violence in a qualitative or quantitative manner, being B. When looking at the context surrounding A, the focus will be not only on *why* it happens, which is highly likely to be contingent, but also on *how* and *when*. We aim to investigate what causal links have been argued to exist, and seen to exist in empirical studies and theoretical contributions to explain the crossing of thresholds in armed conflict involving a state and rebel actor. The hypotheses will be generated based on the material brought together in the chapters that follow. The concluding chapter will attempt to bring them all together in a comprehensive overview.

The approach has inherent scientific shortcomings. As scholars in the field of international relations have noted, the hypothesis approach is important and increasing in importance (Mearsheimer and Walt 2013). However, hypotheses make sense only if there is an underlying theory that is able to explain the causation: 'a theory explains why a particular hypothesis should be true, by identifying the causal mechanisms that produce the expected outcomes(s)' (Mearsheimer and Walt 2013, 432). One of the main drawbacks of hypothesis-focused research is a failure to build cumulative knowledge, which is a particularly pressing problem in the field of civil wars studies where the niche and micro-level have dominated over broader ideas and larger theories. This criticism and these concerns are fair and will be addressed in the concluding chapter, where some building blocks for a theory of escalation and de-escalation will be presented. The following chapters will provide us with the necessary foundations for some measure of conjecture as to the causality of the crossing thresholds in civil war. While borrowing heavily from the hard work of colleagues working on micro-level questions, this present investigation positions itself at the meso-level, with a focus on theoretical propositions of conflict escalation and de-escalation.

This study will thus be based on insights from the existing theoretical literature combined with some empirical material. Without aiming to be exhaustive, the present study is intended to help reflect on (de)-escalation. It aims to be a stepping stone in an under-investigated area of rebel violence research: to better understand the process, or the peaks and troughs of violence during the course of war.[3] The empirical material in the shape of short cases or vignettes has been selected based on a series of criteria: firstly, the terrorist and insurgent campaigns have to have a clear beginning and an end in order to draw conclusions about causal processes explaining escalation and de-escalation; secondly, the cases concentrate on examples of rebel violence on national territory and are not focused confrontations between rebels without the state being present; thirdly, a wide variety of examples, both Western and non-Western, have been included. Short elaborations will be used to illustrate the causal mechanisms that have surfaced. By carefully dissecting the causal chains that lead up to, and follow, acts of violence, inferences can be drawn about the action and reaction cycle and about the links between the elements at play. The historian's toolbox, which includes fact finding, process tracing and interpretation, is most suited for this endeavour (Lyall 2015). The comparative aspect will be stressed to generate a more general understanding.

The ambition is to make informed suggestions on the causal mechanisms that might be at play when rebels confront the state and vice versa.

---

[3] For a methodological treatment of the challenges and difficulties investigating non-state actors, see Kruck and Schneiker (2017).

Hypotheses are intrinsically propositions that await further investigation and refinement and require a further test on their tenability. However, based on the presented insights, this study will still make an attempt at theory formulation in the concluding chapter. These theoretical ideas will need to be, without question, also subject of further study.

A second limitation is the role of the state. For the sake of convenience, the state, in contrast to the rebel group, will be conceptualised largely a unitary actor. The research we undertook for this study was primarily focused on increasing the little understood role of rebels in the escalation of violence. A large literature already exists focusing on the state, with a diverse array of theoretical approaches (Allison and Zelikow 1999). The state has a choice to pursue several courses of action prior to and during engagement with rebels. Where possible and where available, we have incorporated the considerations and information relating to the decision-making on the part of the state. Unfortunately, this has not been possible in all cases. We have also paid little attention to the collusion between the state and the rebel group. There is only one small example below in the case of Sri Lanka, but for the focus of our investigations, it was only of secondary importance. With these limitations, we have attempted to develop the arguments with as much depth and breadth as possible and based on the evidence at our disposal.

The aim of this book is to take a closer look at the interaction between rebel groups, such as terrorist, insurgents, guerrillas and the state. As Clausewitz has stipulated, the development of war is unpredictable and largely a product of chance. Our case studies only underline this truism. However, several very notable mechanisms have surfaced in the material under investigation. The mechanisms we identify later relate to important routes to escalation and de-escalation, such as social mobilisation, provocation, substitution, group processes and interaction dynamics. We detail these mechanisms as starting points for further discussion. Without wanting to be exhaustive or present the final word on escalation, these mechanisms help to further understand what happens after an armed conflict breaks out and before it terminates.

The structure of this book is largely chronological in the sense that we operate from an idea that violence breaks out at a certain point in time. Before the outbreak of war, the discussion about the context and political opportunity is relevant. This is where Chapter 3 takes off. Subsequently, violence has a starting point and the ideas of provocation, force and concession will be dealt with in Chapter 4. Chapter 5 will focus on the capabilities that are necessary to sustain a conflict. Here we will further dig into the hypotheses that relate to the capabilities; first a discussion about rebel strategies will be presented. In Chapter 6, a treatment of operations and tactics will follow. Chapters 7 and 8 will reflect further on the development of a violent campaign from the perspectives of the group and the individual level and the issue of public support and legitimacy, respectively. In a separate chapter, Chapter 9, we will focus on insights into de-escalation. The final chapter will attempt to draw conclusions, present ideas for a further theoretical development of the concepts of escalation and de-escalation and paint some avenues for future research.

3

Political Opportunity and Rebel Violence

In the previous two chapters, escalation has been argued to theoretically develop along two axes: via an increase in political will and an increase in capability. In this chapter, we will start by taking a closer look at the environment in which the political will in particular gestates, that is the political opportunity structure. How does the political opportunity structure develop, and how does mobilisation emerge? Social movement scholars have noted that violent political struggles require at least to some degree social mobilisation (Goodwin and Jasper 2009; Alimi 2011). Social mobilisation thus provides an important condition for escalation. The aim of this chapter is to look at this process of the production of violence and escalation from the perspective of such a conducive environment. The material in this chapter points out that social mobilisation is far from a linear process. Moreover, violence importantly occurs when the political opportunity structure is closing and even when political opportunity and mobilisation of the population are absent.

THE POLITICAL OPPORTUNITY STRUCTURE

Social movement theorists and scholars of contentious politics, in their attempts to explain political violence, have brought forward the political opportunity structure as a crucial focus (Tarrow 1994; McAdam, Tarrow, and Tilly 2001; Fearon and Laitin 2003). While this research has, for a long time, investigated protests and demonstrations with an emphasis on Western experiences, only recently the study of contentious politics has turned towards including the use of violence (Alimi 2011; Della Porta 2013; Bosi et al. 2014).

Collective action emerges in the context of a conducive opportunity structure, which refers to 'the opportunity structures that create incentives for movements to form; to the repertoires of collective action they use, to the social networks on which they are based and to the cultural frames around which their supporters are mobilized' (Tarrow 1994, 27; also Busher et al. 2019). Crucial for action is this political opportunity structure, which is not of the groups' own making but is deemed necessary for mobilisation and action. Restricted access to the political domain forms an important and dominant approach to explain violence.[1]

Political opportunity structures can be very diverse. Two ideal polity types will be discussed here, following Max Weber: patrimonial and legal-rationalist structures (Weber, Roth, and Wittich 1978). The discussion here is not aimed at being exhaustive, but it aims to set the stage for a further investigation of political will and escalation in state-rebel confrontations.

Patrimonial Structures

Patrimonialism can be seen as a specific form of authority and legitimacy based on the idea of patrons and clients and reciprocity between them (Chabal and Daloz 1999; Duyvesteyn and Murphy 2010; Bach 2013). Patrons safeguard the interests, both material and immaterial, of their clients, who in their turn act as patrons for others. In this way, a hierarchical structure develops in society, signifying a specific way of organising political power and accountability. As long as favours, such as allegiance, money and food, flow up and down the system, it will remain stable. When the oil that keeps this machinery going dries up, as happened, for instance, at the end of the Cold War with the termination of the patronage of the United States and the Soviet Union, the system becomes unstable, and in many cases collapses. This occurred for example in the case of Somalia, which was among the first post–Cold War failed states and continues to be one to this day. Patrimonialism was the dominant form for organising the political domain in Europe before the French Revolution, and it continues to mark many political systems across the globe today.

---

[1] For a discussion of the shortcomings and problems of the political opportunity structure approach, see Della Porta (2013).

Neo-patrimonialism, as distinct from patrimonialism, is argued to possess a guise of a rational legalistic system through the presence of a bureaucracy. While earlier scholarship interpreted the presence of patrimonialism as a continuation of pre-existing patterns of leadership and authority, more recent interpretations stress a lack of leadership and economic underdevelopment (Pitcher, Moran, and Johnston 2009). Scholars have pointed out that we need to be careful to equate dictatorship and patrimonialism. For the case of Africa, a distinction is useful; a type of authority is not necessarily a type of regime (Pitcher, Moran, and Johnston 2009).

In the case of patrimonialism as regime type, previous studies have shown that authoritarian regimes transitioning towards democracy have a high propensity to become engaged in political violence, both internally and externally (Mansfield and Snyder 1995, 2005). In particular, semi-democracies leave uncertainty about the 'rules of the game' and thereby potentially facilitate escalation (Pierskalla 2010). Authoritarian regimes experiencing a transition towards democracy have been qualified as rather inept at stopping violent activities; 'semi-repressive state reactions often contribute to the evolution from political mobilization to terrorism because of their inconsistent mix of repression and reform' (Weinberg 1998; Richardson 2006, 7).

With patrimonial regimes exhibiting inherent weaknesses, a debate ensued about failed states in the 1990s. The concept of the 'failing state' was introduced by Gerald Helman and Steven Ratner in 1992 (Helman and Ratner 1992). The major problem with what has become known as the failed state discussion is that it is very normative; is there such a thing as a successful state? (Ezrow and Frantz 2013)

The occurrence of violence within patrimonial regimes has been studied extensively. Violence has been argued to be very likely in these patrimonial systems because alternatives for peaceful transitions of political power are scarce (Duyvesteyn 2005). One of the main unanswered questions is whether the weakness of the state caused rebels to establish themselves, or whether the existence of rebels caused the state to fail. Perceptions notwithstanding, the patrimonial state in Africa in most cases appears to 'work' for most involved (Chabal and Daloz 1999). The state, or absence of the state, does not prevent people from going about their daily lives. Historically, the African state has never been a very strong institution. The central dilemma of the African state of how to rule and claim authority over distant and sparsely populated territory predates colonialism (Herbst 2000). The dominant role and outward claim of rule based on control of the state capital continues to exert an influence not only on the legitimacy of African states but also on conflict patterns (Herbst 2000; Duyvesteyn 2005).

Patrimonialism has been successfully applied as a lens in recent years in studies of civil war and rebel groups (Murphy 2003). The patrimonial logic applies to the leadership structure, for example, in the case of the Liberian civil war and the warring groups, which were the main protagonists in that conflict. The militia leaders in return for the fighting capacities of their followers, often legally minors, awarded them with nourishment and opportunities for loot (Murphy 2003). Further application of the patrimonial political model to rebel groups followed. The patronage network has in many cases been built along the lines of charismatic authority of the leader (Hofmann and Dawson 2014), ethnic, clan or social identity.

Also, in studies of the global jihad, it has been found that patronage holds significant explanatory power:

> [T]he jihad is a variant on a traditional Middle Eastern patronage network. It is an intricate, ramified web of dependency and, critically, the patterns of patronage and dependency are its central defining features, rather than the insurgent cells or their activities. Analysts have sometimes seen the marriage relationships, money flows, alumni relationships and sponsorship links in the jihad as secondary, subordinate to a military core of terrorist activity. But fieldwork analysis indicates that jihadist military activity may actually be merely one of the shared activities that the network engages in, while the core is the patronage network. (Kilcullen 2005, 603)

Patrimonial structures of authority, as political opportunity structures, are not only important for the environment in which violence occurs, but also for understanding the inner workings of rebel groups. To this latter issue we will return in Chapter 7. Suffice it to note at this stage that patrimonialism as a regime type has inherent weak points that could facilitate violence; limited access to political power except through the patron network or co-option, little accountability and limited scope for peaceful transitions of power, before and during violent campaigns. Patrimonialism as authority type is a common organisational structure for rebel groups, often with a role for charismatic authority and with a measure of stability but it possesses these same weaknesses.

Rational Legalistic Structures

There is an important argument that democracy, as the most prominent example of a rational legalistic type of regime, can both facilitate and act as a brake on political violence. It is prohibitive for political violence because of the open political opportunity structure. Democracy can defuse the potential recourse to violence because of alternatives to voice discontent. Civil liberties, freedom of speech and association offer opportunities for political participation (see discussion in Li 2005; and in Chenoweth 2013).

Democracy has, at the same time, been found to facilitate political violence for exactly the same reasons (Kydd and Walter 2006, 79–80). From a quantified perspective, fully functioning democracies tend to host more rebel groups using terrorist strategies compared to fully authoritarian societies (Eubank and Weinberg 1994, 2001; Weinberg 1998). Freedom of political organisation, freedom of association and freedom of speech are the most notable features found in the literature (Ross and Gurr 1989, 409); it is a consistent finding that 'terrorist groups tend to target societies with the greatest number of political alternatives, not the fewest' (Abrahms 2008, 84). Also, the freedom of association can breed rebel violence; 'nations in which there were many political parties … also had a higher number of terrorist groups. The latter were relatively scarce in countries without visible political parties and in one party systems' (Weinberg and Eubank 1992, 129). Freedom of speech has been argued to promote terrorism, even attracting rebel groups from outside: 'In a liberal democracy, terrorists are more likely to receive the media attention that they seek. … Thus, Western Europe has served as a venue for terrorism from other regions, such as the Middle East' (Enders and Sandler 2000, 309).

Fully authoritarian regimes are generally less susceptible to terrorist strategies (Wilkinson 1986; Weinberg and Eubank 1992; Weinberg 1998; Enders and Sandler 2000; Laqueur 2003). The repression possible in authoritarian regimes is largely seen as the explanatory factor why these states witness little rebel violence (Art and Richardson 2007, 570). Non-democratic states are thus allegedly better at instituting necessary and stringent countermeasures because of a lack of limits on repression (Merom 2003; Mandel 2015; Ucko 2015; Byman 2016).

There is an interesting debate, importantly informed by the left-wing political violence experienced in Germany and Italy in the 1970s (Della Porta 1995b, 2013). Evidence from these cases points out the following. The political opportunity structure, specifically the unwillingness or inability to address the political discontent, the experience of a decreased space to voice discontent, as well as a lack of confidence in the existing democratic structures, contributed to the emergence of violence by the German

Rote Armee Fraktion and the Brigate Rosse: 'Escalation was the product of polarization in the political culture, of reciprocal misunderstandings between elites and oppositions, each of whom feared the other would betray the principles of democracy' (Della Porta 1995b, 189). Furthermore, '[e]scalations resulted often because of the state's lack of confidence in democratic protest combined with the protestors' lack of confidence in the democratic state institutions' (Della Porta 1995b, 73). When the political culture developed more extremes and the state closed political opportunities, violence increased (Della Porta 1995b). This development we will also see later in the case of the Montoneros in Argentina in the same period. Furthermore, the establishment of violent counter-movements, such as the neo-fascists in Italy and other right-wing radicals, as a response, led to further polarisation (Della Porta 1995b, 2013). A similar development of polarisation, outbidding between social movements, has recently occurred between jihadism and right-wing extremism (Busher and Macklin 2015). These are some of the pathways of the emergence of opportunity structures in rational legalistic polities for violence. Moreover, as a result of violent activity itself, the political domain tended to become more closed (Wilkinson 1986; Neumann and Smith 2007; Abrahms 2011).

Similar to the patrimonial structures, distinguishing rational legalistic regime type and authority type are important for understanding the background of, and the conditions in which violence comes to the fore. Contrary to the patrimonial authority structure, not many studies have appeared that detail the rational legalistic inner authority structures of rebel organisations (Bakke et al., 2012). This appears as an interesting niche for further research. As regime type, rational legalistic opportunity structures have features that can pave the way for the creation of an opportunity structure conducive for violence: freedoms of association, organisation, speech and movement. A (perceived) restricted access to the political domain and political polarisation can shape the environment in which a violent campaign develops.

Both patrimonial and rational legalistic structures can facilitate the emergence of political violence. The options the political opportunity structure offers inform the choice for the rebels to cross the first threshold of violence. The discussion, so far, has hinted, furthermore, at possible correlations between political opportunity structures and preferences for particular strategies (Clapham 2003, 8). Patrimonial authority structures are linked to a choice for insurgent strategies. When the regime type has a propensity to exert lesser control over territory, insurgency becomes an option in light of its territorial component in the shape of liberated zones. Rational legalistic structures are more closely linked to the strategy of terrorism. When the state is perceived to strictly control territory, terrorism is a more likely option. To what extent rebels are indeed free to choose their strategy will be reserved for further discussion later. Within the boundaries of these developing political opportunity structures, the state and the rebel group will have to operate.

At this point, two short vignettes will be presented to detail the process of the opening and closing of the opportunity structures and the behaviour of rebel groups preceding and during the course of an armed struggle. Firstly, we turn to Argentina in the 1970s and subsequently to Sierra Leone in the 1990s to see where and how social mobilisation took place or failed to materialise.

Vignette 3.1 – The Montoneros: Social Mobilisation and Political Opportunity

Social mobilisation in the case of Argentina in the 1970s occurred along the lines of broad opposition against a repressive, authoritarian state that offered very limited inroads for political participation or change. Argentinian society has had a long tradition of military intervention in politics. Between 1930 and 1976 there were six military coups. In 1955, President Juan Peron was ousted by a military coup, but his ideology of 'Peronism', a mixture of socialism, nationalism and Catholicism with an important role for the labour unions, continued to influence politics. After the ousting of Peron, opposition against the military dictatorship emerged at the grassroots level. Large parts of Argentinian society were excluded from political access and the ideology of Peronism filled the niche (Pion-Berlin 1989).

The military junta, which called itself, slightly ironically perhaps, the Argentinian Revolution (1966–73), attempted to establish an authoritarian regime based on conservative social values with control over social life and cultural expression, including the relations between the sexes. Peronism started to form the backbone of social protest from the 1960s onwards. From the start, however, Peronism was not institutionalised. It idealised the guiding role of the exiled Juan Peron and revolved around his charismatic leadership,

Vignette 3.1 (cont.)

resembling something of a personality cult (Pion-Berlin 1989; Le Blanc 2012).

On 20 May 1969, a joint labour and student protest spiralled out of control when one protestor was killed by police in Cordoba, giving rise to what has become known as the Cordobazo. For two days rebels controlled the city, followed by similar uprisings in other cities around the country. The first response of the military junta was to increase repression. This repression led to further polarisation when the so far uncommitted groups in society started to join the rebellion against the dictatorship. On the brink of collapse, the military decided to hold elections, and in the ballot of 1972, Peron won convincingly (Le Blanc 2012).

Since Peronism was weakly institutionalised, upon assuming power, the fissures that had held the different groups together against a common enemy, the dictatorship, started to appear in the open. On 20 June 1973, Juan Peron returned to Argentina and among the crowd welcoming him at the airport, a firefight broke out. What has become known as the Ezeiza massacre, after the name of the airport, pitted two main factions of Peronism against each other. The right-wing faction sought the route of authoritarianism and the use of established channels of politics. The left-wing faction wanted to pursue social revolution and aimed for a complete overhaul of the political system.

The Montoneros had first appeared as a group in May 1970 with the abduction and revolutionary trial of a former member of the military junta General Arambu. The name Montoneros derives from the word 'monton', meaning 'a lot' and 'fighting in a loosely organised fashion'. The group was part of the left fringe of Peronism (Le Blanc 2012). They had taken the lead in an attempt at mass mobilisation and aimed to pursue extra parliamentary measures which went against the spirit of democracy in order to attain economic and military power with the ambition 'to control the fulfilment of the popular will' (Le Blanc 2012). Their idea was to attain national liberation through a class struggle based on a vanguard that would lead the masses in a revolution. This idea was, not surprisingly, very much inspired by the Cuban Revolution, where some core members, such as Fernando Abal Medina, Norma Arrostito, and Emilio Maza, had received training.

The conflict in Argentina developed as an internal conflict within the Peronist movement, where the social mobilisation which had previously benefited from opposition to a widely despised authoritarian regime now shifted towards different interpretations of Peronism. Juan Peron himself increasingly sided with the parliamentary social democratic interpretation rather than the revolutionary strand within his movement. When Peron passed away a year after the return to democracy in Argentina, the struggle for control over the Peronist movement increased. Under Peron's control, a death squad had been organised: the Argentinian Anti-communist Association (AAA). The AAA was used to intimidate political opposition, but after Peron's demise it was increasingly used to target the revolutionary Peronist left, specifically the Montoneros and their perceived supporters. While before 1974 the Montoneros' violence came largely in the shape of armed propaganda, this symbolic violence made them popular and elicited support for the group. The violence by the death squad, however, pushed the group underground and led to radicalisation. At the same time, they had lost any legal means of expressing political discontent. With political and forceful repression rife, the Montoneros saw violence as the only way out of the situation. It was expected to help mobilisation and serve as a vehicle for politics. Neither worked very well.

Peron's widow, Isabel Peron, who had taken over from her deceased husband, lacked the political acumen to keep the Peronist movement intact and further fragmentation ensued (Pion-Berlin 1989; Le Blanc 2012). On 24 March 1976, the armed forces intervened again and took over power from Isabel Peron. The Process of National Reorganisation (PRN), as the military junta called itself, started a campaign of systematic state terror to eliminate any remnants of political and social opposition. After the loss of the Falklands/Malvinas conflict, this period came to an end in 1983 with the reintroduction of democracy.

In the case of the Argentinian social mobilisation and violent expression, the role of the state and the repression of protest, which was at least initially non-violent, is illuminating. The violent repression of the Cordobazo had a rallying effect on society to make a choice between the dictatorship and the forces of change. The Montoneros appeared in a time of political turmoil. Interestingly, the support for the Montoneros agenda declined the moment the Argentinian political system returned to democracy both at the end of the Argentinian Revolutionary regime and at the end of the Process of National Reorganisation dictatorship. They failed to capitalise on the opposition to these two repressive regimes and failed to build a substantial base in order to provide an alternative in a democratic setting. They were highly effective in rousing popular opposition and justifying their use of force, but as soon as the political tide turned, they suffered the consequences and displayed a glaring lack of political skill to deal with it.

Their main challenge consisted of organising a mass support base that could serve as a shadow state or stepping stone towards political power in an urban setting where detection by the state's repressive forces was a prevalent risk. They could not rely on liberated zones either in the country side or in the city. Their idea of finding cover among a sympathetic population was proven wrong when the leadership decided to meet one day for dinner in a popular pizzeria called 'William Morris' in Buenos Aires. What would later be dubbed the 'Day of the Montoneros', ended with a group of high-ranking militants, who had not taken any security precautions, being betrayed and killed in a fatal shoot-out with police in the restaurant (Le Blanc 2012). Their failure to organise, either as a formal organisation or in a base area, contributed to the ultimate demise of the Montoneros.

The continued confrontation between the Montoneros and the state repressive apparatus led to a decline in the supportive social movement, which did not continue to see the Montoneros actions as politically self-evident, as they had done in the past. The decline in the social movement due to the transition to democracy coincided with the radicalisation of the Montoneros themselves (Pion-Berlin 1989; Le Blanc 2012). The separation between the political opportunity structure and the Montoneros interpretation of it underlines the importance of the link between the rebel group and a supportive social environment for its activities.

Interestingly, in this case, the social mobilisation for the rebels occurred predominantly during the course of violent action against the ruling dictatorship rather than preceding it or even afterwards. The Montoneros' violence was very discriminate and effective in mobilising the population. However, the successful mobilisation was not translated into a structured organisation or institutionalised power the rebels could rely on in changing times. This proved a costly failure the moment the opportunity structure opened up.

Specifically, at times when the political opportunity structure was closing rather than opening, we see a rise in the level or spread of violence, conforming the existing insights from the literature discussed earlier. We are seeking a deeper explanation: how can we understand this? According to Clausewitz, the vigour with which war is fought is dependent on the significance the belligerents attach to it (Clausewitz 1993). In important contributions to the debate about the drivers of insurgency and counter-insurgency wars, Andrew Mack in the 1970s, and Ivan Arreguin-Toft more recently, have pointed to the significance of the weight attached to the perceived issues at stake in armed conflict (Mack 1975; Arreguín-Toft 2005; also Bosi et al. 2014). Mack explained that the disparity in strategic weight can explain strong power defeats in irregular war. When survival is at stake, high costs will be incurred. When war is not about survival but forms a peripheral interest, the stronger side presents a vulnerability that is exploited by the weaker side. Furthermore, Toft stipulates that the weight of the issues might increase because the desired aim or goal of the conflict threatens to be delayed. Duration then becomes a key motivator and past investments need to pay off (Arreguín-Toft 2005).[2] The closing of the political opportunity structure and thereby the raising of the price increases the weight the rebel group attaches to the issues at stake. With repression and resistance experienced by the rebel group, it is logical that the weight of the issues for the rebels is reinforced rather than downplayed. This is a form of escalation. We see this played out in the case of the Montoneros. The organisation opts for violence and acquires significant standing when the opportunity structure closes in 1970. This is the process whereby developments in the political opportunity structure reinforce the saliency of the conflict issue. In Sierra Leone in the 1990s, there is a completely different dynamic at play in the political opportunity structure.

---

[2] This has also been a feature in the wider field of international relations, see for example George and Simons (1994).

Vignette 3.2 – Sierra Leone and the Rebel United Front

In March 1991, the conflict that had broken out two years earlier in Liberia spilled over into Sierra Leone. A small group of fighters crossed the border between Liberia and Sierra Leone and attacked some strongholds in the Kailahun border district. The small group of men hoped to imitate and emulate the success of the National Patriotic Front of Liberia (NPFL), which had managed to oust the president and take control over large parts of the country. The recipe the NPFL promulgated was an attack against a remote region where a lot of ready resentment against the regime would be present (Duyvesteyn 2005). This would be activated by example. The Sierra Leonean War in its current historiography is most notable for excessive cruelty perpetrated by the fighters, which included women and children. This cruelty has been variously explained by concepts such as greed, grievance, war systems, active rivalries, rebel culture, performance and cultures of shame (Richards 1996; Keen 2005; Mitton 2012, 2015; Fujii 2013).

Sierra Leone was a patrimonial state ruled, since independence from the United Kingdom in 1961, by President Siaka Stevens, who had come to power in the late 1960s (Reno 1998). His one-party dictatorship stifled opposition, which was co-opted by the patronage machinery, incarcerated, if not killed. The regime oiled its machinery largely with the income from alluvial diamond mining in the interior of the country. The only way to effect political change in this highly closed system was violent overthrow, attempted several times, also by the population in the diamond districts, who were bereft of the profits of the trade, which were siphoned off to the capital Freetown.

When economic difficulties arose in the 1980s, the legitimacy of the system became further compromised (Aning 2010). Opposition did materialise from among university students and the young urban unemployed. The worsening economic situation functioned as a bridge between these previously highly distinct social groups. There was a convergence of ideas and agreement on the unjust nature of the regime. Ideas met opportunities for action in the shape of training some members of this disparate group received in Liberia, Ghana and Libya.

Violence started on 23 March 1991 in Kailahun district in the heart of the diamond mining area. Social mobilisation did not come off the ground as the Rebel United Front (RUF) had hoped when a group of around 150 men, consisting of both Liberians and Sierra Leonean veterans of the Liberian War, started out. The group included Foday Sankoh, a one-time army corporal in the Sierra Leonean army and later employed as a freelance photographer. He was among those trained in Libya in 1988. He operated with two comrades Rashid Mansaray and Abu Kanu, who were also trained in Gaddafi's Libya. The small group did not know any formal organisation or hierarchy (Abdullah and Muana 1998, 177). However, Sankoh presented himself as spokesperson and became the public face of the RUF.

A well-thought-out ideology was absent, and the aim of getting rid of the president and making a dash for power was the main driving force for the rebels. Later, one of the main mottos of the RUF became 'arms to the people, power to the people, and wealth to the people' (Abdullah and Muana 1998, 191). They did manage to recruit some of the local opposition leaders and eliminate the representatives of the regime. The RUF resorted early on to recruitment of children. The recruitment that occurred was generally driven by 'the reversal of social hierarchy through the possession of the means of violence' (Abdullah and Muana 1998, 178), which meant that the RUF was seen as an opportunity for liberation and individual assertion. The RUF was mainly attractive for the illicit diamond miners and unemployed youngsters, which formed the bulk of the first wave of supporters, rather than the settled urban population in the region (Richards 1996). What alienated most ordinary people was the looting that in particular the Liberians engaged in and which the RUF leaders allowed as a way of repaying them for their support (Abdullah and Muana 1998, 180).

The RUF failed to establish a base area or capture a zone in which they were in control, contrary to the 'prescriptions' of the Liberian War, and were subsequently cornered in a small inhospitable zone on the border. A completely separate development led to what the RUF desired most, the removal of the president; a group of young officers from the regular army of Sierra Leone went to the capital in April 1992 to complain about pay and lack of supplies. Their action ended up in the removal of President Momoh, Stevens' successor, and a military junta was established, the National Provisional Ruling Council (NPRC), led by a junior commander Valentine Strasser. The RUF, however, was suspicious of the NPRC and accused it of being a continuation of the previous regime in a new guise. The NPRC in its turn saw a need to enlarge the army to deal with the RUF violence and started a large recruitment drive, attracting the same kind of recruit as the RUF – the young unemployed from both the city and the countryside with little education and prospect. For the general population the army and the RUF became almost indistinguishable. The term 'soldier-rebel' or 'sobel' was coined to describe the phenomenon (Abdullah and Muana 1998, 182). Without a base area, drying up of recruits and lack of public support, RUF forces retreated further into the dense forest of the Sierra Leone-Liberian border area. There had been no general uprising or significant social mobilisation either for or against the RUF.

Regrouping and rearming by raiding army depots, the RUF managed to emerge somewhat re-invigorated in 1994. They had organised in a more structured fashion and managed to gain a territorial foothold. The number of bush camps grew and were used as launching pads in a hit-and-run struggle against the NPRC government. This development can be explained by the fact that the new government under Strasser could neither take over the previous patrimonial system nor set one up itself. Furthermore, the economy was in tatters and the recruitment drive for the Sierra Leonean armed forces led to 75 per cent of the annual budget to be allocated there, leaving them still underfunded and taking funds away from health care and education for the general population (Reno 1998).

The attacks the RUF carried out, often by only platoon-size groups, were aimed at intimidating government control and scaring the local population.

Civilians in the war zone became familiar with two-phased attacks: first a lightening raid by RUF forces in which weapons, medicines and young people might be carried away, and then a second wave in which defending troops would descend on an area with trucks to carry away heavy items, including zinc roofing materials, abandoned by fleeing civilians (Abdullah and Muana 1998, 184).

A turning point in the war was the appearance of self-defence militias, the Kamajors, organised on a local basis, with superior knowledge of the surroundings and with support from the local population. This was possibly the only and most significant social mobilisation in the course of the conflict. The Kamajors started to protect their villages and attack the RUF. The Kamajors were drafted by the South African private military company, Executive Outcomes (EO), which had arrived in the country in March 1995. Allegedly based on a deal involving mining rights (Reno 1998), the company managed to retrain some parts of the armed forces and assisted in creating a secure environment. The capital was cleared and the mining areas were brought under control by mid-1995. The RUF was forced to sign the Abidjan Peace Accord in November 1996, all but defeated by the highly effective joint operations by EO and the Kamajors.

At the same time, there was an upsurge in the practice of mutilation and torture by the RUF. Individuals were targeted at random, hands were chopped off so people could not vote nor work in the diamond mines. Furthermore, forceful marking of bodies with the RUF acronym carved into the skin was a widespread practice that prevented those individuals from returning home, and assured compliance with the RUF wishes. Commensurate with the theories presented above about the occurrence of indiscriminate violence, these practices took place in a phase of the conflict when rivalry between warring actors was at a high point and alternative means to elicit compliance were absent.

In March 1996, a democratically elected government, as part of the Abidjan Peace Accord, came to power, lead by Ahmed Tejan Kabbah; and the contract with EO was not renewed. This led to an upsurge in violence in the country. A little over a year later, the government was deposed in a military coup, which was supported by the RUF. What they did not manage to achieve themselves by

---

military force was accomplished by latching on to the initiative of the armed forces – control over the capital Freetown. The new regime, the Armed Forces Revolutionary Council, was led by Johnny Paul Koroma. The conflict ended through international mediation and the signing of the Lome Accords in 1999, which gave the vice-presidency to Sankoh and his group control over the diamond mining. Violence, however, did not completely end. An intervention by the United Kingdom terminated the conflict by early 2002.

Social mobilisation for the RUF did not get seriously off the ground in any phase of its existence, but still it managed to operate and survive for a significant period of time. It did not espouse an ideology such as nationalism, ethnicity or social justice, nor was it based on a predatory urge, such as in neighbouring Liberia where the warlords ended up as extremely wealthy individuals. Violence continued, according to some interpretations, because a life outside of the RUF was unimaginable and a continuation of the system of war was a safe fallback position (Keen 1998, 2012; Reno 1998). Furthermore, a rebel culture facilitated its prolongation, as well as opposition against their activities. Social mobilisation did occur on a limited scale in support of the Kamajors, the local self-defence militias. Since they protected the population, close to the areas they were most familiar with, they became very popular and received significant support. The mobilisation occurred thus well after the start of the conflict, within an opportunity structure that seemed consistent in its absence of any substantial role for a centralised state power. This case does not confirm the claims in the existing literature that the political opportunity structure shapes the expression of violence. Notably for its absence and, also importantly, inability, the state had limited shaping power. Moreover, mobilisation was limited and still significant rebel violence emerged.

The two cases bring forward a series of important points. Firstly, most individuals affected by the violence in Argentina and Sierra Leone were forced to make a choice when violence arrived on their doorstep rather than before the outbreak of conflict. Both rebel groups operated from a more or less expressed belief that action would generate an uprising and create a revolutionary situation, rather than using propaganda and indoctrination as a precursor to the first use of violence. This echoes some of the earlier twentieth-century revolutionary war thinking, most notably Focoismo.

Secondly, ideology or ideological concerns played a role in Argentina for the social mobilisation but was largely absent in the case of Sierra Leone. Different interpretations of Peronism were at the heart of the conflict and Peron himself played a rather dubious role, as he could be the most credible arbiter of defining the core of Peronism. In fact, by raising the AAA, he substantially contributed to worsening the situation, and a polarisation of the political landscape took place. Ousting the Sierra Leonean patrimonial elite and a reversal of power relations were ideas behind the conflict in the West African country. Interestingly, these goals were shared by many, namely the accidental coup by Strasser, but it did not prove to be a sufficient rallying call to bring the population together. Subsequent opposition to the RUF, among others by the Kamajors, also led to a measure of political polarisation.

Thirdly, with a very thin ideological content, the role of political entrepreneurs rather than ideology was more pronounced in the Sierra Leonean case. Foday Sankoh and his comrades willingly tried to activate the resentment in the border areas where diamond mining took place and where previous opposition to the regime was strong, and which he hoped to activate as resources for the struggle.

Fourthly, the activation of local grievances to boost mobilisation occurred in both cases. In Argentina, the grassroots organisations that had sprung up as alternative for political opposition channelled the local grievances, such as lack of sanitation, health care and education into a wider movement of political discontent. The fact that the grassroots organisations managed to improve the conditions for the local population won it significant support. The close links between the grassroots and the Montoneros created a broader opposition front. Similarly in Sierra Leone, the fact that the border regions where the resentment was largest were attacked first shows that the idea of linking local grievances to mobilisation potential played a role for the RUF as well.

Fifthly, the role of the political opportunity structure and the divergence and convergence of the rebel activities within that context are illuminating. Initially the Montoneros had made a correct assessment of the opportunity structure and how violent expression could play a role in it. They were highly successful with the attacks against targets that contained a clear political message. However, when the opportunity structure

changed, they found it hard to adapt. In the end, the Montoneros dis-
banded ten days after the return to democracy in 1983. They had failed to
build up a political base and legal representation when circumstances
allowed; they lost all means of entering the opened up political opportunity structure with the advent of democracy and made themselves redun-
dant (Le Blanc 2012). In the case of Sierra Leone, the closed patrimonial
system was one of the reasons for the RUF to use violence. The RUF did
not manage very well to adapt to changes in the opportunity structure
with the changes in regime. Even though attempts were made to introduce
a measure of democracy, the RUF let most opportunities, such as during
the Kabbah regime, pass by. The RUF failed to integrate into the political
system as a way out of violence. There is only one exception: the co-option
of Sankoh in the Koroma regime and assigning him control over diamond
mining. A lack of proper organisation and anticipation for an alternative
future is what reduced both organisations to ultimate irrelevance in the
post-conflict period.

ESCALATION: THE SALIENCY SHIFT

This chapter has critically assessed the roles of the political opportunity
structure, social mobilisation and their development in the initial stages
of conflict. We have used the distinction between regime type and
authority type, patrimonialism and rational legalistic structures, to
identify where the opportunities and constraints lie in the first production of violence. Closed opportunity structures, political entrepreneurs,
local issues of discontent and, most importantly, violent interaction
between the rebel group and the state formed important ingredients
to understand the opportunity structure. The case material of two
highly divergent cases has pointed out that the political opportunity
structure is important to understand conflict escalation. However,
social mobilisation does not necessarily form a precursor to violent
action, nor is it a condition for the occurrence of violence overall. It
is neither necessary nor sufficient to explain the initial aggravation of
armed conflict.

Significant for understanding the development of the conflict escalation
is the violence itself that acts as a catalyst for mobilisation (Kilcullen
2009). The short vignettes in this chapter have illustrated the pathways
of mobilisation as a product of the emergence of violence. Social mobilisation occurs when the political opportunity structure closes, as argued in
the existing literature and illustrated by the Argentinian case.

Furthermore, mobilisation can be initially absent, for example the case of Sierra Leone. The use of violence forces a choice on the population, underlining the prescription by insurgency thinkers, such as Marighella and Guevara, that a vanguard can create a revolution. Furthermore, other studies have already shown that ongoing violence forces a choice on the affected population, especially when there is a rivalry between state and the rebel or between rebels. Indiscriminate violence occurs, when it is unclear who is in control. This forces the population to choose sides (Kalyvas 2006; Metelits 2009). Furthermore, the group mobilisation triggers more mobilisation of other groups, hitherto not mobilised, who disagree with, or feel threatened by the mobilising group (Carter 2017, 40). This appears to be a self-reinforcing process, also visible in the two cases by the emergence of more conflict parties.

Aligning with existing insights but offering an explanation for escalation specifically when the rebel groups meet passive and active resistance or opposition, their perceived conflict issues gain in significance. In the case of Argentina, we witness this in the closing of the opportunity structure by the Argentinian dictatorship and their treatment of protesting students in 1969. In Sierra Leone, the raising of issue salience is visible in the opposition of the Stevens regime but more significantly in the emergence of the National Provisional Ruling Council (NPRC) of Valentine Strasser, who started to compete for the same prize of control over the state. We will take a closer look in the next chapter at the exact form of the contestation and the raising of the issue salience, by zooming in on the repertoires of the state to address the opposing rebels.

The raising of issue salience is an important form of escalation and makes up our first proposition. The importance and weight attached to the perceived issues at stake increase when the opportunity structure to voice discontent or opposition is contested. This insight lends itself to the formulation of a first hypothesis: a saliency threshold is crossed when the weight attached to the issue or perceived issue at stake rises. This can be explained by changes in the opportunity structure in which the rebels and the state operate or the emergence and confrontation with violence. This hypothesis conforms with the second approach to escalation, discussed in Chapter 2, which proposed to see escalation as resulting from the crossing of a threshold of commitment. The participants become more attached to the conflict issue when it is contested.

This chapter has attempted to show that especially the violent interaction itself can contribute to mobilisation and, furthermore, that mobilisation of the population is not always a necessary nor sufficient precondition for the outbreak of violent conflict. A changing perception regarding the issue of contention, a shift in conflict saliency is the first causal proposition brought forward in this chapter. We will now shift attention to the subsequent stages of violence in state-rebel confrontations, where we will see more variations of the saliency threshold and provide more detail.

4

Political Will

Provocation and Concession

At the start of an armed challenge, for instance in the shape of a bomb attack or skirmishes in the countryside, the state has largely four options available (Berry 1987; Neumann and Smith 2005). First is a moderate response, a prevalent course of action in many rational legalistic regimes (Berry 1987). The state responds by repression of the armed challenges, and at the same time, it tries to take seriously the underlying grievances. Second, the state can respond with overwhelming and outright force. This occurs in all types of political regimes, provided the state has the capacity to respond forcefully. A third course of action is to abstain from a violent response and place emphasis solely on non-violent measures. The state refuses to heed calls for stringent and repressive countermeasures and can, for example, opt for negotiation with the rebels, directly or indirectly and offer concessions. A fourth course of action would be abstaining from responding all together. There are examples of state inaction actually leading to escalation of rebel violence, which will be addressed later.

This chapter will take a closer look at these response options. We will start with a discussion of the use of force, either moderate or outright, for both the state as well as the rebel group, as this turns out to be a very common course of action. In particular, the provocation mechanism will be illustrated by two case examples: the Moro National Liberation Front in the Philippines and the Provisional IRA and the Northern Ireland conflict. Subsequently the chapter will focus on concessions and negotiations and their link to the aggravation of conflict and finally the use of the non-response option. The chapter will bring forward not only that the state may itself initially provoke the rebel group to pursue violence. Paradoxically, both coercive and compliant state responses are related to more violence. State actions in whichever shape can contribute to reinforcing the salience of the issues of contention. This chapter will present a second variation of the issue saliency threshold directly caused by state countermeasures. This chapter compliments the previous one, which more emphasised the phenomenal or structural perspective. The present chapter presents arguments with a focus on the actor and agency perspective.

PROVOCATION AND REPRESSION[1]

The Rebel Group

It is both a central idea of 'propaganda by deed' practitioners and a consistent finding of empirical investigation by scholars that the conduct of a violent campaign by rebels is very often dependent on the counter-measures taken against it (Alimi et al. 2012, 2015; Della Porta 2013; Bosi et al. 2014; Carter 2016; Piazza 2017). Very few rebels are initially powerful enough to deal one decisive blow to, or to conventionally attack and defeat, the state to realise their aims. There are interesting theoretical prescriptions on how to rely on provoking the state into overreacting in order to play into the cards of the rebel group (Petersen 2011). They focus to a large extent on the state giving in to the mechanism of provocation (Fromkin 1975).[2] By attacking a weakness of the opponent, for example, its civilians, its infrastructure or its leadership, the militants aim to trigger the state into acting. They benefit when the state, out of its own doing, starts to show its 'repressive side', which confirms them in their claims that the state is illegitimate and needs to be undermined and replaced.

Some notable insurgency thinkers, such as Carlos Marighella and Franz Fanon, formulated as a central prescription for a successful insurgency strategy the provocation by an avant-garde of an overreaction by the state to mobilise the population (Marighella 1974; Fanon 2004). In order to achieve provocation, the media is indispensable. Typically, the media give more attention to the spectacular and extreme and to those events that directly touch a large number of people (Clauset, Young, and Gleditsch 2007, 59). A provocation campaign craves media attention. The premise here is that the rebel campaign is closely linked, if not

---

[1] This section is based on Duyvesteyn (2014).

[2] See also discussion in Angstrom and Petersson (2019) about provocation as part of escalation processes in interstate conflict.

largely dependent on the activities of others, including the state and the media. Indeed, '[t]he coupling of significant constraints on the use of force with incentives to respond observably to threats leads democracies to be especially prone to a strategy of provocation' (Carter 2016, 137).

The State

Despite the theoretical prescriptions of provoking an overreaction by the state, there are many examples of the state more or less independently using violence first. Several studies point out that a provocative tendency is present in state behaviour towards potential rebels (Kalyvas 2006; Morgan et al. 2008, 118–119; Lyall 2009, 331). In a straightforward fashion: when the state has an important role in social interaction, it influences the development and outcome of this interaction. Based on a mathematical analysis, '[t]he regime ... turns out to be the key factor that influences opposition activity because it alters the cost of an opponent's tactics' (Lichbach 1987, 289). Others have also argued that the response of the government is crucial to understand terrorist strategies (Fromkin 1975; Crenshaw 1991; Zirakzadeh 2002; Siqueira and Sandler 2006).

The provocation mechanism works when the state, through its violent responses to non-violent protest, triggers violence from the rebel group. When the state feels severely challenged by the presence of strong opposition groups, it can decide to use force first. There are many examples showing that the start of violent interaction was triggered by violent action by the state. In the case of Argentina, discussed in Chapter 3, we saw that violence first emerged after the killing of a protestor by the police. There are many other examples; we will highlight just three: the African National Congress (ANC), Euskadi Ta Askatasuna (ETA) and the Irish Republican Army (IRA). Nelson Mandela argued that the South African government's attitude and response to ANC protest formed an important cause for violent action: 'the fact that the government had met non-violence by force and had barred all channels of peaceful protest [had] left African nationalists with no choice but to embark on violent forms of political struggle' (Guelke 1995, 173). In the case of the Basque ETA movement, only '[a]fter a popular ETA activist was killed by the police in 1968, ETA claimed its first victims by assassinating an inspector of Policia Nacional and a Guardia Civil' [sic] (Barros 2003, 402). Also for the case of the IRA, it has been suggested that state activity drove the violence in the 1970s (White 1989; Asal et al. 2015). For example, one recruit Tommy Gorman, who joined the IRA in 1970 described the activities of the British army as a crucial recruitment mechanism: 'We were creating this idea that the British state is not your friend ... and at every twist in the road they were compounding what we were saying, they were doing what they were saying, fulfilling all the propaganda ... the British Army, the British government, were our best recruiting agents' (Cited in: English 2005, 122; see also White 1989). An officer of the 'Green Jackets' also described the counterproductive effects of British actions:

> Yet is was these widespread imprecise operations that so strongly alienated the section of the population that were not involved with the terrorists but were inevitably treated as though they were. Nothing could have been more calculated to drive the non-committed part of the population into the arms of the terrorists from a sense of personal outrage and humiliation. (Evelegh 1978, 29)

The IRA example will be further elaborated shortly. An anthropological study looking into reasons for participation in violence, based on field work in the El Salvadoran civil war, has also unearthed this provocation mechanism (Wood 2003). Provocation compounds the conflict issues. Adam Roberts has called the use of violence bringing about escalation and countermeasures, the rebel equivalents of blitzkrieg and war of attrition (Roberts 2005). There are some statistical findings that rebels tend to engage in war as a reactive enterprise, for example as a result of state provocation, rather than a proactive undertaking (Katagiri 2013). Furthermore, it has been claimed the targeting of military instead of civilian goals is more likely to trigger the provocation mechanism (Carter 2016).

This mechanism will be further illustrated through the vignettes provided later in the chapter. The provocation mechanism might be more important for those rebels who operate from a starting position of limited power, both in political will and capability. The provocation by the state can both reinforce the political will to resist (raise the conflict saliency) and augment the capability to do so via increased opportunities for recruitment and material input. This seems to be, in particular, the case for rebel groups using terrorism as strategy of choice. The effectiveness of the state using repression against groups using terrorism cannot, statistically, be correlated to a pacifying effect (Piazza 2017). By raising the cost of engaging in terrorism via repression, the activity is not curbed. Moreover, when the rebel group has strong organisational cohesion and significant support, repression is even less likely to work (Matesan 2018). These factors will be further dissected subsequently.

The provocation mechanism works in close conjunction with the countermeasure imperative. It is the commonly observable chain of events after an attack against unarmed and unwitting targets. A public outcry occurs, to which political decision-makers are forced to respond. A non-response is often not an option in terms of political capital and electoral consequences at least in most rational legalistic systems. James Fearon has called this 'audience costs' in the context of international crises (Fearon 1994; Pierskalla 2010). He has argued that violence is more likely in states where the audience costs for backing off in a crisis are high.[3] Even though the state 'may be aware that crackdowns are counterproductive, in the sense of increasing mobilization ... [it] may have no other reasonable option for increasing security' (Bueno de Mesquita and Dickson 2007, 377). To be seen to be weak is deemed a sign of a political lack of strength, both in patrimonial and rational legalistic political systems. Therefore, there is strong pressure, if the capacity is present, to respond forcefully.

Repression, the use of force, incarceration and criminal prosecution are just a few of the instruments, which can be used by the state as countermeasures. The way the state behaves and responds has far-reaching consequences for the further development of the conflict. A notable finding in the discussion about these interaction processes is that there is evidence of congruence in state responses and militant counteraction. In separate studies, it has been found that when harsh measures are taken, militants are more likely to use violence. Confrontation and repression elicit a like-minded response (Lichbach 1987; Della Porta 1995b; Vinci 2008; Cf. Lyall 2009, 331). Furthermore, state responses that alternate between extremely severe repression and leniency also encounter more violence (Crenshaw 1983a). Such inconsistency forms a problem: 'semi-repressive state reactions often contribute to the evolution from political mobilization to terrorism because of their inconsistent mix of repression and reform' (Richardson 2006, 203; Eubank and Weinberg 1994).

To confirm the working of the provocation trap and the countermeasure imperative, we need to look for further evidence of a preference for harsher policy responses. This does indeed find confirmation (Malvesti 2003; Heiberg, O'Leary, and Tirman 2007, 499). Furthermore, in a large

---

[3] There has been a discussion in the journal *Security Studies* about the merits of the audience cost concept and its relevance. Some scholars doubt the validity of both Levy (2012) and Schultz (2012).

cross-case comparison, a team of researchers has concluded that 'in the early phases of a conflict ... repression nearly always leads to an escalation in violence' (Heiberg, O'Leary, and Tirman 2007, 411). Finally, another large-scale study concludes that when the state adopts a repressive approach 'escalation ... usually works to the irregular adversary's advantage' (Morgan et al. 2008, 154; see also discussion in Eastin and Gade 2016). In short, state actions hold important, if not crucial, clues to the first development of violent interaction and conflict escalation.

We will now take a closer look at two specific examples to detail the provocation–repression mechanism. The first case focuses on the Philippines. The initial use of violence by the rebel group was preceded by a highly provocative measure by the government in the 1970s. This will be followed by a short case of the IRA and the working of the provocation–repression mechanism in the first stages of the violence there.

Vignette 4.1 – The Moro National Liberation Front (MNLF) and the Imposition of Martial Law in the Philippines

The conflict in the Philippines occurred in the context of a closed political opportunity structure based on the authoritarian rule of Ferdinand Marcos. In contrast to the majority Christian population of the Philippines, the island of Mindanao in the south of the Philippines contained a large Muslim population. Not only religious fissures marked Mindanao and its surrounding area of the Sulu islands but also clan and class divisions played a role. The Muslim population of Mindanao were called Moros, a word used by the former Spanish colonisers. The Moros constituted a tribal society. The three largest tribes were the Tausūg, the Maguindanao and the Maranao. The Muslim communities were organised according to a structure of sultans and datus, the traditional rulers within the communities. On top of the clan divisions there were social distinctions between the elite and lower social strata of mostly landless peasants working as wage labourers in the large plantations, which formed a source of friction.

The idea of secession of Mindanao because of its unique Islamic identity in the Philippine archipelago surfaced in the 1960s. In 1963, just off the end of the Sulu islands, the British protectorates Sarawak and Sabah gained independence, becoming part of Malaysia. In the past Sabah had been part of the Sultanate of Sulu aided by the government in Manila, an attempt was made to gain control of Sabah. The plan was to recruit and train a local Mindanao force in secret and provoke and destabilise Sabah. The plan was aborted prematurely when a mutiny broke out ending in the group's members being killed in what has become known as the Jabidah massacre. The Philippine government manipulating parts of the local population to settle a territorial claim did not go down well and created substantial animosity towards Manila (Reed 2013, 283–284).

A group of young Muslims, who had been educated outside of the region in Manila and Cairo, forming a new and ambitious generation, became preoccupied with a Muslim awakening in Mindanao. They saw an opportunity to receive training in newly independent Malaysia. While abroad, these young men set up the Mindanao National Liberation Front. On their return the group settled in the western part of Mindanao and established a base in the Cotabato and Lanao regions. Some initial skirmishes in 1971 were mostly between Muslim and Christian elite groups contesting power in an area of mixed religious allegiance. Violence flared up in the run up to the local elections in 1972 but remained largely contained and targeted against opposing political candidates. Subsequently, communal clashes occurred, which in many cases were seen as attempts by the local population to intimidate opponents and defend themselves. With the local elections over, in which Christian candidates were successful in increasing local representation, some semblance of calm returned to the region.

However, in Manila, things started to heat up on the eve of national elections due in November 1974. Two months before the elections, in late September, President Marcos declared martial law applicable to the whole of the Philippines. Even though events in Mindanao were given as a reason, the level of local violence had, by the end of 1974, substantially reduced. The declaration of martial law proved to be the fuse that set the tinderbox alight: the 'imposition of martial law was, in fact, the proximate cause, not the consequence, of an armed Muslim insurgency against the Philippine state, and it led to an unprecedented level of violence and disruption in Cotabato and all of Muslim Mindanao' (Reed 2013, 298; McKenna 1998). One of the measures under martial law

---

was the collection of private weapons from among the population. Furthermore, martial law curbed political activity. The Moros strongly felt that the only option available was armed opposition against the government. The conflict escalated here as a result of the declaration of martial law, which was instigated by the government (Reed 2013, 299). Only after the imposition of martial law, the MNLF rose to prominence as the predominant organisation representing the secessionist agenda. Even though they had been making preparations for conflict in Mindanao, the developments initiated by Manila sped up their plans.

We see here that the authoritarian Marcos regime played a crucial role in the outbreak and initial escalation of the conflict in Mindanao. The political opportunity structure closed with the imposition of martial law and the action of the state specifically provoked the rebel group to cross the threshold of violence. Provocation also played a role in the development of the armed struggle of the Provisional IRA in Northern Ireland. Here we also see that the role the state adopted towards the conflict was of key importance to understand its further development.

Vignette 4.2 – Northern Ireland: Sending in the Army

The violence in Northern Ireland, starting in the late 1960s and leading to a period of violence lasting for over thirty years, demonstrates the power of the provocation mechanism. While the roots of the problems in Northern Ireland go back centuries, the violence starting in 1968, which pitted the Catholic and Protestant communities against each other, can be clearly linked to the Irish civil rights movement. People started taking to the streets to protest against the disadvantaged position of the Catholic population in regard to employment, housing and representation in Northern Ireland's institutions (Kennedy-Pipe 1997; Moloney 2007; Thornton 2007, 75).

The first state response was employing the Protestant-dominated Royal Ulster Constabulary (RUC) to halt and prevent communal clashes. This triggered even more violence from among the Catholic population. The latter perceived the RUC as biased, with instances where the RUC actively assisted in attacks by Protestant mobs on protesting Catholic civilians (Kennedy-Pipe 1997; Moloney 2007). The provincial government, dominated again by Protestants, decided to deal more forcefully with the rioting and called for the help of the armed forces in 1969. Initially the army was welcomed by both communities, the Catholics perceiving them to be less tainted and perhaps the third-party they had been hoping could safeguard their security. However, the army started to operate based on the perception that the Catholic community was the main source of violence, to the relative neglect of the Protestant groups as fermenting the 'Troubles'. This led to the loss of the perceived status of the armed forces as an impartial force in the conflict. This position could not be regained.

While initially the main task was policing, the Conservative government in London from 1970 onwards decided on a military defeat of the Irish Republican Army (Coogan 2002). Hopes of quick defeat were short-lived; the army made several crucial mistakes, which ended up helping the recruitment for the Irish Republican Army and substantially raised the level of violence in the province (Neumann 2003; Thornton 2007; Dickson 2009, 485–486). In particular the confrontation on 30 January 1972, which has become known as Bloody Sunday, had counterproductive effects. On that Sunday, a march by Catholic protesters ended in police shooting dead twenty-six people, five of whom were shot in the back.

A lack of overall political direction and a carefully thought out strategy to deal with the problems of Northern Ireland were missing from the beginning. The army was sent to Northern Ireland one year after the civil rights marches had started leading to violence on the streets. The move from Westminster to deploy the army seemed a swift and decisive measure. What was lacking was, first, a clear and coherent understanding of the underlying drivers of the provocations. No political goals were formulated, nor guidance provided, on the end state to be achieved. The army took over policing roles from the RUC together with the local reserve police force, also known as the B-specials, who were both distrusted and despised by the Catholic community. Secondly, unity of command was a problem. The army in fact had to report to three political masters: not only did it fall under the Ministry of Defence, because of its policing duties, it had to report to the Home Office and because of its deployment in Northern Ireland, also to the Parliament at Stormont (Neumann 2003; Thornton 2007, 76–77).

Left to its own devices, the British army in Northern Ireland made several errors that led to a substantial aggravation of violence in the early 1970s (Kennedy-Pipe 1997; Neumann 2003). The combination of being seen to be a partial force and doing little about Protestant violence were very costly mistakes. It substantially reinforced the opposition against British rule and aided in recruitment for the IRA. Sending in the army led to a situation where road blocks, armed patrolling, surveillance and personal checks became a fact of daily life. They restricted the freedom of movement and confronted the population with a wealth of curbing and repressive measures (Hoffman and Morrison-Taw 2000, 45–46; Donohue 2008). Internment without trial and direct rule from London did not aid in de-escalating the violence. Stringent countermeasures led to a very significant increase in violence.

In both cases we see that the state used repressive measures with the aim of pre-empting significant violence. Martial law in the Philippines was intended to both prevent an outbreak of war and help Ferdinand Marcos fortify his reputation as strong ruler before the elections. By sending the army to Northern Ireland, it was hoped that further violence could be prevented. The political opportunity structure in Northern Ireland closed further, and the political domain became polarised. This leads us to conclude that the role and response of the state to violence holds the key to further understand the development of the rebel campaigns (Carter 2017). In both cases, it confirmed the rebel groups and their supporters and potential supporters in their belief that the state was illegitimate, non-representative and would only listen to the language of force. As outlined in the introduction to this chapter, after the initial outbreak of violence, the state has several options to respond; a course of action we will now turn to is the outright use of overwhelming force. The more conciliatory approach and the non-response trajectory will be discussed subsequently.

OVERWHELMING FORCE

The Rebel Group

Rebel groups can and have used overwhelming force to gain the upper hand in their confrontation with the state. Several notable rebel groups have in the past managed to attain the third phase of Mao's Revolutionary People's War and defeated their opponent: the Indochina war fought by General Giap against French colonial occupation, with the defeat of French colonial forces at the battle of Dien Bien Phu in 1954; the war of independence in Guinea-Bissau in the 1970s, where the African Party for the Independence of Guinea and Cape Verde (PAIGC) insurgents led by Amílcar Cabral at its peak controlled almost two-thirds of Portuguese Guinea (Katagiri 2013). Another notable example forms the Liberation Tigers of Tamil Elam (LTTE), which will be detailed in Chapter 5, which at its peak controlled substantial territory in the Jaffna peninsula. Later we will focus in more detail on the strategic choices and approaches of rebel groups. Here it suffices to conclude that overwhelming force has been witnessed in the past but forms an exception. This cannot be said of its use by the state.

The State

Regardless of what strategy the rebel group has adopted, several notable thinkers have put forward arguments for the use of overwhelming force against rebel groups. Several scholars have put forward that repressive force, collective punishment and targeted killings work against rebels (Peters 2004; Van Creveld 2006; Luttwak 2007). It should be noted that overwhelming force and repression are by no means the exclusive domain of authoritarian states or closed political regimes (Ucko 2015). Appearances notwithstanding, the use of this approach is independent of regime type. Both rational legalistic and patrimonial regimes have in the past used this route to quell rebel violence (Connable and Libicki 2010; Ucko 2015). It tends to be a popular approach because it conforms with the expectations of many: 'military combat requires no concessions, grants no legitimacy, and is consistent with the norm of punishing illegal violence' (Pruitt 2006, 373).

Overwhelming force has been argued to work towards reducing the effectiveness of rebel operations, the creation of disaccord between the rebels and the population and the demonstration of shortcomings in rebel claims; 'state violence reveals that the insurgency cannot credibly protect the population nor respond in kind, feeding the perception that the insurgency is both likely to lose and is endangering the locals without bringing tangible benefits' (Lyall 2009, 331). Following this logic, it would mean that the population is expected to automatically support the state.

For fighting a rebel group using terrorism, generally two approaches have been distinguished: the war model and the criminal justice model (Pedahzur 2009). The war model has been adopted, for example, in the case against Al Qaeda and the 'War on Terror'. The criminal justice model followed in many cases of largely domestic terrorism (Ganor 2005; Weinberg 2008, 180). The use of the military can take different forms. In the case of Al Qaeda, a war has been fought in Afghanistan to combat terrorism and punish those who harboured terrorists. Also, the armed forces can carry out a campaign of targeted killing and take out those individuals who have crucial leadership positions in rebel organisations (Byman 2006; Carvin 2012). This issue will be further addressed in Chapter 7. While the death of Osama bin Laden in 2011 has been lauded as a success, it has not signalled the end of the organisation. The war in Afghanistan has turned into the longest American armed engagement.

In contrast to the discussion about rebel groups using terrorism and the effectiveness of overwhelming force, the latter has for a long time been discounted in the discussion about insurgents. When rebel groups use a strategy of insurgency against the state, a hearts and minds approach has dominated as a prescription to the debate (Thompson 1966; Petraeus and Amos 2006, 282). While part of an historical pattern (Hack 2009), using overwhelming force in fighting an insurgency has, recently, started to receive more attention. A few contributions have investigated specifically the effectiveness of repression and overwhelming force (Josua and Edel 2015; Pampinella 2015; Ucko 2015; Byman 2016). Some scholars have found evidence that coercion and repressive force have been effective in the past against insurgents in particular, but not against terrorists. Insurgents also have, in several cases, been defeated by force (Clancy and Crossett 2007, 91). This, again, seems to go directly against the emphasis on hearts and minds approaches in the currently dominant counter-insurgency discourse. There are significant problems, both morally and ethically, with the adoption of measures of overwhelming force.

When it comes to the overall evaluation of these practices, the record is decidedly mixed (Mandel 2015). Do forceful measures help to curb violence or resolve conflict (Brophy-Baermann and Conybeare 1994; Byman 2006)? Gil Merom, in a study into counter-insurgency, raises the argument that democracies are inherently weak in facing rebel groups because the violence that, he deems, is required to combat the phenomenon is politically unacceptable (Merom 2003; Mandel 2015).

On the one hand, there are examples of states using outright repressive force, which have been successful in defeating rebels. The Russian approach in Chechnya is an example of an almost exclusive reliance on an all-out repression and has defeated, to date, the Chechen resistance (Lyall 2009, 331; Zhukov 2012; Mandel 2015).[4] In Chechnya, overwhelming and repressive force has been argued to work: 'Whereas selective counterinsurgency tactics are more successful than indiscriminate force in suppressing nationalist violence, they have little to no effect on Islamist violence' (Toft and Zhukov 2015, 236). Specifically looking at its effectiveness, 'indiscriminate violence can have suppressive effects [which] helps explain the otherwise puzzling persistence of these practices among the world's militaries' (Lyall 2009, 357). In an overview article, however, it is not a unidirectional effect: 'violence, repression, and the non-mediation of grievances do not necessarily escalate the insurgency, at least not in the short term' (Ucko 2015, 32).

On the other hand, scholars have contested these effectiveness claims. Some find, based on case studies, that harsh repression always elicits further violence and thus forms a very powerful escalatory mechanism in civil conflict (Kalyvas 2004a; Hultquist 2015). Based on a mathematical model, others have contributed that repression is a counterproductive method to de-escalate violence (Toft and Zhukov 2012).

In order to crack the puzzle why repression sometimes works and other times proves ineffective, the specific context in which it is used deserves more attention. Some scholars have pointed out that in those cases where terrorists were successful in attaining their stated political goals, there was a significant measure of public support (Charters 1994, 227; Cronin 2006; Paul 2010; Wood 2010; Schuurman 2013). Also, when the state political system that instituted particular measures against rebels was perceived as legitimate and representative, the room to manoeuvre seemed to be relatively larger (Wood 2010). Alternatively, when public support and legitimacy were lacking, countermeasures of whatever nature seem to be much harder to institute. This insight will be further developed in Chapter 8.

---

[4] This case will be further discussed in Chapter 9.

Could alternative courses of action be envisioned? Out of the courses of action outlined at the start of the chapter, in most contrast to overwhelming force, are the ideas of negotiation and concession. What insights could be gained from these debates?

NEGOTIATION AND CONCESSION

The Rebel Group

Presuming that underlying issues of contention cause the continuation of conflict, it would seem logical to take a closer look at negotiation. We know, so far, that there is a statistical correlation between regime type and the propensity to engage in negotiation. Democracies, in general, are more inclined to seek negotiation compared to authoritarian regimes (Walter 2002, 10–11). In a study into the experiences of negotiating with rebels, a willingness to join the negotiating table has not been clearly linked to a desire to pursue peace (Duyvesteyn and Schuurman 2011). Negotiations have often been engaged in for the paradoxical reasons of gaining breathing space, to re-group and re-arm, for a new round of fighting, or to gain legitimacy. Furthermore, negotiations can cause splits within rebel groups and lead to elevated levels of violence caused by hardliners. The LTTE in Sri Lanka, for example, has consistently used ceasefires as breathing space to re-arm and re-group rather than as a mechanism for peace or to attain political gain (Bloom 2003, 72). Also, M-19 in Colombia, discussed in Chapter 8, used a lull in fighting to re-group. Most problematic is the repeated finding in the literature that negotiated settlements, as outcomes of these processes, are very brittle and a majority of conflicts that ended via negotiations resumed within a couple of years (Licklider 1995; Toft 2006, 52; Walter 2015). There are examples, of course, of successful negotiations and they continue to be seen as one of the important ways out of terrorism (Cronin 2009). Negotiations themselves are not necessarily escalatory or de-escalatory. The mechanism by which negotiations do directly contribute to elevated levels of violence is through the creation of spoilers. This mechanism will be further described in Chapter 7 when we discuss group and individual dynamics.

In general, rebels using terrorism are not very likely to accept concessions; a finding in the terrorism literature is that rebels using terrorism are not likely to compromise even though a strategic logic would consider this the most logical course of action (Abrahms 2008, 87). There is no satisfactory answer to this problem apart from the high exit costs out of the struggle for the terrorists even after accepting concessions. Conversely, the state for its part is more likely to make concessions when the rebel group is strong. Likely because of a belief in the ability of strong rebels to command compliance from its supporters and to adhere to the agreement (Cunningham, Gleditsch, and Salehyan 2009, 578). Or, alternatively, this can be explained by fear that the rebel group will become stronger and demand more at a later stage. Later we will see an example of the Canadian Front de Libération de Quebec stepping up its campaign after the government offered concessions.

Two explanations are offered for the occurrence of violence after concessions: concessions are accepted by moderates, leaving the radicals in need to make their mark and control the remnants of the organisation (Ross and Gurr 1989; Bueno de Mesquita 2005); a second explanation is that governments can suffer from credible commitment problems when making concessions (Walter 1997, 2002; Fearon 1998; Crenshaw 2000). There is uncertainty whether the state will stick to its promises and the rebel group has reasons to distrust its counterpart. This crisis of confidence in government action can possibly be remedied by enlisting the help of those moderates or third parties (Walter 2002) which have accepted the government concessions (Bueno de Mesquita 2005).

The State

Several experts have suggested that instead of a focus on the violent effects of rebel activity, attention for its political causes would be more productive (Crelinsten and Schmid 1993; Alexander 2002). Dialogue, negotiations and concessions would form logical avenues to pursue. Here, however, we also find largely contradictory evidence as to the wisdom of such a course of action.

There is a very vocal school not only of politicians but also of scholars who strongly advise against talking to terrorists because it could act not only as a conduit for recognition and legitimacy but it could also be seen as encouragement for violent means (Wilkinson 1986). In this perspective, violence is awarded with a seat at the negotiating table.

Looking at the state of the art, assessments of the effectiveness of negotiations and state concessions are highly divergent. Firstly, some scholars claim no positive correlation exists between negotiations, concessions and increases in violence (Crenshaw 1983a, 1991): 'A widely accepted if unproven "lesson" of terrorism is that granting terrorist demands encourages more terrorism' (Crenshaw 1983a, 11). Secondly, based on the case of Israel, there is evidence that concessions are linked to an actual decrease in violence (Dugan and Chenoweth 2012).

Thirdly, others claim that there is a more or less consistent evidence of a clear increase of the level of terrorist violence, after concessions are made by governments under attack (Hewitt 1984; Wilkinson 2000). Concessions can encourage rebels to demand more or become more violent. Experts point to several examples, among others to the Action Directe in France. A partial amnesty by President François Mitterand in 1981 led to a hunger strike by those not affected by the pardon and an increase of severe attacks by those released. 'Some members of Action Directe, particularly the two "historic leaders" returned to the underground and initiated a strategy of political assassinations, whereas before the group had restricted itself to relatively harmless bombings' (Crenshaw 1991, 83).

Fourthly, yet others point out that the evidence goes both ways. Dealing with underlying grievances by ways of concessions might be highly contingent. Richard Art and Louise Richardson conclude that 'Turkey and France made no efforts to deal with underlying factors, yet the two governments were successful' in curbing violence (Art and Richardson 2007, 576).

Concessions can be expected to work in a situation where a resumption of violence is unattractive. These conditions have been suggested to relate to the negotiating position of the rebel group. As already discussed in Chapter 2, William Zartman has identified a 'mutually hurting stalemate' as the primary enabling condition for negotiations to become feasible (Zartman 1989). There are indications that, in particular, negotiation from a position of strength is more likely to be successful than when the state or the rebel group is on the losing end. Statistical analyses have found that 'terrorist conflicts in which concessions have been made are more violent but shorter' (Bueno de Mesquita 2005, 171).

One of the ways in which rebel violence has ended in the past is through a transformation of the organisation into a political party and integration into the existing political structure (Ross and Gurr 1989; Cronin 2009). Not only the IRA but also the ANC and the Palestinian Liberation Organization (PLO) have undergone this transformation process. What these cases have in common is the specific nature of the contests: decolonisation or nationalist struggles (Wilkinson 1987, 460; Sederberg 1990, 277; Hoffman 1998; Laqueur 2001; Cronin 2009).

What is important for this study is that when political concessions, both as a bargaining tool and a conflict resolution measure, are made, this can lead to both more and less violence. Violence can materialise as a result of choice by hardliners in the rebel group, the spoiler problem, or as a result of credible commitment problems by the state. The likelihood of negotiations taking place and leading to concessions has been linked to the positions of relative strength of the belligerents. The last course of action the state and the rebel group can enact, as put forward in the introduction of this chapter, is not responding and doing nothing.

THE NON-RESPONSE OPTION

The Rebel Group

Not all social movements cross the threshold of violence. Even in cases of prior violence by the state against opposition, there are non-state actors refraining from the use of force, either by choice or resulting from a lack of capabilities. In a comparative study, looking at the outcomes of violent rebel campaigns as compared to the outcomes of non-violent resistance to attain political change, the record for violent resistance is not very good. Non-violence has a higher pay-off regarding the attainment of strategic aims. Non-violent campaigns have in the past been indeed twice as likely to succeed in attaining political change compared to violent campaigns (Chenoweth and Stephan 2011).

The State

The non-response option does not feature prominently in any discussion about effective state countermeasures when confronted with terrorist or insurgency groups (Mueller 2005). However, it is a clear alternative and there are several examples of a non-response: after the attack in 1983 of the Marine barracks in Lebanon, the World Trade Center bombing in 1993, the Oklahoma City bombing in 1995, the Khobar Towers bombing in 1996, and the USS Cole suicide attack in 2000. These examples illustrate that the non-response option might, in fact, occur more frequently than recognised. It is obviously among the least desired effects from the perspective of the rebel group.

The non-response option could be interpreted by the rebel group as a sign of weakness, and therefore elicit escalation. A case can be made that the World Trade Center bombing can be linked to 9/11, as can the Khobar Towers and USS Cole attacks. An alternative reasoning would focus on the fact that indeed no reprisals were taken and subsequent violence diminished, for example the Oklahoma bombing in 1995.[5] A clear-cut

---

[5] Monitors of right-wing extremism have, however, noted that the activities and recruitment in these circles in the United States have substantially increased in the period after the Oklahoma bombing (Southern Poverty Law Center Unknown).

absence of violence after state inaction, however, cannot be observed. John Mueller has argued that for the state, the 'non-response' option should be more seriously considered: 'experience suggests that politicians can often successfully ride out this demand [for forceful action] after the obligatory (and inexpensive) expressions of outrage are issued' (Mueller 2005, 501). For the state, there is to date too little empirical evidence to further substantiate this discussion. The non-response, similar to negotiation and concession, can thus both lead to more and to less violence and the link is therefore not linear.

THIRD-PARTY INTERVENTION

In the discussion of agency in the processes of escalation, a treatment of the role of outside forces is warranted. There is an increasing trend over the course of the last century for foreign intervention in ongoing civil wars (Grauer and Tierney 2017). Today, there are very few active rebel groups that do not receive some form of foreign aid. There is a large body of literature devoted to dissecting the role of third parties. Some of it focuses on the reasons for meddling in the affairs of others, some of it looks at the practices and yet others study their role as mediators and facilitators in conflict transformation and resolution. The most important outside actors in ongoing civil wars are states (Byman et al. 2001; San Akca 2009; Connable and Libicki 2010; Byman 2013). To a lesser extent, organisations among diaspora populations and other rebel groups intervene in ongoing armed conflicts. The last group of non-state actors is increasingly active as intervenors (Grauer and Tierney 2017; Moghadam and Wyss 2020).

Motivations to support or work with rebels may vary widely from increasing regional and local influence, destabilising neighbouring states to keep them weak, revenge, promoting regime change, national security, prestige, support to ethnic and religious brethren, irredentism, ideological affinity and opportunity to obtain natural resources (Byman et al. 2001). These intentions seem as diverse as the reasons offered in the causes of conflict debate.

Third parties do not necessarily act in an impartial manner. Many studies that focus on third-party intervention are often premised on the belief that the good offices of these parties can be effective in containing and resolving armed conflicts (Walter 2002; Kydd 2003; Fortna 2004). However, there are a few notable studies that question these premises and point to escalatory tendencies in third-party intervention (Betts 1994;

Regan and Aydin 2006; Duyvesteyn 2009). Even interventions that are carried out under the banner of an impartial international organisation, such as the United Nations, tend to be strongly biased towards the state (Gent 2008). This bias can, and does, trigger more and stronger violence from the other parties involved in the conflict.

While this study does not directly aim to address the conflict dynamics of third-party involvement, its potential escalatory role warrants attention. During the period of the Cold War, there were largely two sets of arguments that supported the view that outside states could, in fact, be pushed into conflicts in order to secure their direct or indirect interests. Conversely, pull factors played a role as well, with the state or rebels having an interest in soliciting outside support for their cause (Latham 2010). For rebels, biased third states involving themselves in the conflict could provide political, financial, military and/or logistical support, which could all facilitate the rebel group. The large and profound impact of foreign intervention on rebel conflict has been noted earlier: 'foreign assistance – which often significantly bolsters insurgent capabilities- increases violence' (Wood 2010, 612; Lockyer 2011; Wood, Kathman, and Gent 2012). Humanitarian aid provision as a specific form of inter- vention directly influences patterns of violence (Wood and Molfino 2016). Intervention has also been found to increase violence beyond the borders of the original conflict, in the shape of transnational terrorism (Chenoweth 2013; Kattelman 2020).

Furthermore, it is widely recognised that foreign support is the single most important factor to explain insurgent success (Record 2007; Connable and Libicki 2010; Grauer and Tierney 2017). Foreign interven- tion can come in the shape of political support, recognition and conferring of legitimacy. We will see in Vignette 8.1 that the visit of French President De Gaulle to the World Expo in Montreal in 1967 provided a major boost to calls for Quebec independence, when De Gaulle expressed his support for the aim. Apart from legitimacy, other forms of intervention are eco- nomic or military aid, or the provision of sanctuary or safe haven. The effects of foreign intervention, as found in the literature, are that conflicts tend to last longer, witness more casualties and display an increased chance of success for the rebel group.

Foreign intervention constitutes escalation by the simple measure of an increased number of conflict participants. More interesting and important are the more qualitative aspects of the intervention. External intervention can contribute to a shift in saliency of the issues at stake of the rebels.

Escalation ensues when outsiders reinforce the rebel agenda, their legitimacy, or support the group with military or economic aid or sanctuary.

ESCALATION: THE SALIENCY SHIFT

This chapter has attempted to address the reinforcement of political will based on the multiple pathways of conflict in its first stages with a focus on agency. The actors under consideration in this study, rebel groups, usually start in an environment marked by a large power disparity. It has been estimated that around 90 per cent of all rebel groups are weaker than their state opponent at the outset of conflict (Jo 2015, 219). The state, generally, has the instruments of power under its command and the rebel group is attempting to build up instruments of pressure and coercion to force its demands. While important thinkers have proposed the working of a provocation trap to draw out the state in a battle where its disadvantages are played at, this chapter finds that the state is often prompted to use violence first after which the rebel group follows suit. There is little evidence that the state carefully considers its options and plans ahead, once force is used (Silwal 2017).

The ideas discussed in this chapter of provocation, overwhelming force, negotiation and concession are very close to the idea of political resolve that has emerged already in the previous chapter. Dealing forcefully and decisively with a rebel group would show strong will and commitment. Many states continue to harbour the belief that it might hold the magical key to dealing decisively with unwanted and unwelcome opposition. Instead, it has a tendency to harden resolve.

It is clear that the response option matters for the development and dynamics of conflict. While, so far, the literature seems to point out that the effect of the countermeasures is largely contingent, we propose that provocation, overwhelming force, negotiation, concession and non-response possess escalatory potential in the raising of an issue's saliency. In other words, these countermeasures can all provoke a reinforcement of the saliency of the perceived issues at the core of the conflict. When the state responds in a manner that for the rebel group causes a recalibration of the importance or weight attached to the perceived issues of contention, this crosses a threshold in the conflict. This is a form of escalation. This recalibration can, of course, occur multiple times before the conflict terminates.

The mechanisms unearthed in this chapter have focused on escalation as deriving from political will. It is clear that these initial stages are of paramount importance, not only to set the conflict on its course, they also act as a political resource to create or augment social support and legitimacy. These mechanisms can both fortify and jeopardise political capital, actor legitimacy and popular support, which are all significant for the conduct of any war. These ideas will be taken up again in the following chapters.

5

Capabilities

Strategy

So far, this study has focused on only one of the parameters for escalation: increases in political will. Reinforcements in political will have not only been discussed in the shape of the political opportunity structure and mobilisation, which provide the context for violent action. Also, the dynamic interaction and the various political decision points and instruments, such as adopting a repressive approach or engaging in negotiations and offering concessions, have been discussed as pathways of conflict. Both these domains have provided a specific form of escalation in the shape of a saliency threshold, a reinforcing of the significance of the issue of contention.

This chapter will turn to capabilities as a second parameter of escalation. Here we will focus on strategy. As noted in the Chapter 1, the strategies rebels generally adopt have a tendency to play on the political will of the opponent rather than its capabilities. This has been the justification for discussing political will before capabilities.

At the outset of a campaign, there is usually a large power disparity between the actors and the rebel group tends to operate from a limited power base. We have seen in the previous chapters that adopting local issues and provocation can contribute to strengthening the rebel group position. Furthermore, the choices and activities of the state can aid with recruitment and resolve, based on the measures instituted against the political challenge posed by the rebel group. This chapter will focus on rebel strategies and the strengths and weaknesses of the two predominant strategic approaches: terrorism and insurgency.

STRATEGY

'[S]trategy is about choice', according to Lawrence Freedman,

[i]t depends on the ability to understand situations and to appreciate the dangers and opportunities they contain. The most talented strategists ... will always be thinking about the choices available to others and how their own endeavors might be thwarted, frustrated or even reinforced. It is this interdependence of choice that provides the essence of strategy and diverts it from being mere long-term planning or the mechanical connection of available means to set ends. (Freedman 2006, 9)

Strategy is inherently dynamic.

To what extent are rebels calculating strategists and active in their choice of particular strategies? Several notable insights have been offered to understand strategic choices. Firstly, there is a degree of parallel or like-mindedness in response and an increasing congruence of approaches during the course of rebel–state confrontations.[1] Rebel groups tend to be adaptive and agile opponents who select their optimum approach, importantly informed by the options selected by the state opponent (Katagiri 2013; Farrell 2020). When rebels attempt to fight the state using a similar strategy as their opponent, they tend to run a higher risk of losing (Arreguín-Toft 2005; Katagiri 2013, 2014). When rebel groups use a non-conventional strategy, they are generally more likely to be successful in attaining their stated goals. This has been the case for around half of all rebel conflicts (Arreguín-Toft 2005). As already noted, only in a few cases in the past have rebel groups managed to transition to the last phase of the Maoist model, a conventional confrontation.

Secondly, apart from congruence, several scholars have noted that the choice for a particular strategy is closely linked to outside or foreign influence (Katagiri 2013). When outside states provide advice and support, rebels are inclined to think of themselves as possessing sufficient capability and are more likely to choose, for example, a conventional strategy. Rebel capabilities are closely correlated to the level of violence (Wood 2010; Wood, Kathman and Gent 2012).

Thirdly, the choice of strategy is not only linked to the particular dyadic relationship and outside influence. The issue at stake has also been found to bear on the choice between conventional and irregular strategies. When

---

[1] This is a well-known phenomenon in international relations with Kenneth Waltz, for example noting that 'Competition produces a tendency toward the sameness of the competitors' (Waltz 1979, 127). See also the discussion about the work of Thomas Schelling and norm convergence in Chapters 2 and 3.

territorial considerations play a role, or when self-defence is at stake, conventional strategies seem to prevail. When liberation from colonial oppression is a main goal, irregular war has been more popular (Katagiri 2013). This is likely linked to the need to exercise territorial control to defend against a (potential) occupier or to create a fait accompli for nationalist claims. Earlier we have also seen that ideological claims are linked to defined modi operandi in jihadist groups (Drake 1998; Asal and Rethemeyer 2008; Moghadam 2008; Sanín and Wood 2014; Toft and Zhukov 2015).

Overall, the state approach, outside support and the issues at stake have all been linked to the vectors of choice for the strategies rebels adopt. Two strategic approaches predominate in the practice of state-rebel confrontations (Cf. Kalyvas 2011). Why and how do rebels choose one over the other? Existing arguments have mostly looked at structural or contextual conditions. In the discussion in Chapter 3 about the political opportunity structure, we have already seen that the choice for either a terrorist or an insurgency approach is linked to the prevailing political conditions. Agency, or conscious choice, has been relatively downplayed in order to understand the adoption of either strategy.

Firstly, some have argued that terrorism is predominantly used as a strategy in democratic states and insurgency has been commonly used as a strategy in partly democratic or authoritarian states (Art and Richardson 2007, 8). The existence of a functioning democratic state with a monopoly of force, it is argued, makes it difficult for an alternative social organisation to act as a rival for social order. When a malfunctioning state exists, it becomes attractive to organise an alternative or shadow state.

Secondly, others have proposed that it is the role of territory that affects the choice for either terrorist or insurgency strategies (De la Calle and Sánchez-Cuenca 2012, 2015). When the state is in full control of its national territory, terrorism becomes an option to contest control. When the state is not in control of its territory, insurgency becomes possible. This is an argument used to explain, for example, the relative absence of terrorism in large parts of the African continent. Terrorism becomes attractive 'when there is not enough space for guerrilla warfare' (McCuen 1966, 32; Clapham 2003; Kalpakian 2003). There is a related argument that terrorism is predominantly, if not exclusively, an urban phenomenon and insurgency a rural activity. While the insurgent operates in the countryside, to establish safe zones and shadow institutions, the terrorists operate in the city to directly target the state opponent in its political heart (Laqueur

2001; Kilcullen 2009, 2013: Le Blanc 2013). Urban guerrilla, a term frequently used in the 1970s, presents in this perspective a challenge. While terrorism thrives by secrecy and aims for a large impact in densely populated urban environments, insurgency and its requirement of organisation and recruitment runs a large risk of detection in urban centres. This is also called the dilemma of the urban guerrilla, which will be dissected further shortly. Others have suggested that such a distinction between urban and rural contexts does not really exist (Marks 2004, 125).

Thirdly, it might also be the combination of ideology and grievances that explains the choice for either strategy:

[I]n studying insurgency, we are not faced with an either/or proposition as concerns the role of ideology and grievances. If a movement has only the first, it invariably remains small and becomes a band of terrorists. If it has only the second, it survives as rebellion. That it links the two in symbiotic fashion not only describes the reality of insurgency but also in large part explains its passion and staying power. (Marks 2004, 126)

This idea is corroborated by several studies into the development of rebel violence. The pragmatic use of local grievances, combined with ideology, political entrepreneurs and feasibility, as discussed in Chapter 3, form important ingredients in explaining the durability of civil conflict (Kriger 1992; Fearon and Laitin 2003; Duyvesteyn 2005; Biggs 2007; Weinstein 2007).

Fourthly, the choice for terrorism or insurgency might be a function of size and strength of the group (Hoffman 1998; Art and Richardson 2007, 639; Lockyer 2011). Martha Crenshaw has argued that terrorism is 'the resort of an elite when conditions are not revolutionary' (Crenshaw 1981, 384). However, there are some insurgent organisations which would qualify as strong, such as the Tamil Tigers in Sri Lanka that at times have voluntarily opted for terrorist activities. Furthermore, there are weak groups, such as the South African Umkhonto we Sizwe, that refuse to use a terrorist strategy (Goodwin 2006, 2027).

The literature thus points out that the choice for a particular strategy is largely informed by structural conditions or context. We will now take a closer look at the strategies of terrorism and of insurgency in turn to assess their strengths and weaknesses.

THE CENTRAL DILEMMA OF THE STRATEGY OF TERRORISM

An inherent escalatory tendency exists in rebel campaigns, which Neumann and Smith have called the escalation trap. The escalation trap has been explained as a situation in which the continued raising of the level of violence is necessary, but at the same time this is detrimental to the achievement of rebel aims. It, therefore, forms a dilemma. The continued need to raise the level of violence to demonstrate resolve and capability will be curbed by the maximum level of force that the rebel group's intended audience is willing to support for the cause (Neumann and Smith 2007). Rebels are often inclined to overestimate their own capabilities, which can lead to escalation spirals, eliciting state countermeasures, which weaken rebel capabilities, and run the risk of eroding public support, and signal the end of the campaign.

The underlying premise of continued escalation is the idea of diminishing returns. The law of diminishing returns, as originally conceived by Walter Laqueur (2001), stipulates that

any attempt to attack targets that are solely of symbolic value will inevitably be subject to a law of diminishing returns, where the publicity and fear generated in each subsequent attack lessens in impact. Added to the likelihood of being unable to attack better-protected targets, a campaign will inexorably seek to widen its targeting attacks toward softer, more-vulnerable targets in order to maintain an atmosphere of intimidation, and this must entail a move toward targeting the civilian populace at large. (Neumann and Smith 2007, 81)

For example, in the case of the Italian Brigate Rosse, which will be further detailed in Chapter 7, the continual raising of the level of violence has been a crucial aspect to understand the logic of the campaign: escalation 'was a consequence of the need [of the terrorists] to attract the attention of the media, which had become accustomed to earlier and less dramatic tactics' (Della Porta 1995a, 136). Furthermore, 'if a campaign of terrorism becomes prolonged there is only one option open to maintain the coherence of the strategy, and that is to escalate the campaign to new higher levels of destruction and indiscrimination sufficient to maintain the sense of terror' (Neumann and Smith 2007, 83). This drive to continuous escalation ultimately undermines the campaign because it compromises the credibility of its political message. We saw this clearly in the case of the RUF in Sierra Leone and the atrocities perpetrated against the population, which lost it any semblance of already negligible popular support.

On an individual level, the law of diminishing returns has also been found. Hans Joachim Klein, a member of the German Revolutionary Cells, together with infamous gun-for-hire Carlos the Jackal, carried out a raid on OPEC in 1975 to press for the release of German Rote Armee Fraktion prisoners. He recounted of 'escalation as a "force of habit" among terrorists' (Discussed in: Hoffman 1998, 177). 'The effect is that terrorists today feel driven to undertake ever more dramatic and destructively lethal deeds in order to achieve the same effect that a less ambitious or bloody action may have had in the past' (Hoffman 1998, 177).

These two related phenomena of the escalation trap and the law of diminishing returns have a counterpart in existing strategic thought. In this discussion, they are called the 'culminating point' in a campaign: the point beyond which more force overshoots its utility (Clausewitz 1993; Luttwak 2001). A good strategist would need to train to recognise this point, even without the benefit of hindsight. In these dynamics we also recognise the Cold War scholars' ideas about escalation as revolving around previous commitment that needs to pay off, the idea of sunk costs, and failures of analysis, discussed in Chapter 2.

To escape the diminishing returns conundrum and the escalation trap, a transition to a different strategy might alleviate the pressure to demonstrate resolve and presence by being physically active among the population. Significant social support and an organised base might act as a brake on the trap and possesses a solidifying effect. It could also provide a stepping stone in the transition to a different political opportunity structure, that is post-conflict politics. We saw this situation in the civil war in Syria, where the Al-Nusra Front, an Al Qaeda affiliate, found itself in a situation in 2015 and 2016 where it was successful in clearing swatches of territory under government control but found it far harder to maintain control and attract active support from the population based on its ideology that found little resonance among the population. In the case of Afghanistan, a similar development occurred:

[J]ihadis are drawn to the front lines and display less interest in governing territory on their own. As a result, areas taken by them are not necessarily run by them. Where they have played a governance role, they generally have done so in collaboration with other components of the opposition, seeking to exhibit discipline and probity while avoiding the impression of forcibly imposing themselves. They have shown a measure of pragmatism in dealing with those who provide services to civilians. (International Crisis Group 2013, 9)

What we observe here is a transition towards a strategy of insurgency. The strength of the strategy of terrorism is its communicative effect contained in the power of propaganda by deed. The weakness is the continual drive for relevance associated with the escalation trap and diminishing returns. Terrorist groups when they grow more powerful can move towards an insurgency strategy.

THE CENTRAL DILEMMA OF THE STRATEGY OF INSURGENCY

Territory holds the key for rebel groups using the strategy of insurgency (Connable and Libicki 2010).[2] This leads to a pressing dilemma. The coercive force the insurgent commands needs to be translated into authority. In general, using purely coercive power is an extremely expensive way of exercising power. Therefore, a transition from coercive power to more authoritative power tends to take place, or the exercise of power will ultimately be exhausted: 'naked (that is, coercive) power always seeks to clothe itself in the garments of legitimacy' (Dahl 1965, 52). These insurgent groups undergo a process that Mancur Olson has described as a transition from a roving bandit to a stationary bandit. The roving bandit has a more predatory disposition and the stationary bandit makes attempts at establishing authority (see also Weinstein 2007; Wood 2010). In the end, 'every stable political order strives to convert coercive into legitimate authority' (Wrong 1979, 86).

The insurgent opts for a route that establishes control over territory and populations and engages in an exercise to provide a measure of social order, predictability in social relationships and social goods, such as security (Tilly 1985, 1990; Taylor and Botea 2008). This process, the construction of a shadow state, brings with it obligations towards the population (Arjona, Kasfir and Mampilly 2015; Duyvesteyn 2017). The provision of order and goods, or opportunities, is rewarded with collaboration, recognition and a measure of legitimacy. This requires resources and capabilities, money, recruits and mechanisms for implementation. A dilemma arises when the cementing of social relations creates a vulnerability: visibility, which poses a potential target for the state (Jardine 2014). The state can try to undermine the rebel group by curbing resources, the provision of alternatives or direct attack.

Control over rural areas is often not enough to attain the desired political change. The case of the Sandinist National Liberation Front (FSLN) in Nicaragua, for example, discussed in more detail later, demonstrated that urban centres tended to become a focal point. In many cases, a political difference can only be made in urban centres (Zurcher 2007, 6). The insurgent dilemma of establishing authority while exercising violence is particularly stark in urban centres.[3] At the start of the twenty-first

---

[2] We have already referred to a small group of scholars who argue for a global or post-territorial insurgency perspective (see also Smith and Jones 2015).
[3] There is, by no means, agreement among insurgency theorists about the role and significance of territorial control in urban areas. See discussion in Connable and Libicki (2010, 36–39).

century, over half of the world's population resides in urban centres. In general, the expectation is that with an increase in urbanisation, armed confrontation in urban centres will become more prevalent (see e.g. Kilcullen 2013). The urban insurgent needs to organise a popular base in an environment in which this is, in most cases, extremely difficult (Connable and Libicki 2010, 93). The state cannot be decisively defeated without the organised support of the population. While tactical independence can be achieved, strategic necessity dictates a close link between the rebel group and the population (Le Blanc 2012). This close link needs to be attained in an environment where state control tends to be strongest and discovery and denouncement are prevalent risks.

Despite arguments to the contrary (Kilcullen 2009; Mackinlay 2009), the Maoist model of revolutionary war still provides an interesting benchmark to study the logic of insurgency. Leaving aside the ideological content of world revolution, the three-phased Maoist model, introduced in Chapter 1, has been adopted and seems to continue to inspire insurgents (Rich 2016, 2018; Whiteside 2016; Philips 2017). The contesting of power in the countryside, the creation of liberated zones and territorial control, and the subsequent development of strength to conventionally defeat the state, remain an important lens through which to view insurgency.

It is true that many contemporary rebels are often organised in a less than hierarchical fashion compared to Mao's ideal prescription and along many different lines of recruitment, which will be further addressed in Chapter 7. The first two phases of the original Maoist model are close to the strategic application of terrorism with its noted vulnerabilities over diminishing returns and the escalation trap. The third phase of strategic offence, territorial control and conventional warfare creates another set of vulnerabilities for the rebel group. Fighting in the open, defending set positions, exposes the group to counter-attack. For the state opponent, this provides an opportunity to engage and defeat the insurgent group.

The lack of territorial control and organisational preparation were key weaknesses in the case of the Montoneros in Argentina, discussed in Chapter 3. They failed to set up an organisation necessary to become, and remain, a force to be reckoned with to takeover power. Organising in a hostile urban environment without any clearly liberated zones was extremely difficult. The Montoneros had only limited success in building up, either during the period of democracy between the Argentinian Revolution and Process of National Reorganisation dictatorship or during the military regimes, any kind of feasible political front organisation that could be seen as an interlocutor or even a political alternative. When these front organisations were attacked, the Montoneros were forced to place their trust solely and exclusively on mobilising rather than organising the population. Their focus on military confrontation and life in the underground lost its public support and led ultimately to their demise. Their position that 'military action was always the superior form of struggle in the conquest of power' proved fatal (Quoted in: Le Blanc 2012, 71).

In the case of Nicaragua, the dilemma was partially resolved, similar to M-19 in Colombia, which will be discussed in Chapter 8, by forging close ties with grassroots organisations that could function as a support base, also in the cities. It was tricky, however, to enlist this support, which was highly successful in the case of the FSLN and less so for M-19, without triggering a repressive response against these organisations by the two governments that were all too happy to find an excuse to curb their influence.

In the case of the RUF in Sierra Leone, it neither managed to achieve substantial territorial control nor prepared the creation of a viable political organisation. In the mid-1990s, they set up a number of bush camps and tried to contest control of the countryside from the central state. This contested control amounted to little, however, without a presence in the capital. In the case of neighbouring Liberia, the opposition forces managed to maintain unity until reaching the capital Monrovia, and when the seat and symbol of political power was within reach, the group broke up into competing factions, nullifying chances of a clear takeover of power but confirming the pivotal role of the capital (Duyvesteyn 2005).

The centre of national power tends to be a focal point in any attempt to take over power. Even in some cases where the state is strong, examples exist where we see rebel groups control territory (Staniland 2010). The IRA had created no-go areas in several cities in Northern Ireland and the Front de Libération Nationale (FLN) in Algeria, fighting for independence from France, controlled large parts of the Casbah in Algiers (Horne 2002). Those rebels active in or around the capital are statistically found to be the stronger ones; weaker groups tend to fight in the countryside (Ruhe 2015, 248). Control and defend territory and populations, under circumstances where discovery and denouncement are continual threats, form the central insurgent dilemma.

STRATEGY IN PRACTICE

So far, a picture has emerged of the rebel group as a highly flexible, if not opportunistic actor. This picture, in fact, provides the common theme in this and the next chapter. We will see that in regard to choices in strategy and operational planning, agility and adaptability are key words. We will first turn to two brief vignettes. In Vignette 5.1, Sandinist National Liberation Front (FSLN) in Nicaragua, the example stands out because the rebel group in this case managed to switch between strategies during the course of its struggle against the authoritarian rule of the Somoza family, which illustrates agency and conscious choice. Subsequently, we will look at the Tamil Tigers confronting the Sri Lankan state, in Vignette 5.2, similarly displaying awareness of strategic choice and consciously using opportunities and constraints.

Vignette 5.1 – Nicaragua: The Sandinist National Liberation Front and Switching Strategic Focus

The conflict in Nicaragua started as an uprising in a closed political system dominated by the Somoza family, which had controlled the country for more than 40 years. The regime was based on a patrimonial logic that bound the elite to the maintenance of the status quo of Somoza leadership. The two decades long civil war ended in 1979 with the violent overthrow of the dictator. The approaches the Sandinista National Liberation Front adopted varied over the course of time. Starting out with a rural insurgency, which failed to attain the desired end, the activities shifted to urban terrain, where they were more successful (Le Blanc 2012).

The Sandinistas, as the rebels in Nicaragua became known, derived their name from the opposition leader, who stood up against American intervention in Nicaraguan politics in the 1930s. General Cesar Augustino Sandino objected to the American presence and interference in politics and paid the price with his life. An incentive to organise opposition against the Somoza dictatorship materialised in 1972, after a massive earthquake had hit Nicaragua, and in particular the capital Managua. The devastating earthquake cost more than 20,000 lives and destroyed large parts of the infrastructure of Managua. The earthquake confronted the population with the total lack of effectiveness of the political system in a time of need. The funds that flooded into the country to help the earthquake victims ended up in the hands of the dictatorship, which personally

Vignette 5.1 (cont.)

benefited. This pitted large parts of the population against the regime. Since political space to manoeuvre was limited, grassroots organisations started to spring up and attempted to organise the population and provide basic services there where the government failed to act. In the countryside, peasants also started to organise as a result of land disputes, when they were driven from the most fertile areas (Kruijt 2008).

The FSLN was the product of a merger of several smaller groups espousing social revolution. The core of its membership consisted of students, and it remained relatively small during the course of the 1960s. A main source of inspiration was the Cuban revolution. The group saw itself as the vanguard in a national liberation struggle against oppression. Armed struggle formed an inherent part of the liberation of the population from this oppression. The group subscribed to the idea of 'Prolonged Popular Warfare', which entailed the rallying of the rural and urban populations and to create a government of popular representation (Le Blanc 2012). The concentration on grassroots organisational work would build the foundations for the large support network on which it could rely in the later stages of the uprising against Somoza. While repression was the regime's answer to the work of the FSLN, this external pressure led to fissures in the group. The group witnessed several splits over the course of its existence; one of the reasons for the breakaway factions was the debate over a focus for the uprising on the countryside or the cities (Le Blanc 2012). It turned out that these disputes over methods did not prove insurmountable. When the insurgency gathered steam in 1978, the different factions found each other again and reunited in the successful overthrow of the regime.

The FSLN started its guerrilla operations in the northern part of Nicaragua in late 1963. Their operation was based on the Foco or column concept, derived from Regis Debray and popularised by Che Guevara (Debray 1973), and was aimed at acting as a catalyst to provoke an uprising by activating the masses into action and creating a revolutionary situation. The application of the Foco idea failed in Nicaragua and the actions of the FSLN in the north gained very little attention. The group leadership realised the necessity of investing in further political ground work.

A second attempt at establishing a Foco, in the late 1960s, gained more traction but this experience was also short-lived. The initial success derived from tapping into very local grievances that spurred the rural population into action. It reached its limits when the guerrillas were asked to operate further away from their home base and the government started to forcefully suppress the Foco in 1967. The publicity the FSLN gained from it was longer lasting; the organisation became well-known and gained more support and recruits for the struggle against authoritarian rule.

The insurgency in the countryside continued and at the same time an urban front was opened up. In 1974, the FSLN went on the offensive; it kidnapped several members of the elite, including direct relatives of President Somoza. The government was forced to release a group of political prisoners and a proclamation of the FSLN was read on the radio. This formed a significant humiliation for the regime and directly triggered a major offensive against the FSLN in 1975 (Le Blanc 2012). The external pressure by government forces contributed to a split in the movement, along the lines described earlier. One faction of the FSLN managed, despite heavy repression, to launch an attack against the Guardia National (GN), the Nicaraguan National Guard bases in the country. In 1978, one of the main opposition figures, Pedro Joaquín Chamorro, editor of the *La Prensa* newspaper, was killed. This led the FSLN, through its grassroots network, to organise a national uprising. An FSLN unit was successful in occupying the National Palace and in taking, in the process, over 1,000 hostages. A series of popular uprisings now took place in urban centres, among others Matagalpa, Masaya, Chinandega, Esteli and Leon coordinated by the FSLN, for which the GN hardly had an answer. GN bases were located in almost every city and were highly visible. For the militants the capture of the GN base meant control over the city. The regime, and in particular the GN, tried to step up their activities by using indiscriminate force, that is bombing raids against urban centres, including the use of white phosphor, which caused large-scale death and destruction among the population (Kruijt 2008; Le Blanc 2012). Using extreme repression in a situation where social mobilisation against the regime occurred was a no-win situation for the Somozas.

Vignette 5.1 (cont.)

With large parts of the countryside under control and the GN hugely overstretched, the final battle concentrated on the capital Managua. The FSLN managed to cut the main supply route to the southern GN flank by capturing the city of Masaya. By ways of a large-scale conventional offensive, the FSLN forces advanced on Managua from the north and south leading to its encirclement. On 17 July 1979, the last of the Somoza dictators fled the country and the FSLN installed its provisional government. The focus on the capital with an urban campaign, which lasted only seventeen months, meant the death knell of the regime, which rural insurgency that had started almost two decades earlier could not achieve. Peace, however, did not return to the country as the FSLN government that came to power had to face armed opposition sponsored by the United States in the 1980s.

The case of the FSLN clearly brings out that rebels consciously opted for a shift in focus for their strategy, in this case moving from the country-side into the cities. This shift is accompanied by the challenge of organising and fighting in an urban environment.

Together with the FSLN, there are several other examples of rebel groups that have shifted to a conventional strategy. The MNLF in the Philippines, introduced in the previous chapter, started operations with a conventional attack against government forces in Sulu province, the heartland of the Muslim community, and with operations in their original base in Cotabato province, where they managed to overrun and occupy twelve cities and threatened the provincial capital itself. The offensive was nearly successful in defeating the government forces, as assessments at the time indicated (Reed 2013, 302–303). The Manila government had to airlift troops into the province to re-establish control. Another rebel group notable for its choice for a conventional strategy is the Tamil Tigers, fighting for independence from the Sri Lankan state. We will now take a closer look at this particular example. We see here again an organisation very agile and adaptable in its approaches, its activities ranging from terrorist attacks to full-scale conventional battle against the state.

> **Vignette 5.2 – From Irregular to Conventional Strategies: The Tamil Tigers and the Sri Lankan State**

The violent struggle for an independent Tamil homeland started in 1983 (Swamy 1994; Joshi 1996). Over the course of its existence, the main rebel group representing the Tamil cause, the Liberation Tigers of Tamil Eelam (LTTE), used several strategies to attain their stated goal of national independence, which ended with their complete military defeat in 2009. Terrorism, including suicide attacks, insurgency and conventional war were used to fight the government of Sri Lanka. The LTTE was a powerful rebel group commanding not only ground troops but also maritime and air forces. The maritime forces, the Sea Tigers, included submersibles. The rest of their arsenal included battle tanks, rocket launchers and anti-aircraft guns and satellite communications. The LTTE was organised as a regular army, with branches and specialisations. A significant proportion of the suicide attacks, around a quarter, were carried out by women, as they could escape detection in Sri Lanka more easily (Hussain 2010, 386).

Tamils live predominantly in the north and east of Sri Lanka and intermixed in the rest of the country, including the capital Colombo. Fractures in society did not limit themselves to Tamils and Sinhalese but overlapped and cut across divisions of language, religion, social-economic class and level of education. The rise of Sinhalese nationalism in the 1950s and 1960s, in the shape of declaring Sinhalese as the official language and Buddhism as state religion, was followed by a commensurate awakening of Tamil national feeling, based on the Tamil language and Hindu religion, although there were also Christian Tamils.

When the 1977 elections, paradoxically, promised to reverse the situation in which Tamil rights had increasingly been curbed, violence broke out between the communities. The LTTE, which had formed as a militant off shoot of a political party the Tamil United Liberation Front (TULF), started violent attacks in the early 1980s. Catalysts for the violence were the Prevention of Terrorism Act of 1979, which included measures such as searches without warrants and detention without trial, which were used predominantly against the Tamil population and the declaration of martial law in 1983 for the Tamil districts in Sri Lanka. Even though uprisings had occurred before, the rioting in 1983 is generally seen as the start of the civil war. In this first phase, several organisations working for Tamil independence cooperated, such as Tamil Eelam Liberation Organisation (TELO) and the People's Liberation Organisation for Tamil Eelam (PLOTE) and all subscribed to violence (Bloom 2003).

This phase is also called the Eelam War I (1983–87) and started out with retaliation against government soldiers for the murder of Charles Anthony, a close aide of LTTE leader Velupillai Prabhakaran. Thirteen soldiers were murdered in revenge, and a backlash occurred against the Tamil population in other parts of Sri Lanka. These activities swelled the ranks of the LTTE, which had previously been rather small and recruited mainly from the lower social strata. Furthermore, the government banned all parties calling for separatism or independence from Sri Lanka, effectively outlawing the TULF and any legal Tamil political representation. Thereby the political opportunity structure closed. This provided another push for the Tamil population into the arms of the LTTE.

The strategy the LTTE adopted was an insurgency against the state, following the basic precepts of Maoist instruction (Hussain 2010, 403). Its stronghold on the Jaffna Peninsula in the far north allowed for a relatively stable base area and an escape hatch, a crossing into Tamil Nadu just a short boat ride away across the Palk Strait to mainland India. Also terrorist attacks in Colombo occurred, such as a bomb explosion at a bus station, which killed 113 in 1987.

This prompted an offensive by government troops against the Jaffna peninsula. The offensive came with great costs in human lives and material destruction. India felt compelled to intervene and organised a humanitarian intervention. India's interest in the plight of the Tamils was driven by Indian politics, and in particular the situation in the state of Tamil Nadu in the south, which housed a significant number of Tamils as well. The sending of an Indian Peacekeeping Force (IPKF) first antagonised the Sri Lankan government, which in its aim to make life hard for the Indians even condoned arms deliveries to the LTTE to fight the IPKF (Dissanayaka 1998, 332). Subsequently, the LTTE itself did not see any benefit in the IPKF for its aims of independence and sent a suicide bomber to kill Indian Prime Minister Rajiv Gandhi in May 1991. In 1993, they also managed to kill the Sri Lankan Prime Minister Ranasinghe Premadasa by ways of a suicide bomb.

When the IPKF left in 1990, the Tamils took over control of Jaffna and the government ended up responding with a large-scale conventional attack on the area, the Eelam War II (1990–95). It employed scorched-earth policies, torture and death squads to cow the population. The indiscriminate nature of the government actions again led to large-scale recruitment for the LTTE. The LTTE in its turn used the civilian population as a cover and used children in its ranks. During this period, the LTTE managed to conventionally confront the government troops and conducted, for example, the battle of Elephant Pass in 1991 with over 5,000 LTTE fighters besieging an army base. The LTTE established significant territorial control in the Tamil parts and organised a shadow state. The most extensive position the LTTE managed to obtain was control over almost three-quarters of the north of Sri Lanka in the early 2000s (Lewis 2012, 315).

A ceasefire that had concluded at the end of this phase broke down and violence re-emerged in the Eelam War III starting in 1995. Government forces tried to retake the northern part of Sri Lanka and focused on the stronghold of Jaffna. The Tigers responded with a series of suicide attacks in Colombo. Suicide terrorism gained in importance among the activities of the Tigers in the mid-1990s (Pape 2005). They, furthermore, reverted to ambushes and hit-and-run attacks against government forces in their areas. The LTTE's most daring attack occurred in 2001 when the Tigers managed to destroy twelve airplanes at the national airport. Eelam IV (2006–09) erupted after the peace process that had been engaged in under the auspices of the Norwegians between 2002 and 2005 broke down irreparably, for which the LTTE was largely blamed.

In 2004, one of the figure heads of the LTTE, Karuna, at that point in command of over 6,000 troops, defected to the government side. He turned informant and provided the government with valuable information as to the positions, strengths and weaknesses of the Tamil groups. This, according to some analyses, caused a turning point in the conflict (Obayashi 2014). What seemed initially the strong point of the LTTE, a well-organised base area with the trappings of a shadow state became its main weakness. A conventional assault against its base area and supply lines is what broke the organisation in 2009. They were still organised as a guerrilla armed force but were forced in a position to defend static positions along the main roads into the north (Lewis 2012, 317). The LTTE 'did not have sufficient strength in depth, either in manpower or in equipment, to fight a drawn-out conventional war, and it was peculiarly vulnerable to a well-planned concerted military campaign that would attack the weaknesses of its conventional positioning' (Lewis 2012, 322). Unable to revert back to the tried and tested insurgency tactics, the LTTE was defeated, its leadership killed, including Prabhakaran. The government placed a large number of militants in camps and the remaining militants in detention centres to control the decaying organisation and prevent at all costs a return to violence.

The Tamil Tigers showed a keen awareness of their abilities and the changing political opportunity structure and devised an appropriate strategy, carefully calculating its chances based on the prevailing structures and conditions to further their aims. We also see in this case the significance of the choices of the Sri Lankan state for the opportunities for the LTTE, repression and provocation were latched upon by its leadership. The MNLF in the Philippines, discussed earlier, exhibited a similar professional outlook. As their first conventional attacks against the Philippine government troops were successful in the Cotabato province. A conventional attack was feasible because of the excellent training and equipment they could rely on. The MNFL attempted positional warfare against the government and gave set piece battle. The areas they conquered, they tried to control before moving on. Despite the MNLF's substantial resource base, the government could resupply faster moving troops from around the country into Mindanao. In April 1974, the MNLF tried their hand at a conventional attack against the capital of Sulu province, Jolo, which signified the largest conventional confrontation of the war. In early 1975, three-quarters of the Philippine armed forces were deployed in Mindanao (Reed 2013, 305–306). This formed the most violent phase of the conflict and it subsequently developed into a stalemate, with the MNLF not being able to mount an offensive of the 1974–75 intensity again in the remainder of the war.

What these examples demonstrate is that for rebels the careful and calculated conduct of strategy is a fact and rebels are, contrary to many arguments presented earlier, strategic actors. At this point it seems logical to revisit the main threshold suggested in the existing literature, atrocity, as forming the predominant, if not exclusive, route to escalation in rebel conflict. The atrocity threshold combines the political will to commit an atrocity with the ability and capability to do so. In other words, the will must exist to cross levels of pre-existing atrocity, together with the means to commit this atrocity against potential victims that are present and which can be reached. Atrocity has formed the dominant conceptualisation of escalation in the existing literature and combines an increased political will with a reinforced capability to transgress a boundary of hitherto unused methods or targets to aggravate the conflict.

THE ATROCITY THRESHOLD

There has been a wide-ranging discussion regarding civilian targeting in civil wars. An important distinction is made between discriminate and indiscriminate violence. The academic debate has investigated the causes of indiscriminate killing. Discriminate violence consists, for example, of targeted killing and kidnapping, which exhibit the important feature of identification of the target of the violence. Indiscriminate violence, conversely, does not display distinction and includes bomb attacks, mop up operations, artillery barrages and aerial bombardment. The atrocity threshold is most notably crossed when indiscriminate killing of civilians occurs.

Four causal explanations have been brought forward for indiscriminate killing. Notably, indiscriminate violence is not necessarily linked to a lack of organisational control. Firstly, as already discussed, contested control or active rivalries among belligerents have been found to trigger indiscriminate violence. Hannah Arendt, in her study *On Violence*, wrote in 1970 that power and violence are not synonymous. Rather, violence is a demonstration of a lack of power (Arendt 1970). More recent scholarship has seemingly built on this idea (Kalyvas 2006; Metelits 2009; Holtermann 2019). Once hostilities are underway, violence can serve a strategic purpose of raising the costs of switching sides. Indiscriminate violence can be logical as a deterrent and control mechanism. It forces people to choose sides: out of fear of further violence, they can start cooperating with the rebel group or defect and join the state or other opposition groups. As noted in the introduction, especially when there is a rivalry between rebels for allegiance of the population, indiscriminate violence can be expected. The function of indiscriminate violence is to force a choice on the population and deter defection (Kalyvas 2006; Metelits 2009).

Despite significant consistency in these findings about the collaboration–control mechanism, they are contradicted by some cases where there has been one dominant insurgency organisation, such as the Tamil Tigers in Sri Lanka. The LTTE has, without much competition from rival rebel groups, engaged in indiscriminate violence against the Tamil population, which was its own supposed natural constituency (Goodwin 2006). There are other explanations for indiscriminate killing.

Secondly, indiscriminate violence can be a function of the resource base of the rebels. Indiscriminate violence can occur when the rebels are not dependent on local resources and experience no incentive to seek support from the local population (Weinstein 2007). When they are independent of local resource bases, there is little need to safeguard popular support and abuses can take place.

Thirdly, indiscriminate violence has been argued to be a function of the ideological foundations of the rebel group. Several studies, already referred to earlier, have found that ideology matters for target selection and specific patterns of violence. In particular, religious or jihadist-inspired groups tend to use this kind of violence (Drake 1998; Asal and Rethemeyer 2008; Moghadam 2008; Sanín and Wood 2014; Toft and Zhukov 2015).

Fourthly, indiscriminate violence has been argued to occur when there is an absence of clear targets. When terrorism entails secrecy and surprise, states can identify few targets, apart from the social base of the terrorist rebel group: 'in the absence of visible enemy combatants, an organisation can hope to cut off their opponent's support by murdering potential recruits'. This can cause 'spirals of violence' (Carter 2017, 45).

Conversely, discriminate violence occurs when there is no contentious control but clarity as to who is in charge, when the rebels are dependent on the support of the population and when clear targets present themselves. Discriminate use of force has also been interpreted as a signal that the rebel group is a serious security actor, in control of its organisation and capable of safeguarding security for the population (Koehler-Derrick and Milton 2017, 915).

The effectiveness of discriminate and indiscriminate violence has also been the subject of investigation. Discriminate or selective violence has been linked to effectiveness, in particular targeted killing, which will be further discussed in Chapter 7.

Several statistical studies have been carried out that show a link between rebel targeting of civilians and the lack of attainment of political goals (Abrahms 2011, 2018). In particular, in cases of rebels fighting democratic regimes, rebel groups tend to use less indiscriminate killing (Jo 2015, 218). The wilful attacks against civilians to elicit compliance from the state towards a desired course of action are shown to work to opposite ends. Governments become less inclined to make concessions when civilians have been wounded or killed as a result of terrorist action (Stephan and Chenoweth 2008, 2011; Gaibulloev and Sandler 2009). Also, it has been found that when civilians find themselves in the crossfire of violence between a rebel group and the state, they can turn against the rebels, blaming the latter for the losses (Kocher, Pepinsky and Kalyvas 2011; Condra and Shapiro 2012; Holtermann 2019).

All the cases examined so far have exhibited this phenomenon, with the most extreme case being Sierra Leone preceding the elections in 1995. Several striking observations can be made about the occurrence of the atrocity threshold. Firstly, the shift of striking at civilians in an indiscriminate fashion is also importantly crossed by the state. In Argentina, the killing by the police of unarmed protesters in the Cordobazo signalled an important aggravation of the conflict, which was caused by the state. Similarly, Bloody Sunday in Northern Ireland displayed a similar pathway of the police shooting demonstrating civilians, causing a major step up in this conflict.

Secondly, the atrocity shift is not linear. The violence did not continue on the same level of atrocity or force the opponent to follow suit. The episodes displaying the use of indiscriminate violence were interspersed with much lower levels of violence. Moreover, the escalation trap of losing supporters does not follow automatically.

Finally, while in the discussion about the increasing levels of atrocity the targeting of the civilian population features prominently, other ways of raising the level of atrocity are available. In the next chapter, we will discuss the introduction of new or more weaponry. Moreover, while a very useful and productive suggestion to address the puzzle of escalation, the atrocity threshold is not unbound. While the logic of the diminishing returns and the escalation trap dictate ever graver and more extreme violence, rebel conflict witnesses constraints. We note, in particular, the choice of not using specific weapons or tactics, and the boundary of what is morally acceptable in the eyes of the claimed constituents of the rebel group. For the purposes of this paragraph, it is necessary to note that important breaks on rebel violence exist and important existing boundaries have not been crossed. We will return to these issues in more detail in Chapter 9.

ESCALATION: THE ATROCITY THRESHOLD

This chapter has put into sharper contrast the picture of the rebel group as strategic actor. The existing literature has emphasised the structural conditions guiding strategic choice of rebel groups. The case material has pointed out that agency also matters in grasping the opportunities offered in the dynamic interaction. Rebels tend to use a variety of means and methods over the course of their existence to further their aims. Again, we find that the dynamic and interactive characteristic of rebel–state dyadic competitions importantly inform escalation. Rebel groups have strategic choices and are strategic actors bound by, just like the state, the environment and structures within which they operate, the opponent they face, the influence of outside actors or sponsors, the issues at stake and the capabilities available. The material circumstances, the political context and the terrain influence the ability to act. Both structural conditions and choice determine the course of action.

We have noted changes and shifts between strategies, between direct and indirect approaches and between urban and rural locations. In urban environments, there are specific challenges and dilemmas related to organising secretly or in liberated zones where state power is often at its strongest or tends to be focused. Strategies of both terrorism and insurgency have inherent weaknesses, that is the drive to action and the exposure of territorial presence and visibility. These potential weaknesses importantly inform the limitations and constraints the rebels face during the course of their struggle. The material presented so far confirms the existence of the atrocity shift, as suggested in the presently available literature. This shift can be explained in a multiplicity of ways; it can be triggered by different causal pathways in which all of the belligerents play a role and does not appear to be linear.

6

Capabilities

Substitution

An influx of new or more military material, weapons, finances and recruits into the conflict all constitute vertical escalation. This chapter will take a closer look at rebel weaponry, targets and tactics. It aims to discuss the escalatory mechanism of substitution. Rebels tend to be very adept at gauging options, when circumstances change, at least in contrast to the state opponent. The substitution, waterbed or risk transfer effect is a prevalent phenomenon (Enders 2004; Frey 2004). Substitution can materialise when rebels shift between targets, tactics, territory or timing of attacks (Frey 2004). Indeed, '[e]fforts to deter terrorist events often displace the attack to other venues, modes of attack (e.g. from skyjacking to a kidnapping), countries, or regions, where targets are relatively softer' (Arce and Sandler 2005; Enders 2004, 184). Substitution can occur on all levels of strategy, that is tactical and strategic substitution, and forms an important form of escalation. While the previous chapter focused mostly on strategic substitution, the switch between strategic approaches, this chapter will unpack substitution via specifically shifts in weapons, targets, tactics, territory and timing of attacks (T4).

WEAPONS

Weaponry enables the rebel group to carry out a violent campaign. The use of more, or different types of, weaponry is a form of escalation (Tishler 2018). Possibly, in contrast to popular perceptions, rebels tend to be quite conservative in their choice of weapons. Among the rebel weapons of choice, we count bombs, remote-controlled or not, firearms, explosive devices, fire and firebombs and sharp objects and knives. In general, the gun and the bomb form the most popular instruments for rebel attacks (Engene 2007; Hoffman 2014). In recent years, there has been an upsurge in the use of improvised explosive devices (IEDs) (Hoffman 2014).

Rebels come across as quite conservative in light of their choice of armoury. In the past, however, rebels have crossed several weapons threshold, for example, the high explosive threshold, the airplane threshold (both as means and method) and the chemical weapons threshold (Tishler 2018; Cronin 2019). The development of dynamite in the 1860s had huge significance for rebel attacks. Preceding this development, the dagger and the highly unstable nitroglycerin were used. Compared to these methods, dynamite enormously increased destructive power of rebel groups (Jensen 2004). The aircraft and its development since the first decades of the twentieth century became a favourite weapon of choice among terrorists in the late 1960s with a large rise in airplane hijacking as a means to gain attention, culminating in the use of aircraft as weapons in the attacks of 9/11 (Hoffman 1998). The use of chemical weapons has only one confirmed example but the threshold has been crossed: the sarin gas attack by the Japanese religious sect Aum Shinrikyō in the Tokyo underground in 1995.[1] Thresholds are generally crossed first by one group and followed by others. Rebels can be learning and adaptive organisations and successful approaches are copied (Midlarsky, Crenshaw and Yoshida 1980; Hamilton and Hamilton 1983; Parker and Sitter 2015; Kettle and Mumford 2017; Veilleux Lepage 2020). We cannot claim that suicide attacks constitute a threshold, despite its renewed popularity in recent decades, they possess a very long pedigree (Rapoport 1984; Pape 2005).

While constrained by limited resources and strategic options, how do rebel groups select their choice of weapon? The predominant choice for the gun and the bomb has been explained by the ease of acquisition and the limited cost of their application (Hoffman 2014; Koehler-Derrick and Milton 2017). Around 96 per cent of all attacks since 1970 were carried out by either of these weapons. The choice for the gun was informed by group goals and size, with large groups aspiring to grand goals of political change more likely to use firearms. More limited agendas sought by smaller groups related to modest political change were more likely to

[1] Other possible examples are the anthrax letters posted in the autumn of 2001 in the United States. The sender(s) of these letters are still to be identified. This makes it questionable whether it could fit in the strategic framework at all. Moreover, the use of gas in the Syrian civil war could fit into this category if it can be proven that the rebel groups used it. So far, the evidence is too scattered to draw any concrete conclusions.

use bombs (Koehler-Derrick and Milton 2017). Larger groups can afford to put their fighters in harm's way, which is a larger risk when using firearms compared to bombings (Carter 2016). Apart from accessibility to and cost of arms, the intended effect has also been linked to informing choice. Paradoxically, rebel groups that intend to create mass casualties and perpetrate indiscriminate violence tend to opt for conventional weapons. Those groups interested in causing fear rather than destruction tend to choose unconventional weapons (Palfy 2003).

There has been a long running concern that weapons of mass destruction might fall into the hands of terrorists. In the literature, there are references going back to the start of the nuclear age: 'warnings about the possibility that small groups, terrorists and errant states could fabricate nuclear weapons have been repeatedly uttered at least since 1947' (Jenkins 1975, 1985a; Mueller 2005, 489; Duyvesteyn and Malkki 2012). To date, however, there are no examples of terrorists acquiring or using nuclear material.

It is commonly assumed that the use of these weapons exceeds their utility as a political instrument because they are too indiscriminate: 'It can be taken for granted that most of the terrorist groups existing at present will not use this option, either as a matter of political principle or because it would defeat their purpose' (Laqueur 2001, 231). Still, Bruce Hoffman claimed two decades ago that

many of the constraints (both self-imposed and technical) which previously inhibited terrorist use of WMD are eroding. The particular characteristics, justifications and mindsets of religious and quasi-religious – as compared with secular – terrorists suggest that religious terrorists will be among the most likely of the potential categories of non-state perpetrators to use WMD. (Hoffman 1998, 197)

Later, we will discuss the idea of constraints, internally and externally induced, under which rebel groups tend to operate.

In some alarmist accounts, cyber weapons are seen as the next threshold which terrorists will cross (Clarke and Knake 2010). Cyber might be an interesting instrument for terrorists: 'waging strategic information warfare might prove most useful ... for actors whose political objectives are limited in scope, who can control vulnerability to retaliation, and who possess a willingness to take risks' (Rattray 2001, 101). However, this requires that the instrument lends itself to repeated and sustained use. In this respect cyber weapons are so far 'insufficiently disastrous' (Liff 2012, 23). Furthermore, 'cyber attacks appear much less useful than physical attacks: they do not fill potential victims with terror, they are not photogenic, and they are not perceived by most people as highly emotional events' (Irving Lachow quoted in Nye 2010, 12). Cyber weapons to date seem to be mainly enablers for terrorist activity, rather than becoming the new weapons of choice.[2]

Efforts to limit the availability of conventional weaponry and explosives have not met with overwhelming success. Weapon embargoes form a very popular instrument to curb violence. The Stockholm International Peace Research Institute has calculated that the United Nations, since 1990, has used the weapon embargo instrument very frequently (Fruchart et al. 2007). Their statistical analysis shows that embargoes generally do not achieve the purpose they are intended for, that is limit the influx of weapons in areas of conflict (Brzoska 2008; Erickson 2013). In particular, neighbouring states tend to be involved with breaking embargo regimes.

An increase in weapons, as well as a change in the use of the weaponry, constitutes escalation. Moreover, the import of weapons from other actors is linked to a lower chance of conflict termination and, by implication, a longer drawn-out conflict (Sawyer, Cunningham and Reed 2017). There is thus a potentially important role for third parties here as well.

TARGETS

Carrying out a strategy requires strategic and operational planning, intelligence collection, gathering required capabilities and, importantly, target selection. Targets can, for instance, be found in airports and airliners, businesses, critical infrastructure, diplomatic representations, educational institutions, government, individuals, institutions, non-government organizations (NGOs), police forces, private property and religious symbols. A very notable trend has been the less and less discriminating nature of the rebel targeting over time (Clauset, Young and Gleditsch 2007). Since the nineteenth century, when anarchists mainly targeted heads of state (Ford 1985; Jensen 2004), a trend can be witnessed towards the selection of more general and random targets. While originally terrorism and political murder were quite closely associated in the phenomenon of tyrannicide, commensurate with the diffusion of state power in more

---

[2] Other noteworthy future trends related to actor capabilities might be linked to advances in robotics, witness the worldwide campaign against killer robots and autonomous weapons. Furthermore, nanotechnology and gen technology might also form the new frontiers in warfare. See also Cronin (2019).

hands than the monarch, targeting widened (Ford 1985; Miller 1995). Furthermore, the symbolism attached to targets moved from highly symbolic, for example political murder, to more general, the continuation of symbolic targeting notwithstanding. Table 6.1 can be helpful to think through the issue of target innovation.

TABLE 6.1 *Rebel Target Thresholds*

Capability		
	New capability Existing target	New capability New target
	Existing capability Existing target	Existing capability New target
	Target	

When the information of the previous paragraph focused on developments in the twentieth and twenty-first centuries is placed in the quadrant (Table 6.2), we see that the supposedly most innovative combination of new capabilities and new targeting has not occurred.

TABLE 6.2 *Target Innovation in the Course of Modern History*

Capability		
	New capability *Dynamite, Airplanes, Chemical weapons* Existing target	New capability New target Existing capability
	Existing capability *Bombs, Firearms, Explosive devices, Fire and Firebombs, Knives* Existing target	New target *Individuals–Groups* *Highly symbolic–Indiscriminate* *Hard–Soft* *Simple–Complex* [3]
	Target	

Existing terrorist targets are focused on symbolic, high value ones selected for an impact beyond the confines of the immediate surroundings of the target. Even the spectacular attack of 9/11 would fit in this description with

[3] This presentation is not suggesting that these target changes are linear.

an existing target, the World Trade Center in New York, which had been unsuccessfully targeted before in 1993. This was combined with an existing capability, an airplane, which has a long pedigree in rebel violent campaigns since the 1960s. The innovative aspect was the new use to which the airplane was put, as a flying bomb. Insurgency targeting also largely appears to comply with the picture of a preference for the tried and tested, for example the continuing importance of the Maoist model (Whiteside 2016).[4]

Target Substitution

Rebels exhibit specific targeting patterns. In particular, when one set of targets becomes difficult to reach, for example, due to countermeasures, rebels easily shift to other types of targets. For example, during the 1970s and the heyday of airplane hijacking, the introduction of 'metal detectors had an unintended consequence of causing a substitution into events in which people got hurt, whereas the opposite was true for embassy fortification' in the aftermath of the embassy bombings in East Africa in 1998 (Enders and Sandler 2000, 327). In the post-9/11 period, substitution of targets has also occurred. According to statistical analysis, shifts from hard to soft targets and from complex to logistically simple targets have taken place, that is bombing campaigns have increased (Enders and Sandler 2005, 275). Attacks, such as in Bali, London and Madrid, have been linked to the hardening of American targets (Rosendorff and Sandler 2004).

In the examples we have looked at so far in this study, it is notable that the targeting in some campaigns was the subject of careful considerations. The Montoneros in Argentina, for example, initially had a highly discriminate targeting policy. In the first phase, when they confronted the authoritarian regime as part of the Peronist movement, their aim of illustrating the inability of the government to protect the interests of the population led to the targeting of representatives of the system. This specific targeting helped to make clear to the population their political message. One example was the kidnapping and bringing before a revolutionary tribunal of General Arambu, figure head of the anti-Peronist forces in Argentina and former military dictator on 29 May 1970 (Le Blanc 2012). The Montoneros initially targeted the oligarchy or the elite members selectively. After repression by the state, they radicalised and broadened their targeting to all ranks

---

[4] Arguments have also been made to demonstrate the continued applicability of the Focoist model (Gartenstein-Ross et al. 2015; Payne 2011) and Marxist revolutionary thought (Kalyvas 2018) to understand the warfare of the Islamic State (2014–17).

of the security forces, focusing on the military apparatus at large (Le Blanc 2012). The Montoneros in Argentina went underground in 1974. Subsequently, their attacks shifted focus; they started to target military garrisons in broad daylight instead of opting for politically symbolic and highly discriminate targets. The population was highly critical of this new development and it led to a loss of support (Le Blanc 2012).

In the case of Northern Ireland, after Bloody Sunday, the Provisional IRA changed targets and became less discriminate, using more violence against civilians, targeting the British mainland and relocating to the countryside because of army activities in urban centres. In the case of the struggle for an independent Khalistan in the Punjab, which will be further discussed in Chapter 7, we see a substitution in the shape of an attack on an international airliner, Air India, in 1985. This target was a curious choice in the further geographically contained struggle in India itself (Reed 2013, 188–189). In the Punjab, the Sikh fighters shifted from an assassination campaign targeted at police officers, mostly Sikh and from the Punjab itself, to a campaign focused on the officers' families as complicit in Indian policies against the Sikh agenda. Their pre-existing political support and legitimacy was lost when the wider Sikh community became a target (Reed 2013). Shifts in rebel targeting can occur frequently.

TACTICS

Tactics of rebels are more diverse than their weaponry: armed attacks, arson, assassination (Mandala 2017, 14–39), bombing, hijacking, hostage-taking, kidnapping and suicide bombing are part of the wide-ranging spectrum. However, the claim by Brian Jenkins thirty years ago still seems to hold true: the 'tactical repertoire has changed little over time. Terrorists appear to be more imitative than innovative' (Jenkins 1985b, 12–13; Cf. Cronin 2019). There has been increased attention for suicide attacks, as a predominant rebel tactic. Several notable features of the practice of suicide attacks have emerged in recent years; Robert Pape noted the perhaps counter-intuitive link between nationalism and suicide terrorism, and its effectiveness in democratic political systems (Pape 2005; Atran 2006). In authoritarian polities, suicide terrorism tends to be focused on regime representatives rather than civilians (Nilsson 2018). Rivalry between rebels and a competition of signalling or commitment can also explain the choice for suicide attacks (Bloom 2007). Based on an analysis of suicide attacks in the civil war in Iraq, scholars have found that perhaps contrary to expectation, the majority of suicide attacks occurred against the Iraqi population and among competing groups internally rather than against the foreign intervention troops and remained largely unclaimed (Seifert and McCauley 2014).

Most rebel activities fall in the category of existing capability with a preference for those tactics that have proven their worth.

TABLE 6.3 *Tactic Innovation in the Course of Modern History*

	New capability Existing tactic	New capability New tactic *Airplane hijacking*
Capability	Existing capability Existing tactic *Armed attack* *Arson* *Assassination* *Bombing* *Explosions* *Hijacking* *Hostage taking* *Kidnapping* *Suicide bombing*	Existing capability New tactic
	Tactic	

Conventional bombing forms the most popular means used. Still, tactics can and do change over time and we witness the rise in suicide attacks, with the phenomenon of the improvised explosive device (IED) recently experiencing an upsurge. There are core features of the tactical practices of rebel groups; we focus in particular on the promulgation of the rebel narrative, tacit coordination and tactical repertoires of contention, and retaliation, before addressing tactical substitution.

Propaganda and Narrative

The rebel message is an important weapon in the struggle against the state, of course, with the intended strategic effect to influence the multiple audiences that are listening. The advent of new media, in particular in the case of the emergence and practices of the Islamic State, has put this aspect very much in focus (Heck 2017; Mahood and Rane 2017). It is a mistake to think this is a particularly new practice (e.g. Re 2017). Apart from the specific newly developed channels of communication, the communication revolution and social media, rebels have always attempted to disseminate their message to the intended audiences. In the past, for example, some of the types of attack were deemed self-explanatory; political murder, attacks on government representatives or institutions, could powerfully and visually communicate the rebel message, that is propaganda by deed (Norris, Kern and Just 2003).

The task of creating, disseminating and dominating the discourse forms an essential part of rebel activities (Freedman 2006). In many rebel struggles, there is a professionalisation of this task, with expertise being specifically sought or developed to deal with the creation of the narrative. However, also for the less able or capable groups, symbolism, legitimacy and communication are of fundamental importance. Some rebel groups are better than others at generating attention and there currently appears a link with the rebel agenda. There is evidence that terrorist attacks carried out by Islam-inspired terrorists tend to receive disproportionately more attention compared to groups inspired by other ideologies (Kearns, Betus and Lemieux 2018). Furthermore, there is also evidence that suicide attacks generate more media attention compared to other tactics, possibly explaining their popularity in the last few decades (Jetter 2019). It is not only propaganda that forms an inherent aspect of rebel activities. Non-verbal communication through examples, but also common repertoires of activities, are also means of transmission of the rebel message. They are aimed at enhancing the effectiveness of rebel operations.

Tactical Scripts and 'Tacit Coordination'

The question has been posed in the introduction to this study: how do rebels, some of them highly fragmented, manage to generate strategic effect? We have already seen that rebels are strategic actors even with limited capabilities. When these capabilities are scarce, rebels can rely on coordination and cooperation, which can act as 'force multipliers' and can increase military effectiveness (Jardine 2012, 2).

A suggestion in the literature is that in the absence of formal coordination mechanisms characteristic of conventional military forces, a form a 'tacit coordination' can surface. Originally developed by Thomas Schelling, in the context of the Cold War scholarship, tacit coordination can arise without an organisational structure, direct communications or common plans of action (Schelling 1980). The idea of a tactical script is that there is some sort of scenario or script that can be copied, adapted and emulated at will in different circumstances. As Thomas Schelling has written, in 'warfare the dialogue between adversaries is often confined to the restrictive language of action and a dictionary of common perceptions and precedents' (Schelling 2008, 141). Schelling talks about a common 'idiom' of 'interaction, a tendency to keep things in the same currency, to respond in the same language, to make the punishment fit the character of the crime, to impose a coherent pattern on relations' (Schelling 2008, 147).

The requirements for tacit coordination are a shared objective, a common geographical location and a limited set of tactical actions available in this geographic location; 'there needs to be a common script or repertoire of tactical-level actions that the various commonly positioned insurgent groups can draw from' (Jardine 2012, 9). These tactically coordinated activities could possibly generate overall strategic effect: 'Tacit coordination between commonly positioned groups with limited tactical scripts results in aggregated strategic outcomes that resemble, but are not a derivate of, a coherent strategic plan' (Jardine 2012, 24).

Tactical scripts and demonstration effects have been prevalent in rebel behaviour (Tilly 1977; Bloom 2007). The idea of propaganda by deed, which surfaced in the nineteenth century and built on the idea of conducting propaganda by demonstration effects, shows the long pedigree of this idea. In recent years, the phenomenon of suicide terrorism has been linked to the demonstration effect. While initially and frequently practised by the Tamil Tigers in their secular nationalist struggle against the Sri Lankan state, other groups adopted the tactic and it subsequently became associated with many other rebel agendas, today most notably the jihadi agenda.

Furthermore, not only can the rebel group rely on tacit coordination and tactical scripts, rebels, in particular terrorist groups, learn and copy from each other (Midlarsky, Crenshaw and Yoshida 1980; Hamilton and Hamilton 1983; Parker and Sitter 2015; Kettle and Mumford 2017). As the strategic plan in most rebel strategies is linked to the will of the opponent, wearing down the state's will to further resist can be served by this tacit coordination and learning behaviour.

There are some examples of this tacit coordination occurring in cases where the rebel group is fragmented. The RUF in Sierra Leone, a highly fragmented rebel group, did exhibit some features of common tactical scripts in the shape of atrocities that projected at least an operational picture (Mitton 2012). Tacit coordination can also be witnessed, for example, in the case of the Taliban in Afghanistan where limited tactical scripts existed that added up to making life very difficult for the intervention forces and tearing at their political will to continue the engagement.

Other examples are the Al Qaeda affiliates operating in diverse battle theatres, such as Yemen, Syria, Iraq and North Africa, relying on similar tactical scripts presenting an image of power and influence far beyond the limits of the specific theatres (Jardine 2012; Simpson 2012). Tactical scripts and 'tacit coordination' are primarily enablers for rebel effectiveness. They can function to augment the operational and tactical level of the strategies of terrorism and insurgency.

Retaliation

Once a violent campaign is underway, retaliation is a common phenomenon. This discussion is closely linked to the use of repression detailed in Chapter 4. Several scholars have argued that retaliation after an attack is necessary and works to curb the activities of rebel groups (Van Creveld 2006; Luttwak 2007). An interesting debate has developed around the American retaliations against Libya in the 1980s. Libya was for a time an important state sponsor of violent rebels.[5] The United States used armed force against Libya in 1986, after the bombing of a Berlin discotheque frequented by American servicemen. The attack killed 3 and injured 229. Some scholars have concluded that the American retaliation with a bombing raid on Libya led to a decrease in rebel activity (Hanle 1989, 218; Prunckun and Mohr 1997). However, other research has found that the American raid led to an increase in terrorist attacks, at least in the immediate aftermath (Enders, Sandler and Cauley 1990; Silke 2005; Lum, Kennedy and Sherley 2006, 505). Attacks increased against American, British and Israeli targets (Silke 2005). These attacks allegedly culminated in Libyan agents downing an airliner over Lockerbie, killing 270 people (Mueller 2005, 491).

There is broader evidence that retaliation often elicits more violence (Kalyvas 2006; Argo 2009; Clauset et al. 2010): 'there was no evidence that violent governmental retaliation decreased the frequency or severity of terrorist attacks. . . . If anything, there was evidence of the reverse: The intensity of terrorist actions increased, or decreased less, following more severe retaliation' (Nevin 2003, 127). This can be explained by those targeted seeking refuge and protection from violence and having incentives to join the rebel group. Moreover, retaliation creates more grievances (Lyall 2009, 335) and can lead to an increase in the salience of conflict issue. Retaliation can also be linked to the strengthening of group cohesion (Kegley 1990).

---

[5] This section is based on Duyvesteyn (2008).

There are also studies that find an absence of more violence or even further compliance behaviour after retaliation (Brophy-Baermann and Conybeare 1994; Sullivan 2007; Lyall 2009, 331; Sullivan and Koch 2009; Miakinkov 2011). For the case of Al Qaeda, a recent study has concluded that after the targeted killing of top-level members, such as Osama bin Laden and Anwar al-Awlaki, there was no noticeable retaliation or step up in the level of violence (Hepworth 2014). Another often studied example is the case of Israeli retaliation after Palestinian attacks. Quantitatively, in this case, retaliation has a correlation with a drop in violence. However, this is only a short-term effect and the policy does not act as a long-term deterrent for violence in this particular case (Brophy-Baermann and Conybeare 1994).

Also, in this discussion links have been proposed with legitimacy and public support (Brophy-Baermann and Conybeare 1994). Repression and retaliation can be effective under specific conditions related to (perceived) state legitimacy and capability (Herreros 2006). This recurrent suggestion in the literature will be taken up and elaborated on in Chapter 8.

Tactical Substitution

Substitution can also occur in the shape of a shift in tactics. If one set of tactics has become more difficult to execute, rebels shift often quite easily to other tactics. Bomb attacks, as noted, prevail in both terrorist and insurgent strategies (Engene 2007).

Statistical studies have found that bombing has a tendency to increase in severity over time: 'the trend we identify for explosives, that is, that such attacks [severe in terms of casualties] have produced progressively more casualties over time, is particularly distressing given the sheer number of explosive attacks in the recent past' (Clauset, Young and Gleditsch 2007, 79; Jenkins 2014, 126). The increase in the number of victims per attack has been specifically linked to the rise of jihadist-inspired terrorism (Hoffman 1998; Rapoport 2001b).

Shifts in tactics are often caused by countermeasures. We have witnessed a downturn in the use of kidnapping and hostage-taking, popular in the 1960s and 1970s: 'hostage-taking events have fallen as a proportion of all terrorist incidents, while deadly bombings have increased as a proportion of deadly terrorist incidents' (Rosendorff and Sandler 2005, 179). Also, regarding the use of IEDs in recent years, we can witness tactical adjustment to countermeasures. The use of IEDs has evolved from simple concealed roadside bombs, which triggered increased armour on vehicles used in Afghanistan, to mounted IEDs: 'the bomb makers adapted and adjusted to these new force-protection measures and began to design and place IEDs in elevated positions, attaching them to road signs or trees, in order to impact the vehicles' unarmored upper structure' (Hoffman 2014, 69). In 2014, the measures against IEDs had cost the United States at least 20 billion dollars (Hoffman 2014). This tactical substitution illustrates the working of a tactical culminating point, where the maximum utility of the instrument has been reached by the development of countermeasures: 'in war a competent enemy will be able to identify the weapon's equally homogenous performance boundaries and then proceed to evade interception by transcending those boundaries' and eventually negating the weapon's original and novelty value on the battlefield (Luttwak 2001, 40; Cronin 2019).

TERRITORY

Attacks can also be relocated to other geographical locales. For example, if the access to a certain terrain has been denied. This is closely related to the phenomenon of conflict spillover. Rebels tend to shift easily between theatres of operation:

> [T]errorists . . . respond to security upgrades in one country by finding less-secure venues or opportunities in other countries. . . . [E]ven though countries may decide their counterterrorism policies independently, the outcomes of their decisions are interdependent. (Rosendorff and Sandler 2005, 172)

One example of geographic substitution is Hezbollah, which purportedly carried out attacks against Jewish targets as far away from the Middle East as Argentina in 1994 (Lutz and Lutz 2004) and more recently in 2012, in Burgas, Bulgaria (Levitt 2013). We have already seen the example of strategic substitution in the case of the FSLN in Nicaragua, switching between rural and urban centres. Territory and territorial substitution play a particularly significant role for the rebel groups pursuing an insurgent strategy (Morgan et al. 2008, 122).

In Chapter 3, we have addressed the role of third-party intervention and the role outside actors can play in a shift in saliency for the rebels or the state. In this chapter, focused on rebel capabilities, intervention has already appeared briefly in the shape of third-party weapon deliveries, which can augment rebel capability. There is one particular feature in the existing literature that has a long pedigree in understanding and defining rebel longevity, which is rebel sanctuary. Providing rebels sanctuary across borders and providing them with an opportunity to hide, recuperate, regroup and rearm forms a key enabler for many rebel groups. There appears to be large-scale consensus that sanctuary across borders is of paramount importance to sustain rebel violence (Thompson 1966; Record 2007; Salehyan 2007; Jardine and Palamar 2014).

There are many examples. In the case of the Philippines and the Mindanao conflict, the safe haven the MNLF enjoyed across the border in Sabah and the indirect political backing of the Malaysian regime, on less than speaking terms with its counterparts in the Philippines, proved essential in the continuation of the struggle (Reed 2013, 295). In particular, the access to external funding and training contributed to the rise of the MNLF as the predominant Moro liberation organisation. Their international contacts, including sponsorship by Libya, meant that they were well equipped, which attracted a steady stream of recruits (Reed 2013, 300–301, 308, 360–362).

In the case of the IRA, the Irish diaspora but also state sponsorship by Libya help explain, among others, the longevity of the violence. In the case of Nicaragua, the FSLN enjoyed sanctuary in neighbouring states but also regional neighbours of Costa Rica, Panama, Cuba and Venezuela, opposed to the Somoza regime, offered help (Le Blanc 2012). The sanctuary the Tamil LTTE enjoyed across the Palk Strait in India's Tamil Nadu was indispensable for recruits, material and smuggling to finance the war in Sri Lanka (Lewis 2012, 320). Indeed, support from India contributed to the LTTE becoming the dominant organisation in the struggle for an independent homeland (Hussain 2010, 403). Cutting off the links with the sanctuary were crucial in curbing the operational effectiveness of the LTTE. Furthermore, the LTTE relied on an extensive diaspora population in Europe and North America that bankrolled the rebel activities through taxation.

Two vignettes in the following chapters in the book will also highlight the feature of the importance of sanctuary. In the case of India, Pakistan fuelled the Sikh dispute but also the many other violent rebels contesting the unity of the Indian state after independence. By deliveries of arms and providing sanctuary, Pakistan aimed at destabilising India by fomenting internal unrest (Reed 2013). In the Chechen case, the sanctuary in Georgia, by no means a supporter of Russian policies in the region, offered the fighters a safe haven away from the battle front. In short, territorial substitution is a common phenomenon and a form of conflict escalation.

TIME

The last form of substitution is time. In many discussions of rebel activity, time is considered an asset, as it is the rebel group that decides through planning and surprise when its next attack will take place (Tse-Tung and Guevara 1961). Time is not an easy factor to investigate in armed conflict (Paquette 1991; Leonhard 1994; Pasco and Navy 2008; Carr 2018; Schmitt 2020). Time has been considered an important factor, for example, in explaining jihadist violence. The role of the religious calendar and the observance of religious feast days has tended to inform the timing of attacks (Hassner 2011; Toft and Zhukov 2015).

Substitution in time can both be time as postponing attacks to a more favourable moment in time and a more favourable period in time. Attacks can be postponed if the group has been compromised and needs to reorganise or resupply to continue operations. To prove that attacks were actually postponed in time is, however, very difficult since it requires information from those making decisions, which even ex post facto is hard to come by.

Attacks can also be postponed for a period of time. To prove that a rebel group opted for a more favourable time period faces a similar investigative challenge. Rebels using terrorist or insurgent strategies tend to have time on their side. They fight a protracted type of conflict and in that sense consider time as available and on their side. They possess what is called strategic patience. In Afghanistan, it was said that the intervention forces had all the watches and the Afghans had all the time, illustrating the awareness of strategic patience (Jardine 2009).

One avenue for investigation would be to further dissect the lulls in campaigns to see whether these can be explained by ideas about more advantageous timing. In particular, the role of negotiations could be informative here. As we have already seen earlier, rebel groups might engage in negotiation for the highly pragmatic reason of creating a breathing space and suspension of armed interaction, which can be beneficial for the group.

A last dimension of the time factor, apart from time as a moment or a period, is the idea of time as duration. In the discussion of the political opportunity structure earlier, we have seen that when the rebel group has invested a lot of time in the struggle, there is a link with tenacity and commitment to the cause, also called sunk costs. All these different dimensions of time can constitute an aggravation of conflict and a form of substitution.

ESCALATION: SUBSTITUTION

Summarising, substitution is a form of escalation. Substitution comes in the shape of shifts in targets, tactics, territory and timing. For the state, conversely, this adaptability can prove challenging. Rebels are similar to the Hydra, the mythological multi-headed serpent which as soon as one head was cut off is able to develop new ones in its place. Substitution ensues when countermeasures are instituted, which inhibit access to targets, compromise the working of previous tactics, challenge control over territory and frustrate the timing of attacks. Rebels tend to have the ability to be highly flexible and adaptable and shift easily towards other or new targets, adopt different or new tactics, move to other grounds and postpone attacks, in particular in comparison to the state opponent. When physical control over a territory is challenged, the key feature of an insurgency strategy, rebels can shift to hit-and-run attacks, ambushes or terrorism. When particular tactics or targets become inaccessible, substituting them for others is relatively easy.

Countermeasures instituted against the rebel group form a significant cause for shifts in targets, tactics, territory or time. Only when targets are hardened or become inaccessible would it become necessary or interesting to shift targeting. When measures are taken to compromise the effectiveness of a particular type of tactics, only then would the importance of maintaining or raising the effectiveness of a particular type of tactics surface as a problem.

It also appears that for groups using terrorism, the flexibility or the likelihood of substitution is higher. For those groups using an insurgency strategy, the flexibility appears less, since these groups have to deal, in many cases, with an organisational aspect, which might require preparation and adjustment in capability and expectations from supporters and the territorial aspect, which creates a measure of commitment but at the same time inflexibility.

Neglecting or denying the rebel group an operational dimension is unwise (Jardine and Palamar 2014). For rebels, it is notable that, in particular, tactical-level actions can generate strategic effects. In fact, tactical engagement within irregular war strategies, while skipping the operational dimension, can bring about strategic success. The most notable example is the Vietnam War, where a powerful strategic effect was brought about by tactical engagement in South Vietnam. This issue will be taken up again in more detail in the concluding chapter in the discussion about rebel victory and defeat.

7

Political Will

Group Processes and Individual Considerations

Although some have claimed that '[e]scalation is possible only after [state] repression' (Pierskalla 2010, 8), there is also strong support for the view that escalation results from internal group processes and individual determinants. This line of argument asks attention for developments internal to the group that account for escalation (see also Bosi et al. 2014). Many studies conducted into the phenomena of non-state actor violence and rebel behaviour find time and again that instead of an ideological struggle, they can also, some claim, much better, be explained by group dynamics and individual disposition. In the study of rebel violence, 'there is a clear epistemic bias in favor of the assumption that most conflicts are motivated by grand ideological concerns' (Kalyvas 2004b, 173). To remedy this shortcoming, scholars have started to look at the interaction between individuals and the development of groups and group dynamics. It has been suggested that 'popular international ideologies spur and catalyze terrorism, but they do not fully define its goals over time' (Cronin 2009, 41). These ideas demand closer investigation.

Rather than political opportunity or ideology, scholars have claimed that social solidarity is the overriding reason for participation in rebel groups (Abrahms 2008). Not only for terrorism but also for insurgency, group formation and behaviour are deemed of the utmost importance to understand it (Kalyvas 2004b, 2006). Rather than ideological idealism, 'the motivations of "ordinary people" caught in the whirlwind of violence and war tend to be mundane rather than heroic: to save one's job, house or family, for instance' (Kalyvas 2004b, 174). For the case of Afghanistan, some have argued that the fighters '[seek] safety, sovereignty, masculinity, and although widely overlooked, a strong bargaining chip through which to enter rather than topple the Afghan government' (Barakat and Zyck 2010, 198). Furthermore, '"fighters" and groups' motives are multifaceted and, in particular, far more parochial, often related to issues of retribution, respect, and access to resources"' (Barakat and Zyck 2010, 196; Thruelsen 2010; Simpson 2012). Based on field work in the Palestinian territories, one study has found that 'communal orientation [rather than strategic calculation] may be necessary to inspire collective action at increasing levels of sacrifice', such as engagement in violent activities (Argo 2009, 659). Ideological justifications might result after joining a group, rather than precede accession. Many individuals active in Marxist-inspired violent groups, for example, only took to reading Karl Marx after they were imprisoned (Merkl 1995, 199). Group pressure can also explain performance in battle. Camaraderie, reputation and leadership can all contribute to fighting potential.

From the perspective of the rebel group, group cohesion is of vital importance. Fragmentation seemingly goes against the utilitarian paradigm predominant in the study of political violence (Abrahms 2008). It does not make sense to split up an organisation when the overall chances of attaining strategic goals are weakened. However, practice shows that rebel groups fragment and split all the time. Several studies have demonstrated that fragmentation of rebel groups can still be explained by utilitarian considerations (Gates 2002; Christia 2012; Fjelde and Nilsson 2012; Staniland 2012a, 2012b; Seymour 2014; Woldemariam 2016). Rational calculations for rebel fragmentation can relate to local leadership interests to pursue a specific advantage, but also the chances of spoils, foreign support, the relative military position, weak state capacity and ethnic fragmentation. Fragmentation can be a result of internal processes or outside pressure, that is by the state opponent, that wittingly or unwittingly breaks up the rebel group. We will now turn to these processes and in particular their link to crossing thresholds in armed conflict.

This chapter is intended to further compliment the picture of escalation and aims to bring together the diverse sets of explanatory factors to create a more comprehensive picture. Escalation can be a product of internal strife, caused by psychological and organisational mechanisms and internal spoilers. Escalation can also result from external pressure on rebels, such as targeted killing and external spoiling. Apart from group processes, the chapter will also focus on individual explanations for increased violence. The examples of the Sikh independence struggle in the 1980s, Germany in the 1970s and Italy in the early 1980s will aid in detailing these processes and mechanisms. We find an important manifestation of escalation in the shape of a group extremity shift.

INTERNAL GROUP DYNAMICS

Internal dynamics in rebel groups have been suggested as key to understanding the development of violence: 'The group plays a significant role in shaping the behavioural processes inherent in becoming a terrorist, but plays perhaps an even more obvious role in terms of sustaining involvement and promoting engagement in violence' (Horgan 2005, 108). Empirical evidence shows that internal pressures can both produce cohesion and fragmentation. In particular, these internal processes of factionalisation and fragmentation, a loss of support and a divorce from claimed constituencies, a failure to incite a successor generation and strategic mistakes lead to group demise (Cronin 2009; see also Ross and Gurr 1989). Several internal dynamics deserve a closer look since they have been specifically linked to escalation: group think pressure and the role of leadership, spoilers, outbidding and organisational survival (see also Thompson 2014).

Group Think Pressure

First elaborated by Irving Janis in 1972, group think exhibits itself in the following way: 'the more amiability and esprit de corps among members of a policy-making group, the greater is the danger that independent critical thinking will be replaced by group-think, which is likely to result in irrational and dehumanizing actions against outgroups' (Janis 1972, 13; see also McCormick 2003). Group think will emerge when there are high levels of stress due to the environmental circumstances in which groups operate, a detachment from society and lack of exposure to alternative points of view, homogeneity among the group members in socio-economic background, a lack of unbiased leadership and transparent decision-making procedures (Tsintsadze-Maass and Maass 2014).

Group think has exhibited the following characteristics: dehumanisation of the enemy, military terminology to describe activists as warriors and the situation as war, which calls for extraordinary measures (Coser 1956; Della Porta 1995b, chapter 7). Furthermore, it is based on the ideas of superior morality of the group, invincibility and invulnerability, illusions of unanimity and collective rationalisation and a censorship on dissent. What can be witnessed in outward activity is seemingly irrational decision-making based on an incorrect impression of reality, a neglect of alternative courses of action and a lack of realistic risk assessment and contingency planning (Tsintsadze-Maass and Maass 2014) Longevity of the organisation increases the chances of group think; '[t]he longer a terrorist organization exists, the more likely that group solidarity will replace political purpose as the dominant incentive for members' (Crenshaw 1985, 473). These suggestions can be linked to the Cold War escalation literature on the emergence of perception biases, failures of awareness and lack of empathy to understand others.

Evidence of the role of group think and outward action is plentiful. Looking into the activities of rebels using terrorism, several scholars have noted that, indeed, these groups, their make-up and activity, often produce outward violence almost regardless of their surroundings or opponent (Crenshaw 1983b, 162, 1985; Della Porta 1995b). Della Porta speaks of 'a vicious circle of irreversible choices, some determined less by reason and will than by chance and "necessity"' (Della Porta 1995b, 22). Outside influences are seemingly limited: '[t]errorism as a process gathers its own momentum, independent of external events' (Crenshaw 1981, 396, 1985, 1991). The political violence in Italy in the late 1970s changed from strategic considerations to internal ones: 'in Italian ... left-wing groups ... engaged in much higher levels of violence than their public constituencies could withstand, in an effort to hold their membership together' (Cronin 2009, 100). Violence was a product of a social learning process and instrumental for internal cohesion and served as a morale booster (Akers and Silverman 2015). The Brigate Rosse (BR), which will be discussed shortly, fell into the escalation trap, where their use of violence exceeded a point of external utility and ended up backfiring by diminishing public support but it clearly did serve internal needs of the group. Group solidarity can thus be a crucial motivator and explains the continuation of rebel violence (Laqueur 1998; Kalyvas 2004a). Over the course of time, these factors have been found to increase in importance. Psychological and relational factors tend to attract more weight over the course of campaigns. In the cases of Germany and Italy, this development had, as important corollary, an increase in casualties (Della Porta 1995b). Moreover, the chances of the group making mistakes tend to grow (Matesan and Berger 2017, 379).

Extremist Leadership

Internal pressures can build resulting from a detachment from society, the necessity to demonstrate group loyalty, to boost morale and promote unity, to establish control and eliminate dissent and to demonstrate leadership. This shift in the extremity of the points of view that members hold occurs not only when the group becomes more inward looking but also when more militant leadership comes forward (McCauley, Segal and Hendrick 1987). Once the struggle is under way, more militant leadership tends to come forward (Coser 1956; Deutsch 1973; Pruitt and Rubin 1986). Whereas group think focuses on the identification with fellow group members, there are several scholars who have noted the central role of identification with the leadership for understanding group action (Johnston 2009). In a study into group leadership, the workings and outward activities of rebel groups are explained by leadership performing indispensable roles (Freeman 2014). Two main functions can be identified. Leaders can be providers of inspiration and operational direction.

Leadership can inspire by ways of charisma and ideological vision. Over time this inspiration, borrowing from Max Weber, tends to become routinised through procedures, symbols, rituals and ceremonies. An example is the role of Shoko Asahara, leader of the Japanese Aum Shinrikyō sect responsible for the sarin gas attack on the Tokyo underground in 1995. The role of individual leadership can produce violence based on charisma and the desire among group members to please the leader. Operational direction is provided by the leadership through the development of plans and directing the followers to carry these out, through the maintenance of the organisation and the forging of external contacts (Freeman 2014).

Shifts in the extremity of points of view can occur within the rebel group, which produces outward violence (Silke 2008). The leadership can have far-ranging influence in regard to the practices and tactics employed by the rebel group (Bastug and Guler 2018). Group pressure and militant leadership can thereby result in more and heavier violence.

Apart from group pressure and extremist leadership, larger movement processes can also contribute to conflict aggravation. Rebels can try to balance against their rivals to prevent being dominated. Rebels can defect or switch sides. Spoiling behaviour can also be used to make life difficult for rival groups. Outbidding is also a method that can be used in the shape of offering a better deal to supporters, which comes often in the shape of public goods. Alternatively, outbidding can occur via more effective or convincing violence. In particular, the last form of outbidding and the idea of spoiling have, in the literature, been linked to escalation. The emergence of spoilers and the practice of violent outbidding, together with group pressure and extremist leadership, are two dynamics that can also lead to an extremity shift, which constitutes escalation.

Spoilers

The level of violence in armed conflict can significantly be affected by spoilers from within the ranks of the rebel group. Spoilers are those actors involved in armed conflict who try to sabotage dialogue and de-escalation and often actively seek escalation. In his 1997 benchmark study on spoilers, Stephen Stedman argued that the logic of spoiler behaviour demands a visual, physical display of violence in order to make known the existence of the spoiler party (Stedman 1997). Spoilers are not exclusively an accompanying phenomenon of rebels; also the state can give rise to spoilers from its ranks, such as South American death squads and extremist groups in South Africa seeking restoration of the status quo.

Firstly, violence can be a signal for others of the existence and the commitment of the breakaway faction. Spoilers can use violence in a signalling function and as a means to demand clarity from their potential supporters of where they stand. This can force moderates to choose sides. This factionalisation is often linked to ideological extremism (Hafez 2020). The emergence of these splinter groups is linked to the original organisational parameters of the group, that is pre-existing structures and fissures (Burch and Ochreiter 2020).

In quantified studies, spoiler behaviour is correlated with violence in cases where resources are abundant and moderates are not co-opted by the government to act against the rebel group. In other words, they can still be won over (Bueno de Mesquita 2005).[1] There are several examples of the signalling function of violence (Kydd and Walter 2006). At the start of the Good Friday peace process in Northern Ireland, there was a marked upsurge in IRA violence mainly intended for consumption of the Republican supporters to show that despite its place at the negotiating table, the IRA had not forfeited force and there were parts of the organisation still espousing the armed struggle. The 1998 Omagh bombing in Northern Ireland was intended to spoil the peace process between the warring parties and the British government but, in fact, ended up attaining the opposite effect, strengthening the resolve of those seeking to end violence.

---

[1] This argument is similar to the collaboration-control literature on the function of violence as forcing a choice on the population in case of unclear control (Kalyvas 2006).

Secondly, violence can also rise, after the initial termination of conflict, as a sign of attempts to establish dominance over parts or remnants of an organisation. In an attempt to explain the resumption of violence after initial termination of rebel violence, several authors have suggested that splits occur as a result of disagreements over the spoils of war (Atlas and Licklider 1999; Boyle 2009, 2014). The outcome, often based on compromise peace, does not meet with expectations of members of the victorious rebels. Capabilities have not been downgraded and a renewed claim on power and a chance of control becomes attractive. This follows largely the logic of patrimonial authority dynamics. In post-conflict politics, however, there is uncertainty over who is in charge of the rules of the game.

Thirdly, parts of the formerly united rebel group can give rise to spoilers who might feel the need to follow suit and use violence. This has been called chain-ganging, a mechanism whereby more violence is preferably avoided, but since others have engaged in it, as in a chain gang, there is no other option (Krause 2014, 82). This occurs when spoilers have arrived on the scene and other parts of the movement are left with no choice to follow suit.

A specific form of spoiling is defection to the side of the government. There is evidence that goes both ways as to the causality of defection and violence. One study finds that defection to the government side has, as in the case of Sri Lanka, led to more violence (Obayashi 2014).[2] A reduction of uncertainty as to the whereabouts and the capacity of the rebel group has in this case led to emboldening the government to take offensive action and defeat the group. Others have argued that a reduction in uncertainty lessens the chances of violence because of reduced necessity (Fearon 1995).

Most of the rebels discussed in this study have witnessed spoiler behaviour. Some rebel groups ended up with offshoots or even multiple factions during the course of their existence. Splits do seem to occur when external pressure is lessened and there is room for a dissenting voice, political openings occur or negotiations are conducted, fissures are likely to come to the fore that the rebels are unable or unwilling to deal with internally. As noted earlier, the FSLN in Nicaragua experienced splits related, among others, to the strategy that the movement pursued to rid the country of

---

[2] However, Mahoney claims that immediately following the split between the LTTE and the PLOTE factions, there was a decrease in violence because of Indian state support for both (Mahoney 2017, 11).

Somoza. The MNLF in the Philippines also witnessed breakaway factions, of those willing to engage with the regime, which had offered a way out of the struggle and those elements within the rebel group that wanted to continue the civil war. Furthermore, in Mindanao, not only religious versus secular but also clans amongst each other, elite versus non-elite groups, and social economic factors played out in the aligning and realigning of the factions during the course of the conflict (Reed 2013, 314–315).

Outbidding

It is an often-observed phenomenon that the more radical section of the rebel group specifically targets the moderate opposition. The former see it as imperative to present themselves as the sole voice of the opposition and other moderate groups that might still be co-opted by the state are seen as rivals. Exclusive claims on legitimacy and representation of the rebel agenda can lead to within-movement violence. This is called outbidding and occurs between different groups within the rebel group or the wider social movement (Kaufman 1996; Bloom 2003; Alimi et al. 2012, 2015; Zuber 2013; Bosi et al. 2014; Della Porta 2014).

Sometimes the mere presence of competing groups can be perceived as a challenge and lead to more violence. A notable example illustrating outbidding is the Tamil LTTE case. Over the course of their thirty-year struggle in Sri Lanka for an independent homeland, the LTTE set out to eliminate its rivals to claim sole authority over the independence agenda. Initially, there were five main organisations, the Tamil Five, espousing violence to further the independence agenda. The Five were made up of the Tamil Eelam Liberation Organisation (TELO), the Eelam Revolutionary Organisation of Students (EROS), the People's Liberation Organisation for Tamil Eelam (PLOTE), the Eelam People's Revolutionary Liberation Front (EPRLF) and the Tamil National Tigers, later renamed the Liberation Tigers of Tamil Eelam (LTTE). (Bloom 2003, 61) Even though attempts were made to form a common front, the Eelam National Liberation Front from 1984 till 1986, the LTTE instituted an assassination policy to rob rival organisations of their leaders. In this quest, it was strong enough to confront both the state and the rival groups at the same time. The LTTE first managed to neutralise the EPRLF by eliminating its leadership. It was subsequently clear that any leader or grouping wishing to split off from the Tigers would face elimination. Despite its harsh treatment of potential defectors, the most significant split that signalled the end of the LTTE was the breakaway faction led by Colonel Karuna, who in 2003 during the peace process chose to distance himself from the LTTE leadership (Lewis 2012, 315). His main support base, the eastern part of the island was where the first government advances against the LTTE were successful, ending ultimately in the defeat of the rebel group.

Outbidding also occurred in the case of the Algerian war of independence, where the Front de Libération Nationale eliminated the moderate opposition which had formed as an interlocutor of the French government. Starting right after the Second World War, the insurgents tried to develop the FLN as the sole legitimate representative of the nationalist agenda. In the process, others, striving with more peaceful instruments for the same ideal, were assassinated (Horne 2002; Krause 2014). A similar development occurred during the Spanish civil war, where rival Republican political entrepreneurs were targeted and the moderate voice was eliminated (Herreros and Criado 2009). There is evidence that this violent form of outbidding against rivals works even when it involves the killing of civilians (Alimi 2011; Mahoney 2018). It is not so much the violence but rather the size of the group after the splintering that influences its chances of success (Hafez 2020). Outbidding in the shape of suicide terrorism as a bargaining tool among different factions or groups has found far less agreement in terms of its effectiveness. There are experts who have found that outbidding can act as a form of currency to increase rebel group legitimacy (Bloom 2004). This apparently applies in particular to groups in the Middle East. Others are far less certain and claim that outbidding does not make suicide terrorism more popular or necessary (Findley and Young 2012).

Outbidding is another form of an extremity shift. The drive to eliminate rivals leads to a more extreme stance of the overall opposition. For the case of rebels espousing a nationalist agenda, one hegemonic group among the family has been found to increase the chances of strategic success: 'hegemonic movements are more likely to be clear, credible coercers with cohesive strategies of violence than are united or fragmented movements, and are therefore more likely to yield strategic success' (Krause 2014, 84). When the hegemony over the specific movement and agenda remain unclear, infighting and outbidding overrule strategic considerations, according to these insights. This is closely related to an action imperative; once a more radical stance has been adopted, the pressure mounts to demonstrate this to the outside world.

Organisational Survival

Organisations possess a natural tendency to grow when attempting to achieve their aims. This is a central idea in rational choice theory (Olson 1994). Rebels can adopt two routes to deal with growth (Freeman 2014). Firstly, the rebel group can centralise, organise and create a bureaucracy and/or a territorial base. This is generally the direction followed in the insurgency strategy. The rebel group develops into a shadow government or shadow state to prepare itself to eventually take over power.

Secondly, the rebel group can decentralise and devolve decision-making to smaller and smaller units operating in a network structure. This has been the route adopted by many rebels using the terrorist strategy. To safeguard operations and escape detection, this is an attractive course of action. However, a decentralised organisational structure can hamper operational effectiveness because supporters expect specific benefits from powerful organisations. The most extreme form of devolved power is the form of leaderless resistance, a format popular among right-wing radical groups but also among jihadis.

The challenge most rebels face is that they need to 'pursue strategic objectives that benefit their larger social movements while they simultaneously pursue organizational objectives that benefit the groups themselves' (Krause 2013, 290). Can these objectives be pursued simultaneously? How can we explain which consideration is dominant at what point? What is pursued when and what happens when they contradict, for example in light of the achievements of strategic goals that might require the disbanding of the group? One study concludes that 'organizational objectives ... play the dominant role in group motivations for violence and perceptions of its political effectiveness, rather than the strategic objectives on which existing scholarship relies' (Krause 2013, 291).

Continued existence can become a primary and overriding concern for small groups.

[A]cts of terrorism may be motivated by the imperative of organizational survival or the requirements of competition with rival terrorist groups. Terrorism is the outcome of the internal dynamics of the organization, a decision-making process that links collectively held values and goals to perceptions of the environment. (Crenshaw 1985, 473; Dixon 2020)

The quest of organisational survival is fed by the participation of the members of the group, their social identity and the identification with the group's goals. Organisational objectives are claimed to play a dominant role when the survival of the rebel group is challenged by the state or by competitors from among the social movement family (Krause 2014). An example is the successor generations of the German Rote Armee Fraktion, which will be further elaborated later. When the founding members of the group, among them Andreas Baader, Gundrun Ennslin and Ulrike Meinhof, were behind bars after 1972, the group was severely weakened. A new campaign of violence started with an increased level of violence and with the two-pronged goal of carrying the ideals of a Marxist world revolution and pressing for the release of the first generation from prison. The idea of a fundamental threat to organisational survival forms the most extreme form of a saliency shift. As a saliency threshold, it therefore constitutes a form of escalation.

This chapter has brought forward several propositions. We identify three main processes based on endogenous rebel group developments that are a form of escalation: group dynamics, including group think and the emergence of extremist leadership, spoiling and outbidding. Firstly, an internal radicalisation of the positions adopted towards the cause and the advent of radical leadership can create pressures. Internal group processes, independent of external circumstances, can produce outward violence. An extremity shift can also ensue out of internal spoiler behaviour. The signalling of dissidence or continued commitment, fighting over the spoils of conflict or simple chain-ganging are forms of spoiling activity that are linked to crossing thresholds in war. Within the wider social movement from which the rebel group can derive, an elimination of the moderate voice can take place. This outbidding also signifies an extremity shift.

Apart from the extremity shift, another variation of the saliency shift has surfaced, augmented saliency caused by challenges to group survival. A fundamental threat to the survival of the group is a saliency shift. Apart from these purely internal dynamics, external pressures on these internal processes can give rise to escalation, which we will now discuss in the following section.

ESCALATION AND EXTERNAL PRESSURE ON REBEL GROUPS

External pressure can come in many different shapes and guises. The importance of protest policing has been noted as well as its effect on the hardening of the stance of the rebel group members (Della Porta 1995b). Furthermore, arresting members of the group of supporters or sympathisers and surveillance by the security services are other means of increasing pressure on the rebel groups and can result in violent outbursts. What are the effects of outside pressure on internal rebel dynamics?

Three generations of scholarship can be distinguished devoted to the question whether external pressure increases internal rebel cohesion (McLauchlin and Pearlman 2012). The first generation observed the phenomenon of increased internal unity and cohesion as a result of external pressure (Coser 1956; Benard 2012). Solidarity among group members was strengthened as most important effect of the application of outside pressure, specifically violence. The second generation placed emphasis on the fragmentation of movements as a result of outside coercion, pre-existing fissures and problems were brought out into the open and subsequent disintegration was the result (Tilly 1978). A third generation has proposed that integration or disintegration could be linked to the idea of satisfaction with pre-existing decision-making structures within the rebel movement (McLauchlin and Pearlman 2012). If there is a dissatisfied section in the movement, outside pressure might further the specific interests of this group and defection results. However, if the institutional arrangements are satisfactory to all tiers and members of the group, outside pressure will more likely reinforce internal cohesion (Pearlman 2012; Warren and Troy 2015). However, some recent scholarship, using quantification, has concluded that overall state violence, as a specific form of outside pressure, does not have any significant effect on the cohesion of the organisation (Asal, Brown and Dalton 2012, 111).

External pressure can affect rebels in two ways: their internal dynamics and their production of outward violence. In the following sections, we will take a closer look at several aspects of the working of external pressure: divide and rule, targeted killing and third-party spoiling. These forms of external pressure are focused on affecting the inner dynamics of rebels, playing different sections against each other, generally, in the hope of weakening the rebel group and gaining political benefit.

Divide and Rule

A very common approach by states on a course to repress rebels is to exert pressure by ways of playing different factions, parts or individuals within the rebel group against each other, that is a divide and rule approach. Active promotion of splits within terrorist and insurgent movements has been prescribed as a recipe to weaken rebels. Many states have consciously tried to wean moderates away from the core rebel group in order to divide the membership. Choosing this course of action, however, has been linked to more violence (Bakke, Cunningham and Seymour 2012; Walther and Pedersen 2020), the prolongation of conflict (Bakke, Cunningham and Seymour 2012; Obayashi 2014) and also to difficulties in ultimately resolving the conflict (Horowitz 1985). The Indian government, as an example, promoted tensions between the different parts of the Sikh movement and adopted a divide and rule approach. They played the pre-existing factions within the movement against each other, leading to divisions and the adoption of diverging goals. The result was a variety of groups with a variety of violent agendas. It made tackling the Sikh challenge much more difficult and negotiating a settlement a far-fetched option (Reed 2013).

For the rebel group, divide and rule is not only a challenge but it could also provide an opportunity to deal a blow to weaker factions within the opposition movement and take the lead or strengthen its bargaining position vis-à-vis the government. This is of interest because not only, as already noted above, is the state more inclined to make concessions to a stronger opponent (Cunningham, Gleditsch and Salehyan 2009, 578). Also, there is evidence that a strong rebel group possessing internal cohesion is linked to an increased chance of attaining goals (Akcinaroglu 2012).

Targeted Killing

Targeted killing has been the subject of a polarised debate in recent years. This has, among others, been inspired by the killing of Osama bin Laden in 2011 and the rise of the practice by using drones in a variety of conflict settings. Targeted killing is aimed at undermining the operation of rebel groups by focusing on its leadership and core membership. It is, however, by no means a new phenomenon.

Taking out the leadership of rebels has been proposed by a host of scholars as effective for the state in curbing rebels (Art and Richardson 2007, 639; Harmon 2008; Jordan 2009; Tierney 2015). When the leadership is weakened or eliminated through the use of military measures, a follow-up generation cannot be established. The existing supporters become disillusioned and can decide to quit. The lack of a second generation has been identified as an important cause of the demise of rebel violence (Cronin 2006). Several examples have surfaced in the literature: 'the ambush of the Black Panther leaders in Chicago in December 1969 and the attack on the Symbionese Liberation Army headquarters in Los Angeles in May 1974. In both cases the "revolution" was terminated by a single lethal act' (Hanle 1989, 216). But also with groups espousing other agendas, we see the practice as prevalent. Examples are the arrest of the leadership of Sendero Luminoso and the Kurdistan Workers Party (PKK) (Cronin 2006; Harmon 2008). There is supposedly a 'profound cumulative effect of targeted killing on terrorist organizations. Constant elimination of their leaders leaves terrorist organizations in a state of confusion and disarray' (Luft 2003, 3). The specific targeting of the leadership overall leads, arguably, to a swifter conclusion of the civil war and substantially reduced levels of violence after the targeted killing (Johnston 2012).

Yet others have pointed out that targeted killing might only possess a partial and temporary effect rather than a permanent one (Cronin 2009). The complete opposite, a consistent and lasting rise in violence has also been argued to exist. There is evidence that after targeted killing there is an upsurge in violence (Gross 2003; Luft 2003; Byman 2006). The reasoning followed here is that targeted killing of the leadership leaves lower ranking members of the organisation in charge with a lower threshold for indiscriminate violence, thereby causing at least short-term escalation (Abrahms and Mierau 2015; Abrahms and Potter 2015). Furthermore, a substitution effect has been found in the shape of less effective and sophisticated violence against those held responsible for the targeted killing (Wilner 2010).

In an attempt to solve this puzzle, scholars have introduced a more fine-grained analytical framework, investigating the organisational structure and the durability of rebels as variables affecting the targeted killing policy (Carvin 2012). The longevity of the rebel group is one factor; the longer the group is in existence, the less chances of a decapitation of the organisation leading to its fragmentation or its demise (Price 2012, 2019). Furthermore, the specific role of leadership in providing inspiration and operational guidance hold significance for effectiveness. Removing leaders who provide both inspiration and operational guidance could be seen as most effective in leading to the demise of the rebel group. When leadership is based on inspiration, the decapitation of the rebel can lead to ideological confusion and the re-emergence of the collective action problem for the rebel group. When operational guidance is removed, rebels can suffer from a loss of strategic and tactical effectiveness (Freeman 2014, 6).

In the case of the Punjab crisis, which will be discussed in more detail later, we find that at the point when parochial interests started to drive the violence, the targeted killings perpetrated by the Indian state against the most powerful individuals in the movement were highly effective in curbing rebel influence. While there was limited social support for the goal of an independent Khalistan and the rebel group was engaged in large-scale criminal enterprise, taking out the leaders significantly weakened the movement (Reed 2013). The most prominent and richest individuals in the movement were the primary targets of the security forces. The security forces targeted those leaders who had made most money and were closest to the spoils of war. It resulted in a drying up of recruitment because of larger personal risks and a diminished power circle that could be attractive to join for personal advancement.

Third-Party Intervention

We have already seen earlier the role of third parties in the debate about choices of strategy, where they were awarded some influence as to specific rebel strategy. Furthermore, political support and legitimacy, material aid and sanctuary across borders have already been discussed as important for the continuation of rebel violence.

Several studies have looked into the effects of third-party intervention on the organisational cohesion and structure of rebel groups. Their influence has been deemed large; external sponsorship has cohesion-enhancing as well as undermining effects (Lockyer 2011; Olson Lounsbery 2016; Tamm 2016). While fostering or maintaining power relations within rebel groups between leaders and internal rivals, the loss of sponsorship can create chances for rivals to challenge the leadership and splits can occur (Tamm 2016). Similar to the state, outside forces can play divide and rule to serve their own interests. Third parties can thus act as spoilers. We have already seen many examples of third parties offering immaterial and material aid and in particular foreign sanctuary to rebel groups. Third parties can thus affect the rebel group composition, functioning and capabilities. Third-party intervention can hereby contribute to an extremity shift within the rebel group.

Active third-party external intervention in ongoing conflict, as well as targeted killing and divide and rule, can all contribute to a group extremity shift. We now turn to the example of the Punjab conflict, where external pressure on and manipulation of the Sikh movement by the Indian state released a host of unforeseen responses, with an apogee in the killing of the head of state.

The conflict in the Punjab illustrates the ill-thought out consequences of state pressure on the rebel groups, with subsequent
blow back and a contest for control of constituencies. The lack of
anticipation by the state of the reactions of a calculating opponent
importantly marks the development of violence in this case.

At Indian independence in 1947, the state of Punjab was divided
between India and Pakistan. The Sikh East, where the majority of
the Sikhs lived, became the state of East Punjab within the Indian
Union. The predominantly Muslim West became West Punjab
within Pakistan (Dhillon 1990). Within East Punjab, the Sikhs
became a minority. Sikhs define themselves in religious terms, identifying as a group with the teachings of Guru Nanak, incorporating
elements from both Hinduism and Islam. They share a distinct
outward identity based on five symbols: their uncut hair and
beard, a wooden comb, an iron bracelet, a specific undergarment
and a Kripan or sword. For this proud and powerful group in
society, the partition was hard to swallow. Not only had they
contributed disproportionally in number of victims in the independence struggle, because of their wealth, they also paid heavily into the
federal state coffers. While making up only 2 per cent of the Indian
population, the overwhelming number of prisoners taken in the
independence struggle were Sikhs and they covered almost half of
the provincial tax revenue (Dhillon 1990, 18). While dissatisfaction
with a lack of recognition of their religious rights and economic
hardship of Sikh farmers were factors contributing to unrest in the
region, the fuse that lit this already pre-existing tinderbox were the
policies of the Indian government under Indira Gandhi.

Not only did Indira Gandhi try to centralise the Indian state in the
1970s, she also sought political advantage by manipulating Sikh–
Hindu tensions, which had existed in the Indian state since its
inception. Her centralising tendencies and a deliberate testing of
control set her on a collision course with the main Sikh political
party, the Akali Dal, which tried to further an agenda, seeking to
promote Sikh rights. Gandhi wilfully supported the rise of a Sikh
extremist movement to weaken Akali Dal, which she hoped would

---

Vignette 7.1 (cont.)

create space for her national Congress Party to rise at the cost of regionally focused political parties (Chima 2002).

Sant Jarnail Bhindranwale was a respected Sikh preacher who was head of the main institution of Sikh theocratic education, the Akal Thakt. His ideology was focused on promoting Sikh rights and not on the establishment of an independent Sikh Khalistan. Violence gradually rose in April 1978 with the agitation and increasing influence of Bhindranwale. Bhindranwale settled with his followers in the Golden Temple complex in Amritsar, the holy place for Sikhs, which became a no-go area for government officials, including the police. Violence grew into a full-blown confrontation in 1984 when Gandhi tried to forcefully vacate the Golden Temple complex because of its use as safe haven from which attacks were carried out. Gandhi hoped to benefit electorally by winning Hindi votes dealing decisively with blatant Sikh security breaches (Sohata and Sohota 1993).

The end result was a military operation; Operation Blue Star aimed at the re-establishment of control over the complex, which came at the cost of thousands of lives, including Sant Bhindranwale himself and 700 army soldiers (Pettigrew 1995). The Sikh community was enraged and deeply disturbed by the actions of the Indian government –they fed the Sikh misapprehensions about the Indian state. These actions formed a clear conduit for Sikh recruitment into the extremist movement. In revenge for the attack on the Golden Temple, and the subsequent violent mopping up exercise by the Indian government, Indira Gandhi was murdered on 31 October 1984 by her two Sikh bodyguards. The murder led to a wave of communal violence across India against Sikhs and Sikh property. This reinforced the feelings of the Sikh community of alienation that the Indian state was not their home (Dhillon 1990, 210).

Seeking electoral advantage and pursuing policies which were disadvantageous even for the moderate Sikh political parties led to an unwitting rise in violence, which was even more difficult to contain and manage thereafter. By exerting external pressure on the Sikh parties, not only the level of violence between the Sikh factions increased, the subsequent state attack on the Golden Temple complex brought on a further aggravation of conflict. Operation Blue Star forms another example of a case of state reaction triggering an escalation of rebel violence. As one of the main participants, K. P. S. Gill, the then director of Punjab police, has argued that 'Operation Blue Star to clear the Golden Temple complex and the Sikh massacres that followed were "the two most significant victories for the cause of 'Khalistan' . . . not won by the militants, but inflicted . . . upon the nation by its own Government. . . . These two events, in combination, gave a new lease of life to a movement which could easily have been contained in 1984 itself"' (Gill 1999, 3). The provocation by the state and the blowback from ill-thought-through divide and rule actions of playing the different factions against each other importantly explain the course of violence in this case.

So far, the discussion in this chapter has focused on the group. We have seen that an extremity shift in rebel groups is a form of escalation. Group processes, divide and rule pressure, targeted killing and third-party spoiling can all be seen as causing this type of escalation. Individual participation and engagement in violence now warrants a closer look to see where and how these can contribute to escalation. Group processes cannot be understood without some attention for individual dispositions to engage in violence.

THE INDIVIDUAL: ACCIDENTAL GUERRILLAS AND SITUATIONAL ENTRAPMENT

A large scholarship exists related to personal motivations and pathways into violence (Wood 2003; Abrahms 2008; Argo 2009; Ladbury 2009). In many cases, individual engagement in violence occurs by chance (Kilcullen 2009; Arjona and Kalyvas 2012). Moreover, individual routes into violence often leads via family, friends or networks to the taking up of arms. In the case of Nicaragua, for example, the FSLN recruitment largely took place following this pattern; the engagement of the young boys in the neighbourhoods to defend against state repression led whole families to follow suit: '[some] of us thought that the Sandinista Front would appear in columns ... only after [the insurrection] did we realize we were the Sandinista Front' (Cardenal quoted in: Le Blanc 2012, 198).

Both the rebel group and the state aim to influence individual calculations and dispositions to engage in violence. In an attempt to dissect the logic of violence, two types of insurgent actors have been identified –

opportunistic and activist – largely based on their incentive structures (Weinstein 2007; Salehyan et al. 2014). This typology places centre stage the ties between the leadership and the followers. The opportunistic insurgent actor, it is argued, possesses a weak commitment from its supporters and a strong incentive to seek personal rewards quickly. The activist insurgent actor is characterised by high commitment of its participants and a willingness to endure hardship and postpone (altruistic) gains. Opportunistic insurgencies play on the personal benefits for individual participation. These insurgencies are likely to be predatory and use indiscriminate violence. Activist insurgencies, alternatively, display more cooperative behaviour and are discriminate in their use of force. The argument that the resource base of the rebel group holds explanatory power for the development of violence is a wider shared argument (Toft and Zhukov 2015).

This approach, although very valuable, leaves open the questions when and where different constellations of opportunity and activism play out. The dynamic can possibly operate simultaneously; it can differ among parts of the insurgent movement and can change over time. It also omits the possibility that the state is part of the calculation, arguing instead that the state response is part of the larger context from which these groups emerge rather than being a direct contributor to action (Weinstein 2007; see also discussion in Tarrow 2007).

More than one study has found that the individual determinants gain in importance during the course of rebel–state conflicts. There is an observable shift during the course of these struggles from strategic and ideological frames towards other more personal ones (Crenshaw 1985; Weinberg and Eubank 1990; Van Creveld 1991; Della Porta 1995b). Violence can diverge on different levels of the groups (Della Porta 1995b; Kalyvas 2006; Kilcullen 2009; Krause 2013; Busher et al. 2019). For example, in the case of the Punjab crisis, there were two levels of violence. The bottom level consisted of locally inspired violence of the power hungry, the disenfranchised and the criminal. The top level was more ideological (Reed 2013). Over time, we witness, commensurate with an increase in territorial control in this case, more bottom-level violence.

To influence individual recruitment and participation, rebels use material and immaterial incentives. They influence, for example, the opportunities for personal advantage and pecuniary benefit and they co-opt or address local grievances to affect individual considerations.

Material Incentives

Material incentives have been extensively treated in the existing literature and also awarded large importance. Personal opportunity or betterment can form important drivers for participation in armed conflict. A statistical correlation has been found between economic downturns and upswings of terrorist activity (Blomberg, Hess and Weerapana 2004). This could indicate that rising unemployment makes the 'occupation' of terrorist or insurgent gain attraction. This was apparently the case for the Palestinians and the attraction to violence in the 1987 Intifadah (Krueger and Malečková 2003, 128) and the eruption of violence in Aceh in the aftermath of the 1998 Asian financial crisis (Collier et al. 2003) and also for the case of Afghanistan more recently (Bhatia and Sedra 2008).

Personal benefits can start to form part of war systems, in which it becomes of paramount importance to continue the violence to guarantee access to resources (Keen 1998, 2012). Resources, in particular clandestine financing, can be seen as pushing a struggle forward. John Mueller has suggested that most conflicts at the turn of the millennium have been criminal in nature rather than anything else (Mueller 2004). The links between the criminal underworld and rebel violence have traditionally been strong and often form an enabling factor for violence (Piazza and Piazza 2020). Personal self-enrichment, financial incentives, through the spoils of war is important to entice individuals to engage in warfare.

An argument can be made that war as a criminal undertaking increases in importance during the course of armed conflict. Material incentives, promoting participation in rebellion, form one of the main explanations for the continuation of violence, for example, in Eastern Congo (Humphreys and Weinstein 2008; Prunier 2009). It formed also an important but not overriding factor in the war in Sierra Leone (Peters and Richards 1998; Humphreys and Weinstein 2008).

It cannot, however, be discounted that these material explanations are tainted by an unclear separation of conceptual categories. As noted in Chapter 3, the political opportunity structure for many civil wars is provided by patrimonialism. A separation between economic and political power is very hard to make, since the one leads to the other and vice versa (Duyvesteyn 2005). A lack of state capacity can cause economic hardship and the use of violence could compensate for both.

For terrorist strategies, a complete shift towards a criminal organisation is one of the ways in which rebels transform their campaigns (Cronin 2009). Allegedly, some Loyalist groups in Northern Ireland and the FARC in Colombia are examples of this particular transformation process. The conditions for this transformation are provided by the conflict history: easy availability of weapons and a proficiency in raising funds through extortion, robbery, protection money schemes, kidnapping and drugs trafficking. This trajectory of criminalisation can form a barrier to peace. When rebel group members have become rich via criminal activities and have vested interests, they feel the need to protect these.

When criminal activity rises as a proportion of all rebel activity, it can be linked to a loss of popular support. In the case of the Sikh militancy, the main source of legitimacy was overreaction by the Indian state. Increased criminalisation, coupled with more careful and targeted police action, undermined the precarious public support base (Reed 2013).

State measures that specifically target material incentives for participation violence aim to undermine this material incentive structure. Social and economic measures have previously been found to be effective to lessen the threat of in particular revolutionary terrorism (Wilkinson 2000; Manwaring 2001, 41). This would mean that when income inequality is reduced, rebel violence would become less likely. Paradoxically, reducing economic inequality can 'increase *capacities* to organize and carry out terrorism' (Burgoon 2006, 178 italics in original; Freytag et al. 2011). Economic countermeasures, as with so many other countermeasures discussed in this study so far, are not linked in a direct linear relationship to a reduction of violence, as the evidence goes both ways.

Immaterial Incentives

Immaterial incentives can be related to the status of membership of a rebel group or to social goods, such as order, security and safety. Another personal incentive could be the emotional satisfaction of being a group member. In situations of a choice between emotions and rational calculation, emotions have an important role in directing individual considerations for engagement in violence (Pearlman 2013). Immaterial incentives are part of this equation. Membership of a rebel group can offer several types of personal reward and meaning. Social meaning and social regard can be derived from a life as a rebel (Crenshaw 1987). It offers opportunities of assertion of personal dignity and can form a source of pride and identity.

Immaterial incentives can be shaped by social factors (Haer, Banholzer and Ertl 2011; Parkinson 2013). Membership of a rebel group could be seen as a substitute family. The sense of belonging and the strength of social ties form rewards that facilitate and substantiate both recruitment and continued engagement in the rebel group (Abrahms 2008). In interviews with rebels in El Salvador, a 'deeply felt sense of pleasure [was] experienced together by the participants, in their public assertion of dignity, self-worth, and insurgent collective identity' (Wood 2003, 236), that was closely linked to continued engagement in the struggle.

Also, immaterial incentives can be found in the positive (self)-image of a rebel fighter as fighting for a greater cause. The idea of fighting for freedom or the righting of wrongs can form a powerful attraction for recruitment into rebel groups.

Finally, the desire for social order can also provide an incentive for rebel group membership. Analysing the Afghan civil war, a quest for social order and predictability in social relations appeared as important: 'Rather than greed, ideology, or hatred, parties in failed states strive for order' (Angstrom 2008, 379). Similarly, Rupert Smith has contended that 'people seek normalcy ... and that whoever provides it will gain their favour, whilst whoever is deemed to destroy it will become their enemy' (Smith 2006, 407; see also Black 2019).

Immaterial incentives can also be of a more negative nature, such as the desire for defiance, revenge and retribution. Individuals can view membership of a rebel group as a means of expressing a dislike of the existing social order and actively seek an environment with alternative norms and values. Revenge can also form an incentive for participation (Della Porta 1995b; Crenshaw 1999). An example of the dominance of the revenge dynamic forms the German RAF. In the 1970s, after the apprehension of its first generation of terrorists, the activist developed into a band of 'free-the-guerrilla guerrillas' largely motivated by revenge and the desire to liberate jailed comrades (Della Porta 1995b, 134). Revenge has also been a driving force in many other different conflict locales (see also discussion in Kalyvas 1999, 2004a). Revenge can be enacted both internally and externally; in the case of the Italian Red Brigades, internal revenge killings occurred in an atmosphere of suspicion when legislation came into effect in the later stages of the conflict. The fear of becoming a victim of retribution killings might thus have prolonged the violence (Pisano 1980, 9; Dunham 2002, 155; Weinberg 2007, 44). We will now look into these two cases in turn.

In 2015, two separate attempted robberies of cash transit vans in the car park of supermarkets in northern Germany occurred. These incidents would have passed without making much of a mark were it not for the fingerprints that were found of the perpetrators. The German Federal Criminal Office made public that these fingerprints belonged to members of the Rote Armee Fraktion that were still on the loose (Connolly 2016). These activists had continued their life in the underground and were now apparently in need of cash.

The Rote Armee Fraktion, supposedly an offshoot of an international red army, sprang from the youth movement of the late 1960s and turned to violence as a result of what they perceived as a provocation of the German state (Varon 2004; Aust 2008). From 1966 onwards, the German political landscape was dominated by a so-called grand coalition. The two main political parties, the Christian Democrats (CDU) and the Social-Democratic Party (SPD), decided to form a joint government. The rebellious youth found that opposition could no longer take place in parliament and therefore formed the Außerparlementarischen Opposition (APO) or extra-parliamentary opposition. There was reason for concern, they argued, because the grand coalition commanded a two-thirds majority in parliament, enough to change the constitution. Emergency laws, which were introduced in 1968, stipulated that in case of war, natural disaster or other major upheaval, some constitutional rights could be suspended. These emergency laws reminded the students of the authoritarianism of the past. The troubled past was still very much present in German public life. The students claimed that the de-nazification process was incomplete, since many who had dirtied their hands during the Nazi period were still in positions of power. Furthermore, continuities in imperialism even after de-colonisation, in the shape of the Vietnam War, enraged many. These qualms were expressed among others by the German Socialist Students Association and its vocal front man Rudi Dutschke, who was vilified by the conservative press in particular the tabloid Bild Zeitung.

In June 1967, the Persian Shah came to West Germany on a state visit, and the welcome of this controversial figure led to protests on the streets of Berlin. When the crowds became rowdy, police used a measure of force and one student, Benno Ohnesorg, was killed by bullets from a policeman. This outraged the students and triggered further demonstrations. The heavy handedness of the police response proved, according to the students that the state was arbitrary, violently repressive and flaunted its own constitution. Almost a year later, in April 1968, an attempt was made on the life of Rudi Dutschke, who was severely wounded but survived. Several members of what later became the RAF, Andeas Baader, Gudrun Ensslin and two others, fire-bombed a department store in Frankfurt as an act against capitalism.

Baader and Ensslin, a couple, were interested in pursuing an urban guerrilla modelled on the Tupamaros in Uruguay. They were apprehended, however, after the attack in Frankfurt and given prison sentences. The RAF was established in May 1970 by a journalist Ulrike Meinhof, who wrote for a communist magazine, *Konkret*, and Horst Mahler, an activist lawyer, who participated in the APO. Mahler claimed later that the most important reason to establish the RAF was the police violence against the student activists (Varon 2004, 4). Its first act of violence was the liberation of Baader, who was supposed to be interviewed by Meinhof in a library. One of the police guards was killed and Meinhof disappeared in the get-away car together with Baader. A spree of violent activity followed, with a commensurate rate of apprehensions. Bank robberies, arson attacks and shoot-outs with police occurred together with the establishment of action committees in support of the inmates. Paradoxically, RAF violence began at the time when the heyday of public protests declined in the early 1970s (Merkl 1995, 194).

In May 1972, the RAF launched a major offensive that would, they hoped, provide the spark for a revolutionary situation in Germany. The group aimed attacks against the US Army headquarters in Frankfurt, placed a car bomb to kill a federal judge and targeted a bomb at the Springer press, publisher of the *Bild*

Vignette 7.2 (cont.)

Zeitung in Hamburg, and at an American Army base in Heidelberg. The result was: four Americans killed and nearly seventy injured. Within weeks, the main perpetrators were caught: Andreas Baader, Ulrike Meinhof, Gudrun Ennslin, Holger Meins and Jan-Carl Raspe. The scene of action moved to prison, where in early 1973, forty RAF prisoners went on hunger strike to ask attention for their grievances. They demanded prisoner of war status, wanted to be interned together and lifted from what they considered solitary confinement which amounted to torture. The instrument of hunger strike continued to be used off and on, and in 1974, after fifty-four days of hunger strike, Holger Meins died.

With the first generation of RAF members imprisoned, a second generation emerged. In April 1975, the Commando Holger Meins, named after the deceased RAF member, entered the German Embassy in Stockholm and took twelve hostages to press the release of the RAF members in Germany. The timing coincided with the start of the trial against the inmates charged with murder. The RAF had turned into a 'free-the-guerrilla guerrilla movement' (Merkl 1995, 173).

The most virulent phase of RAF activity ended in the hot autumn of 1977. By that time Meinhof had already committed suicide in prison in May 1976. Several attempts had been made to press for the release of the RAF inmates, among others through the raid on OPEC in 1975, an airplane hijacking by Palestinian terrorists in Entebbe, Uganda, in 1976 and in April 1977 through the assassination of the federal prosecutor Siegfried Buback. At the end of April 1977, the court sentenced Baader, Ensslin and Raspe to life imprisonment. In a last-ditch attempt to do something for the sentenced RAF members, a RAF commando kidnapped in early September the head of the German Employers Associated Hanns Martin Schleyer and four Palestinians hijacked a Lufthansa jet filled with holidaymakers from Mallorca and diverted it to Mogadishu, Somalia. A German commando team, the GSG9, established after the Munich Olympic attacks in 1972, was flown to Mogadishu and stormed the plane on the tarmac. The next morning, on 18 October, Ensslin, Baader

---

and Raspe were found dead in their cells. A day later, the body of Schleyer was found in the trunk of a car in Mulhouse, France.

The second generation and subsequent followers displayed none of the fervour of the first generation and were argued to be held together by the mythology of the original RAF group (Merkl 1995, 194). Anti-imperialist violence of the successor generations continued during the course of the 1980s in the shape of attacks against symbolic targets such as American presence in West Germany and NATO. The Supreme Allied Commander Europe, General Alexander Haig was a target, but he narrowly escaped. American facilities in Frankfurt, Wiesbaden, and Ramstein, the US library in Berlin and a Dow chemical plant in Düsseldorf were also targets. Many of the RAF activists received assistance in the shape of cover and safe houses in East Germany, and there is evidence of active involvement of the East German Stasi. In 1998, a RAF document surfaced in which the group announced the cessation of its activities, which is seen as the official end of the organisation.

The case shows evidence of replacement, or at least the mixing of ideological motivations with the emergence of more and more personal motivations over the course of the struggle, including the factor of revenge. We see that the violence erupted with the police repression of student protests was perceived as excessive and which raised the salience of the issue for the protesters. Furthermore, we see evidence of an atrocity shift with the killing of individuals by the group. The next vignette is on the Italian Brigate Rosse, which will show how life in the underground provided constraints, such as a lack of alternatives or a way out of a life of violence.

Situational Entrapment

Once engaged in violence, self-preservation and personal survival often dictate a continued engagement. When the individual rebels are known by name, and are on the police watch list, a departure of the life in the underground and a reintegration into civil society is simply not possible (Della Porta 1995b). This phenomenon has been called situational entrapment and we find that it is visible importantly also on the individual level.

Individuals after initial recruitment find themselves in a situation in which a way out is denied and a continuation of life in the underground is often the only option. Situational entrapment can, on the individual level, cause a shift in extremity.

We will now take a closer look at the example of the Brigate Rosse. The Italian government put in place a specific programme focused on the individual determinants of a continuation of engagement in violence. It attempted to play at the cohesion of the group and appealed to individual calculation for the continuation of the campaign. The specific programme and its timing have been credited with causing a significant degree of de-escalation.

Vignette 7.3 – A Personal Way Out: The Brigate Rosse and the Case of the *Pentiti* Legislation in Italy

Italy, between 1969 and 1983, witnessed a wave of terrorism perpetrated by the Brigate Rosse (BR), a revolutionary extremist group, which has been referred to at several points in this study so far. Not only the Brigate Rosse was responsible for violence in Italian society, during that same period right-wing groups as well carried out political violence. Donatella della Porta has calculated that Italy witnessed '4,362 events of political violence, 6,153 unclaimed bombings against property; 2,712 attacks for which terrorist groups claimed responsibility, 324 of which were against people, with 768 injured and 351 killed' (Della Porta 1995a, 106). At the height of the violence, between 1978 and 1981, Italy experienced on average seven violent acts per day (Dunham 2002, 160). Despite these huge numbers and the political turmoil in Italy during these years, the state was surprisingly successful in ultimately prevailing against the different terrorist movements, and by the mid-1980s the number of incidents had dropped markedly (Hoffman and Morrison-Taw 1992, 27; Merlo and Marchisio 2006, 109; Weinberg 2007, 25, 41, 47).

Italy has traditionally had a strong and large Communist Party, which was committed to participating in mainstream politics. This created room on the left fringe of the political spectrum. It was filled by, among others, the Brigate Rosse. Since the aftermath of the

Second World War, a strong neo-fascist movement also existed in Italy, which initially had also committed itself to pursuing mainstream politics. However, in 1968, it decided to abandon its course of action to realise a strong state through regular politics but instead opted for a strategy of tension, created by putting pressure, including violent pressure, on the regime (Furlong 1981, 70; Weinberg 2007, 29–31). Mutual suspicions and a polarised political domain set the stage for the advent of violent rebels in the Italian political system.

In December 1969, an attack shook Italy. A bomb placed at a bank at Piazza Fontana in Milan killed sixteen people and injured more than eighty. It was likely carried out by right-wing extremists but allegedly framed to look like a left-wing attack. This led to a crackdown on left-wing sympathisers, which in the eyes of many de-legitimised the Italian state. In 1972, the Brigate Rosse first turned to violence with the assassination of a police detective. Subsequently they shifted gear and from 1974 onwards, focused on armed propaganda and attacked symbols of state power, both individuals and institutions. The response of the Italian state was, among others, a series of legal reforms, which culminated in the legislation that was to become vital in ending the BR campaign. Increasing the time of preventive custody, greater powers of interrogation, increased powers to stop and arrest suspects, searches without warrants and increased ability to use fire arms were some of the measures instituted. Beneficiaries of these were two inspectorates that were established to deal with the terrorist threat by surveillance and infiltration. A crucial role was played by Carabinieri General Carlo Alberto dalla Chiesa, who recognised the importance of an integrated and nationwide approach.

In the aftermath of the kidnapping and killing of Aldo Moro, a popular and moderate Christian Democrat politician in 1978, further legislative reforms took place: laws relating to terrorist intent, phone tapping and questioning of suspects without a defence lawyer were enacted. Most far-reaching and most praised for its effectiveness, in contrast to the previous measures, which were generally deemed to have compromised the civil liberties of the Italian state, has been the Penitence law. In effect for just one year (1982–83), it declared association with terrorist activity non-punishable and imprisonment non-mandatory when surrendering to the police, confessing to crimes committed and giving evidence against former comrades. It offered sentence reduction in return for helping the police as the ultimate device against undermining terrorist organisations. It was also applicable to those already imprisoned.

The existing assessments of the Penitence law all point to its effectiveness. Della Porta argues that the number of arrests rose significantly as a result of the coming into force of this particular law (Della Porta 1995a, 118–119). Indeed, de-escalation can be witnessed as a very noticeable drop in the number of attacks from 1983 onwards. The alienation of the BR from their natural support base of left-wing sympathisers after the murder of Aldo Moro, together with increased effectiveness of police work, thanks to Dalla Chiesa, contributed to the decline. The alienation of the BR from its support base had commenced already with a second generation of the organisation becoming increasingly violent, killing a popular member of the labour union (Schuurman 2013). The penitence law is credited as contributing most significantly to the end of the violent campaign (Della Porta 1995a, 118–119; Dunham 2002, 162–163; Cf. Merlo and Marchisio 2006, 102; Weinberg 2007, 53): 'For many brigatisti, the laws on disassociation and repentance must have appeared like a lifesaver to a drowning man' (Weinberg 2007, 55). Without resolving any of the underlying issues that had fed the violence, the combination of a loss of popular support and providing a personal way out for individual terrorists can explain a large part of the de-escalation that was achieved in this particular case.

In the many armed conflicts we have looked at so far, a personal way out of the life in the rebel group has been lacking. The Dirty War during the Process of National Reorganisation dictatorship in Argentina, for example, has been described as excessive. For the individual militants there was no way out of the struggle and continued engagement was the only alternative to being arrested, tortured and killed. There were no negotiating partners on either side and the extreme state repression is likely to have prolonged the conflict beyond its natural course (Le Blanc 2012): 'Members remained militant because of emotional bonds with companions and a lack of alternatives, but not anymore out of a belief in victory or in armed struggle' (Le Blanc 2012, 102). Similarly, in the case of the German RAF, the remaining members still at large attempting to rob a money transport van constitute a form of situational entrapment.

ESCALATION: THE EXTREMITY SHIFT

We quoted Clausewitz in Chapter 1, who noted that the terms of the struggle can change over time and that the factors that explain the outbreak of conflict do not necessarily explain its termination. We see this holds particular relevance at group and individual levels.

When the conflict continues after the initial escalation, internal determinants of the rebel group have a tendency to increase in importance. For the elite of a group, using an insurgent strategy, but also for a terrorist band, group dynamics can gain in significance. Life in the underground changes the conflict dynamics. It often limits the leverage the state can muster in regard to considerations and determinants of rebel action. The underground tends to harden the resolve of the rebel and substantially contributes to the organisational dynamics that provide the conflict with its own group-driven impulse. Past investments need to pay off, and group cohesion and personal commitment prevent defections. A detachment from society can follow, as does ideological radicalisation of the small group. Violence as a means of communicating with the supporting environment and for reasons of survival can exhibit itself prominently. The mechanisms of previous commitment, perception biases, situational entrapment, unwitting sensitivities and failures of analysis are in particular insightful when focusing on the group.

External pressures such as divide and rule, targeted killing and third-party external intervention have also been linked to causing escalation in the shape of an extremity shift. Playing different factions of a movement against each other can serve the purpose of weakening it overall. At the same time, the commitment of parts of the group can increase because of the pressure exerted from outside. Pressure on the leadership, the cohesion of the organisation or the support base might weaken the group but the opposite also occurs.

On the level of the individual, material and immaterial incentives play a role not only in recruitment but also in the continued engagement in the armed struggle. Situational entrapment, being caught in the life in the underground with no alternatives or routes out of a life of violence, dictates a continuation of commitment to the rebel group.

The main threshold we have found in this chapter is the extremity shift, which forms a particular form of escalation. An extremity shift can be seen as, on the one hand, an endogenous process: this type of shift can occur after the rise of more radical leadership or a radicalisation among the group members. Internal spoiling can occur when there is disagreement within the group and factions feel the need to signal dissidence, continued commitment or to fight over possible spoils or simply chain-ganging. Another mechanism by which this shift ensues is as a result of outbidding within the wider rebel social movement. When the group claims the right as primary or sole representative of the perceived cause, outbidding against other contenders leads to an extremity shift within the wider rebel social movement.

On the other hand, an extremity shift can be triggered as exogenous processes: policies of divide and rule by which the state or a third party tries to play different factions of the rebel movement against each other or aims to take out the moderate voice. Targeted killing is a specific method that is employed to threaten the survival of the group. While targeted killing can also logically be linked to a shift in saliency and a shift in atrocity, the direct aim is to weaken the organisation. We therefore propose here to view it as a factor that could lead to escalation in the shape of an exogenously caused extremity shift. On the individual level, we have seen in this chapter that situational entrapment could also lead to a shift in extremity and therefore forms the final proposition. Finally, this chapter has brought forward another version of the saliency threshold. When survival of the group is at stake, this constitutes a specific threshold of saliency.

8

Legitimacy and Support

The rebel group, in order to realise its stated goals, requires credibility and specifically legitimacy and support of a significant number of individuals. Rebels using the strategies of terrorism and insurgency usually operate from a limited power base and need to increase their power to be able to entice supporters and produce outward effects. So far, we have looked at the Clausewitzean trinity by focusing on political will, capabilities and strategy. Moreover, we have investigated the people by zooming in on group and individual factors. The aim of this chapter is to take a closer look at how these factors come together. How do rebels seek legitimacy and gain public support (Wood 2010, 612; Duyvesteyn 2018)?

It is difficult to derive any benefit from crossing thresholds or increasing levels of violence for rebel activities if there is no measure of legitimacy or public support present. The limited available resources need to be employed to maximum effect. Subsequently, power needs to be complemented by legitimacy: 'the power of terrorism is through political legitimacy, winning acceptance in the eyes of a significant population and discrediting the government's legitimacy' (Crenshaw 1983a, 25). The population needs to be won over:

Only when the potential exists for a sympathetic reaction from a politically influential audience will a terrorist organization gain legitimacy. Legitimacy requires recognition by a significant public, and ideally by government decision-makers as well, of the *salience* and the *justice* of the terrorists' cause. What the terrorists want must be seen as both important and right (Crenshaw 1983a, 27, emphasis in original).

The same applies to insurgents aiming to set up organisational structures and engage in some form of rudimentary state-building. Insurgents, because of their greater visibility and the reliance on an organisational structure, are especially vulnerable to the vicissitudes of public support (Matesan and Berger 2017).

As noted several times already, an important paradox exists in this regard: exactly 'the need to escalate', on the part of the rebel group, 'will expose them to a number of adverse responses, which will prevent these actors from acquiring legitimacy *in the eyes of their target audience* or even cause their own destruction' (Neumann and Smith 2005, 574 emphasis in original). The escalation trap and the need to acquire territorial control will demand an increasing level of violence, which at some point might alienate the rebel group from their supporters and potential constituents (Neumann and Smith 2005).

Exactly this reduction in the legitimacy of the rebel group is seen as an important mechanism of de-escalation. 'Military operations that counter the *sustainment* and *legitimacy* of the insurgents and support the *stability* of the general situation seem to be highly influential' (Clancy and Crossett 2007, 98 emphasis added; Parker 2007, 172). Running out of a viable 'strategic narrative' is a way in which de-escalation takes shape (Freedman 2006). Conversely, this also applies to the state. Legitimacy thus forms a central battleground in state-rebel confrontations (Schlichte 2009; Schlichte and Schneckener 2015; Duyvesteyn 2018). It is to this topic that we will turn to now.

PUBLIC SUPPORT

There is significant agreement in the existing literature that public and popular support is crucial when it comes to the use of political violence to realise desired ends (Paul 2010). When terrorism and insurgency are seen as strategies, attaining and maintaining support from the population is a sine qua non for the actors using these means. For the state, conversely, popular support and public confidence in the state's abilities to deal with the violent opposition are crucial for its legitimacy and ability to rule: 'If a state can make its power seem legitimate in the eyes of others, it will encounter less resistance to its wishes' (Nye 1990, 167). Statistically, when rebels are supported by large parts of the population, their chances of winning increase (Connable and Libicki 2010, 176–177; Mason 2016). There are many cases of rebel group demise caused by a lack of support from the population (Charters 1994, 227; Cronin 2006; Schuurman 2013; Matesan 2018).

There are several mechanisms by which public support can come about. These tap into various sources of social support: humiliation, frustration, alienation, hatred, repression, occupation, lack of legitimacy or political opportunity in an existing regime, a desire for resistance, a social movement or grievances. Furthermore, support on an individual level can derive from identity processes, real or perceived kinship ties, cultural and social obligations, revenge, a normative acceptability of violence, cost–benefit calculations, misperception and self-deception (Paul 2010).

Critics, however, have questioned the role of public support. As noted in the discussion about overwhelming force, the case of Chechnya, which will be further discussed later, is often referred to in order to illustrate that a highly repressive campaign can be effective in curbing rebel violence without public support (Lyall 2009, 331; Zhukov 2012; Mandel 2015). Also the case of civil conflict in Guatemala shows that crackdowns are possible even when the insurgents enjoy widespread support among the population. The state in this case was willing to push the repressive approach to its most extreme end and engaged in genocide to quell the uprising (Kruijt 2008). Furthermore, popular support might emanate from highly repressive policies. In the case of the Malayan Emergency, the struggle of the Malayan Communist Party against the British colonial government from 1948 onwards, effective hearts and minds policies were only instituted after a harsh repressive phase of among others population movement (Hack 2009). This created an enabling environment for the softer policy to take effect (Bennett 2009). This leads to the question whether the link between popular support and a conducive operating environment is a linear one (Bennett 2009; Egnell 2010, 288).

These objections notwithstanding, a significant link has been suggested between popular support and the ability to successfully conduct a violent campaign. It therefore warrants further attention. From the perspective of the state, using its instruments to influence the support base, it might find that those actions aimed successfully at the supporting environment of the rebel, at the same time, might harden the resolve of the active terrorists and insurgents (Bueno de Mesquita 2005, 526). This seems to be a central challenge for the state, adopting policies effective against the perceived problem, while at the same time retaining popular support. From the perspective of the rebel group, a delicate balance needs to continually be sought between what is deemed politically and militarily necessary and what is acceptable in the eyes of the claimed constituents. Popular support can flow, importantly, from successful rebel claims to legitimacy. Active or passive support can confirm the existence and acceptance of rebel legitimacy claims.

ROUTES TO LEGITIMACY

Legitimacy is a challenging scientific concept.[1] Some political scientists have identified legitimacy as 'the master question of politics' (Barker 1990, 4). Legitimation can be defined as 'an action or series of actions – speech, writing, ritual, display – whereby people justify to themselves or others the actions they are taking and the identities they are expressing or claiming' (Barker 2001, 163–164). Max Weber identified three main routes for legitimacy creation: rational-legalistic, traditional and charismatic (Weber, Roth and Wittich 1978). These are clearly closely related to the ideal polity types, discussed in Chapter 3. Power that is exercised by a particular ruler needs to be legitimised. Individuals can perceive power to be legitimate based on conformity to established norms or rules (legal validity), beliefs about legitimacy (monarchical, religious or traditional) and actions confirming this belief (pledging allegiance, paying taxes or voting) (Beetham 1991). A ruler can be endowed with legitimacy, for example, via the provision of social goods, such as security and economic opportunity.

Measuring legitimacy is notoriously difficult (Crenshaw 1983a, 32). In the existing literature, legitimacy is generally conceived off as static, and informed by rational choice theory and cost–benefit calculations. Individuals capable of awarding legitimacy are seen as largely self-interested and make rational calculations to decide which actor to award legitimacy. However, closer study indicates that legitimation should properly be seen as a process that is highly subjective and context dependent (Beetham 1991; Barker 2001; Thornhill 2008; Malthaner 2015; Duyvesteyn 2018). It forms a strategic process geared towards the right to rule within a particular normative context and is confined in time and space. Moreover, it is 'a social relationship that translates into particular forms of social interactions with tangible effects, triggering or facilitating forms of social control, and it represents a symbolic resource that both sides can use to influence the other' (Malthaner 2015, 442).

---

[1] See also Duyvesteyn (2017).

From existing studies, four main mechanisms can be deduced which can bestow legitimacy on a rebel group. These mechanisms are not mutually exclusive but can in one sense overlap and in other even, potentially, contradict each other. These mechanisms focus on coercion; control and collaboration; social order and governance; and ideas, culture and beliefs. These routes will be discussed in turn.

Coercion

Coercion is one of the routes to create legitimacy. This is a very straightforward and almost natural route for rebels since violence is an inherent part of their make-up. A certain measure of coercion and deterrent power, rather than compromise and trust, can form the basis for stability. The coercive route to legitimacy is prevalent among rebels (Marten 2004; Etzioni 2007) and particularly appealing to weaker rebels. When capabilities and incentives to entice the population are scarce, rebels tend to more often indiscriminately target the civilian population, compared to cases where rebels are in control of more ample resources: 'capable insurgent groups . . . have fewer incentives to resort to violence to acquire support' (Wood 2010, 612). This is of course paradoxical because legitimacy would be a more cost-effective route to sustainable power. In short, coercion is a means in the legitimation of rebel activities. An example of this mechanism we have seen earlier in the case of the RUF in Sierra Leone.

Control and Collaboration

While coercion is a relatively expensive mechanism to attain legitimacy, the establishment of control, which can result from coercion, is more of a long-term route. Physical control over territory can promote collaboration with the occupier on which a measure of legitimacy can be based (Kalyvas 2006). Pragmatic collaboration, out of fear of possible repression or material inferiority, can also act as a mechanism towards awarding legitimacy (Kitzen 2012). The causal chain would be either control followed by collaboration with legitimacy as a result or alternatively, collaboration, control followed by legitimacy. An example of this mechanism is the case of Nicaragua, where the presence of the Sandinistas explained the pattern of violence and the emergence of legitimacy.

Social Order

The provision of social order can also be a route to establish legitimacy. Based on reciprocity, the ruler comes to be seen as legitimate by the ruled based on the delivery of order (Rothstein 2009). Based on Western experience, 'the convention within contemporary liberal democracies is that it is the act of taking part in elections that legitimates government and secures the obligation of citizens in principle to obey it' (Beetham 1991, 92). In democratic or rational-legalistic authority structures, legitimacy is the result of the exercise of individual freedoms and participation in political decision-making. This is an ordering mechanism.

In patrimonial structures, the rebel group can also provide order and predictability in social relations to establish legitimacy. The establishment of order is rewarded with the allocation of legitimacy and power. In line with social contract theory, legitimacy can be created based on both the output of governance and the creation of social order and predictability in social relations (Lake 2010). The creation of social order is a vehicle by which legitimacy can be awarded to a rebel group. If the state manages to (re-)take the role of providing social order, it can be successful in its confrontation with the rebel group. In the case of the Sikh militants in the Punjab, the Indian state experienced a learning curve and was able to successfully re-establish its role as security and social goods provider. This mechanism became self-reinforcing, where more and more people started supplying the police with intelligence, leading to more effective operations and ultimately to the defeat of the rebel group (Reed 2013).

Finally, legitimacy can also be transferred to a rebel group, not based on quality of its output, but rather based on loyalty and norms or by ideational considerations.

Ideas, Cultures and Beliefs

A final route to legitimacy is claiming religious or charismatic authority. Some political science scholars have claimed that 'in the matter of legitimation it is more illuminating to pay attention to those aspects of politics which involve identity seeking' rather than utility maximizing (Barker 2001, 138–139; Abrahms 2008). Who rules can be of paramount importance for conferring legitimacy rather than the process of how the rule is exercised. The right to rule might, for example, be seen as a God given right and by tapping into religious custom and norms, legitimacy can be obtained.

Ideas and narratives can be seen as routes to establish legitimacy; 'legitimacy lies at the heart of war' and to be seen to be legitimate through the power of the image today is key to success in war (Gow and Michalski 2007, 203). Similarly, strategic narratives have been offered as perspective; these are 'compelling storylines which can explain events convincingly' and 'opinions are shaped not so much by the information received, but by the constructs through which that information is interpreted and understood' (Freedman 2006, 22). These compelling storylines are used to confer legitimacy on an actor in armed conflict. Ideas and narratives lead here to authority and subsequently to legitimacy. Ideology, being part of a larger social movement, for example a worldwide Marxist revolution or a global jihad, also has a legitimation effect for individual and group activity.

Apart from norms and narratives, culture is also helpful to explain rebel legitimacy. In the case of the civil war in El Salvador, rebel culture enabled the operation of the rebel group (Wood 2003). In a study of violence during the Sierra Leonean civil war, the development of a rebel culture was able to link the individual reasons for the engagement in violence with the strategic goals of the leadership of the Rebel United Front (Mitton 2012). A so-called psychology of shame allowed and disallowed certain behaviours during the civil war (Keen 2005).

The reverse, a loss of legitimacy, is very revealing to further our understanding of de-escalation. Two examples will be dissected in this chapter: the struggle by the Front de Libération de Québec (FLQ) and Colombia's M-19. The FLQ witnessed a sudden loss of legitimacy by engaging in a violent activity that went beyond the boundaries of what its supporters could accept in the name of Québec independence. Similarly, M-19 in Colombia lost the connection with its public support base at several junctures in the course of its struggle against the government. However, its ability to reconnect with its supporters at a crucial time towards the end of the conflict led it successfully to attain some of its major goals.

Vignette 8.1 – Legitimacy and the Front de Libération de Québec

During the 1960s and early 1970s, Canada was confronted with a rebel group which derived from the Québécois community, seeking recognition and separation from English-speaking Canada. The armed challenge by the Front de Libération de Québec started in 1963 and reached its apex during what has become known as the

---

October crisis of 1970. The example of the FLQ is interesting because the Canadian state did not buy into the potential provocation of the FLQ. Federal and provincial governments were well aware that alienating the francophone populace would lead to more violence and actively took steps at an early time in the conflict to alleviate their grievances. Conciliation and discriminate violence were integral to the entire approach and the crisis was mainly handled through active police work. Most notably, the violent campaign ended due to a loss of public legitimacy largely of the FLQ's own making. A more powerful counterterrorism instrument can hardly be imagined.

With the benefit of hindsight it can be argued that the FLQ was not much of a terrorist organisation to start with. It consisted of cells and a conspiracy to undermine the Canadian state, and was never so secret, nor so completely devoted to a radical strategic agenda as was made out at the time. Infiltration in the organisation was relatively easy, its goal never quite articulated, as it was clouded in Marxist rhetoric and vague political philosophy of the time (Charters 1997, 139–140, 144). The violence of the FLQ was, in comparison with similar groups, also quite limited. It resulted in the deaths of around eight individuals, of whom only one was premeditated. Bombings were the line of business of the FLQ and these were carried out to threaten the stability and constitution of the Canadian state.

The campaign of the FLQ started with the bombing of an English language radio station in February 1963. Bank robberies, raiding of armouries and constructions sites left the group with the necessary means to continue their violent campaign (Ross and Gurr 1989, 412; Lynd 1996, 42–44; Charters 1997, 141–142; Maloney 2000, 72–73; Clément 2008, 163–164). Escalation of the confrontation was, among others, initially a result of the conciliatory measures instigated by Prime Minister Lester Pearson and the rousing visit of French President Charles de Gaulle in 1967. De Gaulle in a speech in Montreal, while visiting the World Expo in 1967, uttered the now famous phrase: 'Vive le Québec Libre'. This was seen as his endorsement for the Québec independence. Pearson listened to the grievances of the French-speaking community and tried to increase Québécois autonomy in certain policy areas and encourage bilingualism and biculturalism. This road to accommodation produced a split in the Québec movement, with hardliners seeking more radical measures and stepping up their campaign of violence. They were encouraged by de Gaulle, who, with no uncertainty, underlined in his speech the Québec desire of separatism (Lynd 1996, 46–47; Maloney 2000, 75; Bueno de Mesquita 2005, 26–27).

A bombing spree commenced in 1968, which extended as far as the capital Ottawa and was carried out by increasingly stronger devices. In 1970, the FLQ managed to kidnap British consul James Cross on 5 October and Deputy Prime Minister Pierre Laporte on 10 October. Among the demands for the release of Cross was the publication of the FLQ manifesto, which was granted by the Canadian government (Fournier 1984; Cohen-Almagor 2000, 9, 11; Crelinsten 2001, 62, 71–72). This provided an enormous boost for the movement and maximum exposure for their political message. The Canadian government did not budge on the other demands, which included calling off the search for the kidnappers, releasing imprisoned comrades, free passage to Algeria or Cuba and 500,000 dollars. At that point, Laporte was kidnapped by a second cell. This undertaking had been an initiative without prior consultation with the first kidnapping gang. It was intended to strengthen the hand of the first commando and indeed created an atmosphere of all-powerfulness and pervasiveness of the FLQ.

The Canadian federal government, after the first concession, changed course and sent in the army, made hundreds of arrests and instituted emergency legislation in the context of its War Measures Act under the heading of impending insurrection. The provincial government was confronted with an outpouring of sympathy for the FLQ agenda. The declaration of martial law by Prime Minister Pierre Trudeau, in the end on the behest of the provincial government, received a boost of legitimacy when after two days Vice-Premier Laporte was found dead in the trunk of a car. The support for harsh measures against the perpetrators

---

Vignette 8.1 (cont.)

grew – murder was not something the sympathizers were willing to condone in the name of independence. In late November, the hiding place of James Cross was located and in return for his release, safe passage to Cuba was granted to his captors (Charters 1997, 162; Cohen-Almagor 2000; Crelinsten 2001, 64–55).

In the end, it was not so much the increase of powers but rather traditional police work that led to the dismantling of the FLQ cells. While the army was called in aid of the civil power and mainly protected critical installations across Québec and was even prepared for riot and crowd control duties, the FLQ never used this opportunity to trigger provocation. The Ottawa government was at the same time careful to avoid this (Maloney 2000, 82). The mainstreaming of Québec rights contributed to the route out of this crisis.

The route to legitimacy in this case was largely based on the idea of Québec independence, which gained the FLQ support. However, the price to pay for this independence was not worth the life of a politician and the FLQ went into decline. The substantial loss of legitimacy of the FLQ after the death of Pierre Laporte forms a main explanatory factor for the demise of the movement, together with the rise of the Parti Québecois as a mainstream political party to represent the Québecois agenda (Ross and Gurr 1989, 413–414; Ross 1995, 293–294; Clément 2008, 175). The FLQ was 'simply not able to develop a "grievance frame" sufficiently strong to justify its actions or undermine those of the government' (Parker 2007, 169). The failure consisted of making murder seem justifiable for remedying the discrimination and lack of emancipation suffered by the French-speaking Canadians. In the case of Colombia, which will be discussed next, the legitimacy mechanism was based on the idea of opposition against oppression and lack of political access. Further legitimacy for the rebel group was derived from an alternative social order in the shape of grassroots organisation and so-called peace camps where basic needs were catered for. Moreover, coercion was used, with the rebel group M-19 continuing to use violence to press its points.

Vignette 8.2 – Colombia: More Violence, Less Support for the April 19 Movement (M-19)

Colombia's political system was plagued by violence during a large part of the twentieth century. A civil war broke out in 1948, called *La Violencia*, which lasted two decades and pitted against each other the two main political parties in Colombia. The Liberals and the Conservatives were highly elitist political entities and the closed political system they formed excluded large parts of Colombian society from participation in politics. At the end of the civil war, the two parties agreed on a power-sharing arrangement in which they took turns governing and controlling political power. This arrangement, to ensure that no other political power could emerge apart from the two existing power blocks, lasted for sixteen years and further prolonged the exclusionary nature of Colombian politics (Le Blanc 2012).

To give shape to the desire for political participation, grassroots organisations and social movements developed in the 1960s and 1970s. In the countryside, land issues in particular, such as access to arable land, fuelled peasant unrest and fed the organisation of rural guerrilla groups in the 1970s. The Revolutionary Armed Forces of Colombia (FARC), for example, were formed in 1964 as a result of a cooperation between peasant self-defence organisations and Soviet-inspired communist groups (Wickham-Crowley 1991). The National Liberation Army (ELN) was established in 1965 with a base in Castroist thinking and the Cuban revolution, combined with revolutionary Catholicism. The Popular Liberation Army (EPL), founded in 1967, focused on putting into practice Maoist revolutionary thought.

In 1974, the urban guerrilla organisation M-19 appeared, as an offshoot of the FARC. Its name derived from the date 19 April 1970 of supposed democratic elections in Colombia, which were marred by widespread electoral fraud leading to the election of the official Conservative party candidate. A candidate brave enough to run on an independent ticket, on which most of the excluded groups in society (labour, students, grassroots etc.) had placed their hopes, was unfairly defeated. M-19 was a small group that aimed at defending 'the popular will' by using propaganda by deed to voice discontent about the existing political arrangements (Le Blanc 2012). M-19 was inspired by the Montoneros struggle in Argentina and the Uruguayan Tupamaros. However, ideologically it moved from initially a communist-inspired agenda to a more open sovereignty, democracy and nationalist one (Le Blanc 2012).

M-19 first appeared on the scene when they stole the sword of Colombia's liberator Simon Bolivar to 'return it to battle' against oppression (Le Blanc 2012). The strategy of M-19 was to act as the armed representative of all the opposition forces. They were therefore compelled to leave their programme rather vague to attract the largest possible following. In order to act as vanguard, the content of their actions was of extreme importance and they passed up on the opportunity, to their own peril, of organising in any structural or institutional form. In February 1976, M-19 abducted Labour Union leader Jose Raquel Mercado. He was subjected to a popular trial to establish his guilt in collaborating with elite interests. The general public was asked to help reach a verdict and invited to spray-paint yes or no on walls in public places. The public became thus complicit in a guilty verdict. In an attempt to press the government to political concessions, negotiations were started but any movement on either side remained elusive. Mercado was eventually killed when M-19 had manoeuvred itself in a position where it became paramount to prove it was serious.

The Colombian government became very uneasy about these developments and used state of emergency legislation and rule by decree to maintain control, alienating more people in the process. M-19 was part of a panoply of armed opposition groups, and the Colombian government acted against all of them in a concerted fashion, using paramilitary groups in the process (Millett 2002, 48).

In February 1980, the diplomatic representation of the Dominican Republic in Bogota was stormed by M-19. This action, which ended in a siege, forced the government to negotiate and provided M-19 with a large national and international audience to promulgate its message and highlight the shortcomings of Colombian democracy. This further contributed to the spread of their message.

Change was in the air with the election of Belisario Betancur in 1982. He proposed a national dialogue and negotiations with most of the armed groups. During the period of the National Dialogue, M-19 maintained an armed force and even strengthened it, while there was an interlude in the fighting. At the same time, it concentrated on organising alternative structures in so-called peace camps that were set up. As organising in the city remained a challenge, these camps focused on providing food and medical care and self-help groups, including the formation of militias in the countryside. This was largely inspired by the success of the Nicaraguan revolution, in which these base areas were also used before the takeover of state power (Le Blanc 2012). In this case as well, the rebel group needed to organise openly to establish itself as a base for power but the circumstances did not really allow for structured organisation (Le Blanc 2012, 2013).

A cessation of hostilities followed, but violence reignited when Betancur could not live up to the expectations and failed to provide credible commitment in the political overtures. Also, paramilitary organisations, which might have organised as legal civil defence forces, acted to defend particular elite interests rather than provide security for the population. The resumption of M-19 violence was directly linked to the increase of these activities (Le Blanc 2012).

Returning to armed struggle, after the process of the National Dialogue had irreparably broken down turned out to be a strategic mistake. The political opening had provided the population with hope that alternatives to armed force were both available and productive in effecting political change. In November 1985, M-19 attacked the Palace of Justice in Bogota to put President Betancur 'on trial' for his 'betrayal' of the peace process (Le Blanc 2012). The attack was countered by heavy force on the part of the government and more than 100 people died, including several members of M-19 and 11 High Court Judges (Le Blanc 2012). The attack cost M-19 a huge proportion of its public support and led to its ultimate demise (Carrigan 1993; Boudon 2001). Instead of heeding the calls that violence was a deadend street, M-19 continued with violence and organised a military advance on Cali.

Vignette 8.2 (cont.)

With political channels for voicing discontent largely open, of which
FARC, for example, benefited by organising a political party, the
Patriotic Union Party (UP), M-19 decided to use force and thereby
lost a large part of its legitimacy and support base. Non-violent alternatives and protest movements sprung up and contributed to convincing the government to institute reforms. The recognition came slowly
that continuing down the path of armed struggle would end in political
insignificance for M-19. By 1987, the group seized the mood and
abducted Alvaro Gomez Hurtado, an elite representative whose life
would be exchanged for negotiations with the government. This
abduction provided M-19 again with political credit and opened the
doors to the negotiating table. With a declining support base and
a formal offer of negotiations, M-19 decided to abandon the armed
struggle in March 1990. The EPL and a splinter group of the ELN
decided to follow suit. FARC and the main body of ELN continued
their armed struggle. For the FARC, this was a credible option since
during the 1980s they had largely become independent of a social
support base as a result of significant profits from the drugs trade.

M-19 stood out as an organisation that had the ability to gauge the
mood of the population to bring about political change in Colombia.
In the first years of its confrontation, it was quite good at pinpointing
the weak points of the state opponent and successful in carrying out
propaganda by deed. However, once the government under Belisario
Betancur managed to address some of the political points of the rebels,
including M-19, the legitimacy of the use of violence became highly
unpopular. M-19 misread this development, which cost them dearly in
public support. They managed to regain it to a limited extent towards
the end of their campaign, which ended in negotiations and the formation of a legal political party, which participated in elections.

Although the FARC has attempted to overthrow the Colombian government since its inception in 1964, the mutual recognition that armed force
was not going to change the opponent's mind gave rise to a new round of
negotiations. The talks focused on the underlying grievances that were
vocalised by the FARC, and political will ended the decades' long conflict.

A misreading of the opportunity structure, and putting legitimacy on the line, can also be witnessed at the end of the campaign in Italy carried out by the Brigate Rosse, which was discussed in the previous chapter. The group's choice of target, a popular Christian Democrat politician Aldo Moro, like the Palace of Justice attack in Colombia, cost them in terms of the popular vote and contributed to their ultimate demise. The same pattern emerged in the case of Sri Lanka, where the Tamil Tigers killed Indian Prime Minister Rajiv Gandhi, which led to a huge loss of support in the southern state of Tamil Nadu for the struggle of their brethren in Sri Lanka proper (Swamy 2010). In the case of the Rote Armee Fraktion, one of the activists involved later observed that a boundary had been crossed in regard to the killing of individuals in the name of liberation and world revolution: 'we experienced how our sympathizers suddenly became afraid, and many of us did too. . . . The decision to kill had passed a borderline that was simply too much for us and our supporters' (Quoted in: Merkl 1995, 193). A last example forms the Uruguayan Tupumaros, who waged an urban guerrilla campaign in the late 1960s. The high-visibility-armed propaganda campaign provided them with an international following in among others the German Red Army Faction. They also overstepped an unmarked boundary with the murder of the USAID Public Safety Program Director Dan Mitrione in August 1970, which led to the loss of significant popular support and their ultimate demise (Brum 2014). Their armed propaganda campaign

> was part of a delicate and unspoken balance of tactics whereby the Tupumaros's light footprint in violence could not reasonably provoke a much harsher response from the government, because the country was a democracy with checks and balances. It was the escalation in violence that began with the murder of Dan Mitrione, and later continued with . . . the government's own abuses, which dismantled said balance. . . . [T]he Tupumaros essentially saw themselves as having no choice but to escalate their insurgency. (Brum 2014, 399)

In all these examples, we see that the carefully nurtured legitimacy, which sprung from not only coercion but in some cases also from order, example, ideas and beliefs, could be lost in an instant and, importantly often, by the rebel's own making.

GAINING AND LOSING LEGITIMACY

Legitimacy forms a central battlefront in state-rebel confrontations. Based on the material presented in this chapter, we also see that de-escalation exhibits itself in a significant way in the shape of self–de-legitimation. The rebel group can start to overplay its hand and thereby lose the link and support of the populace (Neumann and Smith 2007). This can be a culminating point of success (Luttwak 2001) or strategic miscalculation that causes a decline in perceived legitimacy.

This is not necessarily the same as the escalation trap as discussed in Chapter 4. Strategic mistakes can occur early on in a campaign and escalation need not have significantly materialised for a rebel group to lose the support of the population. An example is the 1985 Palace of Justice attack by M-19, after which the group managed to survive for another five years. This escalation trap is to an important extent based on choices the rebel group makes itself rather than the result of countermeasures of the state or the interplay between the state and the rebel group. The mechanism is not the same either as the atrocity shift. This shift rests on the rebel group wilfully, consciously crossing moral and ethical boundaries, such as killing civilians to exercise control or to engage in moral hazard to trigger intervention. The mechanism that has surfaced here displays the notable features of accident and tragedy rather than choice and wilfulness.

There is evidence that rebel groups are aware of and sensitive to the role of public opinion to such an extent that some have been known to apologise for mistakes (Matesan and Berger 2017). If the costs in public support are very high, the group is likely to issue an apology regardless of the ideological agenda it subscribes to or its type of organisation. The Provisional IRA officially apologised, for example, for the Shankill bombing in 1993 and the Basque ETA movement recently apologised for its use of deadly violence (Jones 2018).

It is important to note that legitimacy and support cannot always be influenced or controlled by the actors that covet it. The discussion in this chapter demonstrates that the creation of rebel legitimacy requires more attention (Duyvesteyn 2017). The problem is that there is only a small theoretical base to explain how legitimacy is created. Several competing ideas exist. Legitimacy can be created by means of sticks and carrots: sticks are coercion and control; and carrots are governance, social order and ideas and culture.

As for the carrots, the provision of basic services, that is governance and an embryonic social contract, form an important mechanism for legitimacy and currently a dominant lens in the literature (Duyvesteyn and Minatti 2020). Most insurgency movements active in the twentieth century have tried in one way or another to set up a rival state structure to wean the population away from the state by providing the services the population requires or demands (Mampilly 2011; Arjona et al. 2015). Examples are not only the Chinese communist party or the Vietminh but also Hezbollah, the Taliban and more recently, the Islamic State. By providing services and social order, legitimacy can be obtained, which is a crucial ingredient for the exercise of sustainable political power.

As for the sticks, coercion has historically been an important tool in colonial warfare to subdue unruly populations that had reverted to covert warfare. In cases such as Kenya during the Mau Mau war in the 1950s against British colonial rule, the Kikuyu population, from among whom the rebellion originated, became subject of communal repression (Bennett 2007). The end result was (temporary) subjugation to the British crown and a restoration of a semblance of order. Coercion helped in the (temporary) creation of legitimacy. This recipe was practiced in many other colonial cases. In more recent times, coercion has been practised by the RUF in Sierra Leone but can also be witnessed in the activities of the Taliban in Afghanistan and the Al Qaeda affiliates in Syria, Iraq and North Africa. There are also significant outliers in the shape of harsh repressive campaigns that counted on little state popular support, either locally or nationally, that achieved a notable effect, for example the termination of the violence in Chechnya and Sri Lanka. We will take a closer look at the case of Chechnya in the next chapter.

What our findings bring forward is a clear ebb and flow of legitimacy and support during the course of conflict. The mechanism of transfer of support from the state to the rebel group or vice versa is in need of further scholarly attention. How legitimacy transfers between states and rebels remains unclear. Whether it is actually transferable or whether different legitimacies can exist at the same time remain important questions for future research. This chapter has brought forward an important suggestion about a causal route for de-escalation in particular: the rebel group de-legitimises itself. The topic of de-escalation processes will take centre stage in the penultimate chapter.

9

De-Escalation

The level, intensity or the spread of violence is not necessarily low or limited at the moment conflict terminates. This phenomenon indicates an absence of a direct, linear link between de-escalation and termination (Staniland 2017). To substantiate de-escalation, we need to look elsewhere. In Chapter 2, we have introduced three important suggestions from the existing literature to explain the occurrence of de-escalation.[1] Deterrence, norm convergence and a mutually hurting stalemate have been put forward to explain the process of a decrease in the level of violence or a reduction of its salience or spread. In this discussion, it was already clear that there are problems with, and objections to, deterrence and the idea of a mutually hurting stalemate. There were doubts about the ability to deter rebels, in particular terrorists. We have not found any specific leads to substantiate a role for deterrence in rebel-state conflicts de-escalation. This might be explained through the escalation dominance disparity. While the state largely has a dominance in capability, the rebel group dominates in the domain of political will. Therefore, the premise that rebels can be deterred via overwhelming capabilities of destruction does not hold. Deterrence via commanding larger political will is more promising. However, the saliency shift, we have detailed earlier, has not indicated a logical end point. In this chapter, we will look further into the limitations of rebel campaigns and how rebel groups limit themselves. At

---

[1] Please note here again (as discussed in more detail in Chapter 2) that de-escalation does not necessarily denote an end or disengagement from violence or de-radicalisation (Cf. Della Porta 2013; Matesan 2018).

this point, the concept of deterrence appears not very productive to explain de-escalation.

A similar problem occurred with the concept of parity and the idea of a mutually hurting stalemate. As noted earlier, these ideas about elusive victory cannot necessarily be linked to de-escalation. Even in situations where objective chances of obtaining the stated goals are remote, rebel groups tend to be tenacious and violence continues (Abrahms 2008, 2011). In the concluding chapter, we will address the paradoxes of victory and defeat for rebel groups, when arguing that for rebel groups victory through the application of tactics or victory in defeat are recurrent phenomena. The concept of victory, we will argue, deserves a rethink (Angstrom and Duyvesteyn 2007, 241).

Since the existing literature, with the exception of the norm convergence threshold, has provided little in terms of precise ideas about the causes of de-escalation (in contrast to termination, e.g. Crenshaw 1999; Cronin 2009; Della Porta 2013; Matesan 2018), we need to look elsewhere. Moreover, there are some debatable claims in regard to de-escalation that warrant attention in this chapter. In particular, the claim that de-escalation is inherently deliberate is in need of correction, together with the dominant view of de-escalation as linear. In contrast to the claim that 'accidental de-escalation is essentially unheard of' (Morgan et al. 2008, 34), we have already found a major de-escalatory mechanism in the shape of self–de-legitimation. This is an almost exclusively inadvertent, if not completely accidental, process. In contrast to the preceding chapters, the following discussion of de-escalation is largely based around the theoretical parameters of de-escalation, that is a reduction in political will and a reduction in capabilities. The two basic Clausewitzean parameters of will and capability would entail that de-escalation, theoretically, follows from either a political unwillingness or a material inability to continue the confrontation. We will logically think through these premises. Preceding this discussion, however, we propose to consider in more detail the restraints rebel groups operate under.

REBELS AND (IN)VOLUNTARY RESTRAINTS

Escalation, according to Herman Kahn, is subject to restraints. He referred in his work specifically to restraints that were accidental rather than wilfully planned: 'the restraints and limitations that were observed in World War II were more often unplanned or even inadvertent than calculated, and there were fewer of them than might be expected today' (Kahn

2012, 34). During the Cold War, the restraints, he implicitly referred to, related to an unthinkable nuclear war. This is indeed very different from conventional war in the example of the Second World War, which appears closer to what Clausewitz called friction, the inadvertent and unplanned restraints that make war in reality so difficult. These are of a different nature compared to the calculated or deliberate brakes in the theorising on nuclear war.

For rebels, the checks on capability, rather than political will, have been argued to explain the limitations to the continual drive to engage in escalation. Their limited means preclude continual escalation. Conversely, as noted earlier, rebels tend to focus on wearing down the political will, rather than exhausting the state opponent's capacities. Restraint can thus be expected to be more a question of will and therefore rational and calculated (see also Busher et al. 2019).

Rebel violence can subside when the group deliberately chooses to do so, or is forced to do so as a result of internal or external pressure, or through insufficient capabilities. These are, respectively, forms of modulated and imposed decline (Becker 2015, 5). The desire to de-escalate might in practice be quite mundane. Deliberate processes of de-escalation can involve the desire to recuperate and recover after a campaign that has cost the rebel group. Alternatively, it might feel the need to lie low after the violence created a backlash among the population. The group may decide to use its resources in an alternative fashion to further its goals. The opportunity structure might have changed and offered openings for alternative means. Finally, there is also an important category of accidental decline.

Even though the means and effects of rebel violence can be seen as subject to restraints, there is very little in the general literature about this aspect. It comes therefore perhaps with a measure of surprise that '[t]hroughout the entirety of the twentieth century no more than fourteen terrorist incidents had killed more than a hundred people, and until 11 September no terrorist operation had ever killed more than five hundred people in a single attack' (Hoffman 2014, 62). This signals that there are relevant restraints to rebel violence and this, to some extent, questions the prevalence of the atrocity threshold as of paramount importance as claimed in the literature.

It is logical to first dissect at this point the restraints on escalation, before turning to de-escalation. Many rebel groups do indeed operate under significant restraints. It is true that a lack of means features heavily in the history of many rebel groups, which have dealt with resource scarcity often as a fact of life. There are also limitations on rebel violence that relate to the unwillingness to use specific means or engage in a level of violence. This is in contrast to the state, which tends to shy away from displaying an unwillingness to escalate, that is it treasures its escalation dominance, as it is assumed in the literature (Daase 2007, 182).

A first set of restraints revolves around political calculation. As noted earlier, rebels are strategic actors making crafty use of circumstances and opportunities to push forward the issues they espouse. Rebel groups, using either the terrorist or insurgent strategies, do engage in an exercise in which ends, ways and means are lined up in order to bargain and coerce the opponent in following its will. Within the parameters of these restraints, de-escalation can be assessed.

Rebels, we argue here, are conscious of restraints. One particular sensitivity of rebel groups is civilian casualties (Abrahms et al. 2017; Matesan and Berger 2017). Around 40 per cent of belligerents in civil wars, since the end of the Cold War, have arguably shown some measure of restraint (Sanín and Wood 2014). In fact, there is evidence that rebel leaders opposed to civilian targeting can elicit restraint from their group members (Abrahms et al. 2017). This is further evidence of rebel groups acting strategically. Mistakes in civilian targeting can cost rebel groups dearly, for example the apologies offered by the IRA and ETA.

A second set of restraints revolves around those imposed by what the outside world will accept and tolerate and also relate to rebel calculations of political will. One of the most significant logics behind restraints on escalation is that 'the level of violence must be kept within the bounds of what the terrorists' "target audience" will accept' (Hoffman 1998, 164; Schuurman 2013). This presupposes that these limitations in regard to the employment of means and effects can be sustained once engaged in a campaign with a living and responsive opponent. In the past, several scholars have observed that violence is indeed constrained; there needs to be 'an effective level of violence that is at once "tolerable" for the local populace, tacitly acceptable to international opinion and sufficiently modulated not to provoke massive governmental crackdown and reaction' (Hoffman 1998, 162). Brian Jenkins has argued that '[t]hey [the terrorists] find it unnecessary to kill many, as long as killing a few suffices for their purposes' (Jenkins 1985a, 6). IRA activist Eamon Collins has written about the parameters for IRA action: 'they knew they were operating within a sophisticated set of informal restrictions on their behaviour, no less powerful for being largely unspoken' (Quoted in Hoffman 1998, 164). Earlier we have seen this type of restraint in the case of the RAF and the recognition that killing people in the name of Marxist world revolution transgressed boundaries. A similar argument applied in the cases of the FLQ and the Brigate Rosse.

The competition in outrage or the crossing of thresholds relating to the level of atrocity, as one of the main escalatory mechanisms identified in the literature so far, and discussed in Chapter 2, are subject to perceived brakes by the rebel group. The rebel group needs to calibrate and recalibrate its plans continually to bridge the 'tension between, on the one hand, using violence as an instrument of strength and a lever of negotiation, and on the other, refraining from excessive levels of violence to avoid destruction, resource depletion, or pariah status' (Becker 2015, 9). In practice, it is evident that the rebel group does so.

A third set of restraints are shaped by capabilities, as emphasised in the literature. These restraints are far less of the rebel group's choosing. While they act as a brake on escalation and the escalation trap, they might also be manipulated consciously to aid in surprise effects. Appearing weaker than they actually are might work to the advantage of the rebel group at certain points. These expectations can be carefully managed. Still, some of the restraints on capabilities are a product of choice. As noted in Chapter 6, refraining from the use of weapons of mass destruction, as too destructive, is a wilful choice. There is a consistent finding in the literature about how to curb insurgency that tackling the foreign ties in the shape of sanctuary, finance or resource bases are highly effective in downgrading the capabilities of rebels to the point of defeat, which presents the first and most direct proposition related to de-escalation in this chapter to which we will return later.

Not only can we identify restraints but also unwillingness and inabilities to continue the struggle, which cause de-escalation. Conflicts in which states and rebels confront each other can de-escalate when the actors are, first, unwilling to pursue the conflict further on the same level or when the use of violence becomes unnecessary or, second, when they are unable to continue using violence. The thresholds related to these two domains will be discussed in turn.

DE-ESCALATION: THE DE-LEGITIMATION THRESHOLD

De-escalation can result when the rebel group is unwilling to further continue its struggle (Busher et al. 2019). Scholars have noted before that the main challenge in dealing with terrorist movements is 'to delegitimize the resort to terrorism as a means of effecting political change and to reduce the opportunities and incentives for doing so. It is to channel the effort to redress grievances into conventional politics' (Richardson 2006, 9). Joel Busher, Donald Holbrook and Graham Macklin have tried to identify the brakes that extremist groups have used to limit violence. They found that alternative approaches, shifts in moral categories, self-identification as a non-violent group and openings to outsiders were among the most significant brakes. These can all be linked to the question of legitimacy. We have seen several groups experience a de-legitimation process; the IRA took this route, as did M-19 in Colombia. The opening up to the political opportunity structure can facilitate this (Della Porta 2013). Democracy can be conducive to mainstreaming violent rebel groups and bring them back into the legal political process. Most Western states, however, do not seem very successful at mainstreaming violent rebels: the Rote Armee Fraktion, Brigate Rosse, the Front de Libération de Québec but also Weathermen in the United States and Action Directe in France all failed to be mainstreamed. The FLQ did see some of its claims represented by the Parti Québecois. The exception forms Northern Ireland.

Norm Convergence

Thomas Schelling suggested during the Cold War that de-escalation is linked to the emergence of common frames of reference (Schelling 1980). When conflict breaks out, norms and expectations diverge and this gap tends to grow during the course of war. When these norms start to converge again, de-escalation can result. Norm convergence could be seen as an inverted saliency shift. In other words, a decrease occurs in the perceived saliency of the issues at stake. The decreased salience might be caused by a changing opportunity structure, by overwhelming force, a reduced social mobilisation potential, changing narratives about the goal of the struggle, changing perceptions of the opponent or an opening in negotiations or offers of concession (Della Porta 2013; Busher et al. 2019). Saliency might also be reduced when capabilities to violently defend the perceived issues are reduced or gone.

When the political opportunity structure opens up, we might expect a drop in violence (Busher et al. 2019). However, there are several challenges to this causal claim. Firstly, there might be a difference between rational legalistic and patrimonial authoritarian structure. There are cases of democracies experiencing rebel violence where the opportunity structure is relatively open, or remains open, and there is no absence of violence. The examples here are Germany and the Red Army Fraktion and Colombia and M-19. In Chapter 3, we discussed the diverse links between polity type and violent opposition. None of these were linear.

Secondly, it is striking that the many of the suggestions offered here about norm convergence focus on the group level (group narratives, perceptions, opportunities). There is evidence, as discussed in Chapter 7, that during the course of a violent struggle more emphasis is placed on the individual or personal levels over the course of time. (Crenshaw 1985; Weinberg and Eubank 1990; Van Creveld 1991; Della Porta 1995b). In other words, the micro level gains in significance the longer the struggle lasts. This creates a paradox where at the later stages in the struggle negotiations and concessions focusing on political grievances might find little fertile ground because the terms of the struggle have shifted to the micro- or individual level. These are some of the avenues worthy of further investigation.

One example of a norm convergence shift, discussed earlier, is Northern Ireland, where some experts have noted the similarities between the Sunningdale agreement in 1973 and the Good Friday agreement (Tonge 2000). The difference is the absence/presence of a shared frame of reference. Norm convergence also materialised in the Latin American cases of Argentina and Colombia, where the opening of the political opportunity structure provided new openings for opposition and recognition of social grievances. More evidence comes from the Palestinian conflict: '[t]he only thing that decreased outrage and support for violence among those with sacred values was the other side's symbolic concession on one of their sacred values (such as recognizing the historic legitimacy of the Palestinian's right of return or of Israel's claim to the West Bank)' (Argo 2009, 675). When the frame of reference incorporates core issues of the belligerents, norm convergence can take shape.

De-escalation will result when common norms and frames of reference emerge that facilitate the communication and understanding between the belligerents. We do note here that the literature to date falls short in identifying the exact routes by which these common norms and understandings are created, which would be an interesting challenge for future investigation.

DE-ESCALATION: THE INABILITY THRESHOLD

While the inability to continue can also be brought about by a lack of legitimacy and public support, there are two main variations on the reduction in capabilities: a loss of foreign sanctuary and a loss of fighters through defection.

The rebel group is unable to continue when its capabilities are compromised or curbed (Thompson 1966). Cutting the material capability of rebels leads to a reduction in its ability to mount violence, either through a lack of resources, recruits or sanctuary, which has a direct link to de-escalation. As noted, one of the most recurring claims is that the most effective measure to curb the ability of rebels to carry out their violent campaigns is targeting their foreign sponsors.

An example of rebels suffering from a decreased capability is the case of Chechnya, which has already been referred to several times in the arguments earlier. Chechnya stands out as a case of counter-insurgency with a significant degree of support and legitimacy for the rebel groups among the population and where Russian forces, to date, managed to defeat it by focusing primarily on the ability of the rebels to continue. A similar route was chosen by the Sri Lankan state in 2009, with similar results. In neither case has the legitimacy of the cause of the rebels been questioned or have underlying grievances been fundamentally addressed.

Vignette 9.1 – The Chechen Civil War: Total Defeat?

Upon the dissolution of the Soviet Union, many parts of the Soviet empire managed to establish independence in a relatively peaceful manner (Zurcher 2007). The new successor state offered a federation treaty to all eighty-eight entities in the territory. All but two signed the document stipulating the new relationship in the federation regarding the level of autonomy and settling tax issues. Chechnya and Tartarstan declined. The nationalist aspirations of the Chechen population turned violent in 1994. The Chechen civil war consists, in fact, of two wars in which the first sowed the seeds for the second. In the first phase, Chechen armed separatists fought the Russians with a defeat of the latter in 1996. The second Chechen war broke out in 1999 when conflict potential was generated by continued Russian rule over the breakaway republic and importantly by the advent of political Islam and in particular Saudi-sponsored Wahabism in Sufi Islam dominated Chechnya.

In the autumn of 1991, when the Berlin wall had come down but the Soviet state was still in a process of transition, the Chechens made a declaration of independence. An organisation sprung up, the All National Congress of the Chechen People, which was led by

---

a former Soviet Airforce General Dzhokhar Dudayev. The Chechen call for secession, based on historical and ethnic grounds, clashed with the Russian claims to national sovereignty. Chechen society is traditionally clan based, with the clan or *teip* as focal mechanism in society. There is debate over the organising capacity of the clan during conflict (Zurcher 2007, 75). Still, the Chechens managed to organise themselves quickly and Dudayev's initiative was widely supported. He subsequently became president of the breakaway republic. In March 1992, the pro-Russian elements in Chechnya attempted a coup d'état which was put down. However, parliamentary rule was abolished in favour of rule by presidential decree.

In August 1994, violence broke out when pro-Russian forces in the north of the republic started a campaign against the Dudayev government. In mid-October 1994, with aid from Russia, these forces launched a direct assault on the capital Grozny. The direct involvement of Russia developed gradually with initially a blockade and only material and financial support. On 1 December 1994, air bombardments were a first direct and acknowledged intervention by Russia to restore order. Despite declarations of intent indicating the opposite, a full-blown incursion started on 11 December with a military advance on Grozny. The support for this direct intervention was negligible in Russia to begin with and this never changed during the course of the war (Lyall 2010, 2). The Russian approach relied heavily on overwhelming force. The morale of the troops, mostly conscripts, was low and they lacked the training and staying power necessary for the confrontation. They relied on indiscriminate shelling, carpet bombing and the use of cluster bombs. While the Russians were successful in curbing the Chechen uprising, they provoked a greater conflict salience effect among the Chechen population, reinforcing the opposition against the Russian presence. As one observer wrote:

The war itself drew a more rigid line of demarcation between Chechens and non-Chechens and heightened Chechens' sense of group solidarity. The warring parties in such a conflict start to 'think' each other, and this thinking is intrinsically divisive. In a sense, *it is the conflict that constructs Chechens, not vice versa* (Tishkov 2004, 10, italics in original).

A siege of Grozny ensued at the end of 1994 and in early 1995, as a result of urban warfare, the Russians managed to gain control over Grozny. In a subsequent conventional campaign, the Russians managed to establish control over the majority of Chechen territory in the first half of 1995.

Chechens changed tactics and focus in June 1995 by taking hostages in a hospital in southern Russia to press their claims. In the city of Budyonnovsk, just north of the Chechen border, a group of separatists took around 1,500 hostages and demanded an end to the hostilities and direct negotiations. Other terrorist tactics were employed in the shape of an airplane hijacking of a flight from Cyprus to Germany in March 1996 and a takeover of a Turkish passenger ship carrying Russian citizens. Both attacks were used to create attention for the Chechen cause.

The airplane hijacking coincided with a surprise assault on Grozny by a significant number of secessionist forces which had infiltrated the city. A renewed round of fighting ensued over the capital. To Russia's surprise, Chechen fighters managed to gain substantial control over Grozny and forced the Russians to the negotiating table. In 1996, the Khasaviurt Agreement was signed, followed by a peace treaty in 1997, which deferred the resolution of the problem to 2001 but implicitly recognised the rights of the Chechen population.

Democratic elections were held and a semblance of calm returned to the region. However, due to a lack of state capacity, coupled with an influx of foreign fighters bringing with them a more radical strand of Islam, which was alien to the region, proved the combination that relit the tinderbox (Zurcher 2007, 86).

In August 1999, a second Chechen war broke out (Souleimanov 2007). Notable Chechen rebel leader Shamil Basayev invaded the neighbouring Russian republic of Dagestan with his International Islamic Brigade to establish a regional 'Islamic Khanate'. The rebels were not welcomed with open arms and with Russian aid were driven back into Chechnya. The response from Moscow was to again invade Chechen territory with military force in October 1999. By 2000, Russian forces were fighting pitched battles

---

Vignette 9.1 (cont.)

---

in urban centres, including Grozny again and Gudermes, against Chechen fighters. In March, the fighters acting in the open were practically defeated by the Russian forces. They shifted to a highly mobile hit-and-run campaign against Russian positions and enjoyed a measure of sanctuary across the border in Georgia. Furthermore, Chechen suicide bombing surfaced in 2000 with attacks inside and outside of Chechnya. Most notable are the hostage-takings at the Dubrovka theatre in Moscow in October 2002 and the Beslan school in northern Ossetia in September 2004. Bomb attacks were carried out on a train in Stavropol in 2003, and on the Moscow underground in 2004. However, the Chechen movement was split between those adhering to the Islamist strand favouring suicide attacks and hostage-taking both in Chechnya and in Russia proper. Strongly opposing this approach were the nationalists.

In May 2000, Russian President Putin introduced direct rule from Moscow to subsequently install his own strongman Akhmad Kadyrov. Kadyrov formed a government and a new constitution was drafted, which granted substantial autonomy to the republic.

In this second phase of the war, the Chechens shifted from a conventional approach that focused on defending territory to a mobile approach. After the rebels were driven from the urban centres, Russia relied on a 'Chechenisation' of the conflict and the use of proxies, in particular the Kadyrov clan to fight against the Chechen resistance. Akhmed Kadyrov became the Russia-backed local strongman, who was succeeded, after his assassination during a Victory Day parade in Grozny stadium, by his son Ramzan. These strongmen enacted the Chechenisation policy to keep the republic within the federation, a referendum and elections were part of this political process. While the secessionist rebels managed to inflict heavy losses on the Russians, by 2005 the rebel group had been reduced to a small band of around 500 men in the mountains in the south of Chechnya.

In April 2009, Vladimir Putin declared the war officially over without any of the underlying issues of secessionist demands nor the Islamist agenda having been met. Despite the official announcements, suicide attacks continued. Current assessments, similar to

> **Vignette 9.1 (cont.)**
>
> the case of Sri Lanka, see the victory of state forces as decisive (Lyall 2009, 331), and while a resurgence of violence cannot be discounted, the heavy-handed approach has contributed to the subsiding of violence twice in this case.

The Chechnya case first illustrates several of the causal mechanisms that we have previously uncovered: 'Chechnya would appear a clear example of indiscriminate repression fuelling an insurgency' (Lyall 2009, 331). By acting forcefully on Chechen territory, using overwhelming and largely conventional armed force, the salience of the issue of Chechen independence was raised among the population. The Chechen case also illustrates the ability of the rebel group, in particular its incarnation as jihadist, to continue the struggle independent from local resources: 'A diversified support base reduces vulnerability to coercion, but also generates incentives to escalate. With sufficient external support rebels no longer need to persuade locals to cooperate, and a selective violence advantage becomes unnecessary' (Toft and Zhukov 2015, 225).

Furthermore, a substitution effect occurred in tactics and strategy with shifts to suicide terrorism, outside of Chechnya and a shift from rural to urban environments and from conventional to insurgency to terrorism approaches. An extremity shift was also notable in the emergence of a reincarnation of the secessionist movement with an Islamist cloak, illustrating the instability of the rebel agenda over time. While the Chechen case can be an example of rebel defeat, a resurgence of the conflict should not be discounted. Rebels can display Phoenix-like behaviour, rising from the ashes for a new round of fighting when new opportunities and/or capabilities present themselves.

The Loss of Foreign Support and Sanctuary

One of the most recurring claims regarding the most effective measure to curb the ability of rebels to continue their violent campaign is targeting their foreign sponsors. There is a recurrent suggestion in the literature that a direct de-escalatory effect can be gauged from cutting foreign ties in particular in the shape of foreign sanctuary. Foreign sanctuary has already been seen to play a large role in the success of insurgencies, the reverse also holds true (Thompson 1966; Staniland 2006; Record 2007; Salehyan 2007). In almost all of the cases, we have had a look at this aspect played a role. Direct foreign support was provided to the RUF by Liberia, India to the Tamil Tigers, the Rote Armee Fraktion by the East German Stasi, to the Chechen rebels by Georgia. International networks of support played a role for the Rote Armee Fraktion and the Brigate Rosse. Diaspora populations reinforced the activities of the IRA and the Tamil Tigers through fundraising or levying revolutionary taxes.

Even though there is a very direct effect between curbing foreign ties and reducing the rebel capabilities, sometimes very little is done. Several reasons present themselves. Firstly, the relationships with neighbouring states might be difficult, for example India and Pakistan in the case of the Punjab and Russia and Georgia in the case of the Chechens. Secondly, there might be physical obstacles in the shape of difficult terrain, monitoring the Palk Straits between Tamil Nadu and Sri Lanka would require substantial capacity. Another example is the border region between Afghanistan and Pakistan. It consists of mountain ranges and is difficult to traverse. The Afghan Taliban benefited in the shape of inhospitable territory and a gateway to federally administered tribal areas in Pakistan, which acted as a safe haven. Not only sanctuary but also trade between rebel-held areas could be the focus of pressure. The Islamic State traded oil that was available in the areas under their control, which provided them with funds to support their struggle (Levitt 2014). It is clear that this insight would provide policy makers with a substantial room for manoeuvre (Record 2007).

Defection

A last mechanism linked to the rebel group becoming unable to continue is via defection of its fighters and a loss of fighting potential. There is a small but growing literature on rebel defection. When and why do individuals defect from rebel groups? In this discussion, both material and immaterial incentives have been brought forward. Presently available research indicates that individuals who participated in rebel conflicts based on ideological or political motivation are less likely to defect compared to those who joined based on material incentives (Oppenheim et al. 2015). This evidence supports the idea that ideology is also important to understand individual trajectories in armed conflict participation. Moreover, the idea of the rebel group as a desirable social unit has also been presented as preventing defection; so far, 'there is circumstantial evidence that terrorist organizations collapse when they cease to be perceived as desirable social collectivities worth joining' (Abrahms 2008, 101). Corroboration of this idea comes from criminological research where defection from life in a gang has been found to be linked to social alternatives:

[D]efection is more likely when the three spheres of politics, family, and work become more distant from one another or, as research on youth gangs indicated, when an individual finds suitable affective substitutes for his or her closest friends that belong to those gangs. On an individual level, exit is facilitated by the development of new circles of support that are sympathetic toward possible signs of abandonment. (Della Porta 2013, 276–277)

Thus, defection is more likely when recruits harbour material or economic incentives and other groups, including the state, might offer a more attractive package (Oppenheim et al. 2015). Scholars have also suggested that legitimacy is reduced, when the rebel shifts from an ideological frame to a more personal frame in the conflict (see discussion in Parker 2007).

Finally, defection can also result simply from an inability of the rebel group to prevent it. The presence of safe havens, in the shape of inaccessible terrain (McLauchlin 2014), foreign sanctuaries, UN compounds or the presence of other rebel groups can facilitate defection (Richards 2018). The inability threshold thus consists of defections, but also as a loss of sanctuary, as major causes of de-escalation.

DE-ESCALATION: THE DE-LEGITIMATION THRESHOLD AND THE INABILITY THRESHOLD

The topic of de-escalation in contrast to escalation is far less developed. While during the period of the Cold War scholarship devoted most attention to deterrence, as the counterweight to escalation, little theoretical and empirical study has been focused on de-escalation as such. Nevertheless, based on existing material, we have proposed several topics worthy of further exploration to get to the heart of the de-escalation phenomenon. Among them we count the loss of social appeal of rebel membership, the loss of foreign support and the convergence of norms between the belligerents. These mechanisms give rise to two major shifts denoting escalation: the de-legitimation threshold and the inability threshold.

The de-legitimation threshold, constituting a particular form of de-escalation, is caused by a loss of legitimacy of the rebel group. This can be caused either by the rebel's own doing or by exogenous pressure. An endogenously caused process, introduced in the previous chapter, has been called self–de-legitimation. It is the result of strategic mistakes, miscalculations and negative fallout from rebel activities, sometimes compounded by the countermeasures enacted by the state. Another form of de-legitimation is the loss of appeal or justification of the use of force. Common norms and frames of reference emerge between the belligerents, and the continued use of violence can no longer be justified or legitimated in the name of the rebel cause.

The inability threshold constitutes a form of de-escalation that is caused by a reduction of rebel fighting capabilities. It also is witness to both endogenous and exogenous causes. A lack of fighters can result from defections that are caused by a reduced appeal of the rebel group or caused by a better deal that is offered by other actors. A loss of foreign sanctuary and/or sponsorship can be caused by choices the rebel group makes or political decision of the foreign sponsor, which can have many different reasons for supporting a rebel group. In the final chapter, we will further reflect on these propositions on de-escalation, as well as on those related to escalation.

10

The Escalation and De-Escalation of Rebel Violence

Following Clausewitz, we have argued that war is like a chameleon, adapting its character to the given context. Armed conflicts between rebels and the state are subject to an interplay between the will and the capability of the actors. Their political logic is changeable and the initial causes of violence do not necessarily explain its subsequent development.

The present study, by using empirical examples, aimed to dive deeper into these causal processes and to unearth some of the often-visible chains of action and reaction responsible for escalation and de-escalation of war. We have found a number of these mechanisms. It appears that time and again, little consideration is given to thinking ahead and keeping an eye on the possible consequences of decisions and effects of particular actions. What might seem a good idea in the short run, be it for political capital or domestic consumption, may end up aggravating conflicts through deliberate acts, structural conditions or accident, via first- and second-order effects. The thresholds we have identified can help us think through the consequences of particular choices and actions. This chapter will present and discuss the hypotheses this study has brought forward, reflect on some theoretical premises for the study of (de)-escalation and the policy relevance of the findings. We will also discuss the limitations of this research project and propose some further avenues for research.

ESCALATION AND DE-ESCALATION: CAUSAL PROCESSES

What can explain sudden rises in the level of violence during the course of conflict? Escalation has been conceptualised in Chapter 1 as the crossing of thresholds. Escalation has been made operational through the

Clausewitzean framework of approaching conflict as a contest of wills, involving political ends which are linked to capabilities which open a distinct number of ways and means to achieve them. Based on a review of the existing literature, several explanations for escalation and de-escalation were identified. The threshold of atrocity is dominant in the existing literature for assessing escalation. Conflict escalates when one of the belligerents opts to raise the level of atrocity by putting to use weapons or selecting targets, hitherto considered out of bounds, in order to outmatch the opponent. During the period of the Cold War, the most dangerous step up was, of course, the introduction of nuclear weapons. In the study of rebel violence, atrocity in the shape of indiscriminate killing has similarly signalled a main threshold.

Crossing the atrocity threshold and transgressing ethical boundaries is risky for the rebel group because of the potential alienation of its supporters. Furthermore, it is a high-risk approach because 'materially inferior actors are sometimes prone to escalate via increasing indiscrimination in targeting, although in most cases this approach remains unlikely to overcome a substantial power differential that will permit them to attain all their objectives' (Smith and Jones 2015, 177). In other words, it puts at risk their legitimacy and chances of success. In the vignettes presented in previous chapters, we saw examples of the crossing of the atrocity threshold in Chechnya with the attacks on the Moscow Dubrovka theatre and the Beslan school massacre. In Argentina we saw the Montoneros move from highly discriminate to more indiscriminate violence. In Germany, while the protest cycle of the late 1960s was winding down, the Rote Armee Fraktion became violent and their campaign started with the killing of a police officer. The crossing of the threshold of atrocity has been highly visible in past rebel conflicts.

In contrast to previous studies, which argued that escalation with the exception of the crossing of the atrocity threshold can only be contingent, we have found several notable and alternative escalatory mechanisms. Based on further testing, these propositions could bridge the gap in our understanding when and how escalation occurs in state-rebel confrontations. It is therefore highly debatable that 'the multiple and contingent factors governing behaviour mean that no predictive mechanism can be formulated to forecast accurately how actors in such situations will escalate' (Smith and Jones 2015, 177). Multiple observable causal chains have surfaced, which substantiate the hypotheses we formulate here. In the process of unpacking the concept of escalation, we have added to the panoply of thresholds and we have uncovered many more indications of conflict aggravation. These can mostly be ascertained only with hindsight.

Escalation and de-escalation possess several dimensions. Conflict can escalate via the number of actors, the number and weight of issues at stake, the number and calibre of instruments used, the widening of tactics and targets, territorial spillover and prolongation in time. These dimensions have been used to make the concept of escalation operational. This study has used both the existing knowledge that has been offered in civil war studies and investigations of rebel groups and a variety of case material to dissect whether and how these thresholds appear in practice. We have found that thresholds tend to be crossed when important shifts in salience and extremity occur, which constitute conflict escalation.

Our findings emphasise the commitment, rather than the atrocity approach, as most viable to trace the phenomenon of escalation. Notably, on the level of the rebel group–state interaction process, the salience of the issues at stake, the reasons why the groups are fighting, play out distinctly. Pre-existing interpretations of escalation, such as previous commitment, perception biases, situational entrapment, tapping into unwitting sensitivities and failures of analysis, played a large role in the explanation of group processes and added to further our understanding of what goes on in the rebel group internally once violence commences. These causal relationships form the propositions this study has brought forward, in an attempt to explain (de-)escalation of rebel-state armed conflict.

De-escalation has hitherto been linked to deterrence, mostly based on ideas from Cold War scholarship, to norm convergence and to the idea of a mutually hurting stalemate. With the exception of the idea of norm convergence, the other two suggestions found little resonance in the material we have looked at but perhaps more detailed investigation can further productively dissect these. As a first step to thinking through de-escalation, we have assessed arguments related to brakes on, and restraints of rebel violence, which have curbed the tendency to cross thresholds. Considerations of legitimacy, public support and acceptability of certain courses of action in the eyes of the supposed constituents are significant in order to moderate the tendency of war to escalate into the extreme. Subsequently, the process of de-escalation has been investigated by looking closer at rebel unwillingness and inability to continue engagement in conflict. We have found a de-legitimation threshold, importantly informed by self-de-legitimation and norm convergence between the belligerents. Moreover, defection and a loss of foreign sanctuary are causally linked to de-escalation.

ESCALATION

Chapter 2 presented the seven dimensions of escalation. We identified four important types of shifts, which can be caused by a variety of mechanisms. Table 10.1 presents an overview of these ideas.

TABLE 10.1 *Escalation Thresholds*

Dimensions	Causes	Escalation
Actors	Situational entrapment Group pressures Spoiling Outbidding Divide and rule Targeted killing Third-party intervention	**Extremity shift**
Issues of contention	Changing political opportunity structure Countermeasures Organisational survival Third-party intervention	**Saliency shift**
Instruments	Indiscriminate killing Retaliation Third-party intervention	**Atrocity shift**
Targets Tactics Territory Time	Countermeasures	**Substitution**

The shifts constitute different forms of escalation, and a shift can occur multiple times during the course of conflict along multiple vectors of causality. The saliency shift, for example, can be experienced multiple times during the course of armed interactions, before a conflict terminates. The extremity shift can, for instance, be caused by different factors, also in conjunction, to explain an increase in severity of conflict.

THE EXTREMITY SHIFT

Extremity shifts within rebel groups have been found to constitute one of the most important forms of escalation. We have identified several main causes of extremity shifts: situational entrapment, group pressures, spoiling, outbidding, divide and rule activities, targeted killing and third-party intervention.

There are several endogenous processes, internal to the group, whereby group radicalisation takes place. Firstly, a causal trajectory for a shift in extremity can be found on the level of the individual, which is called situational entrapment. When there is no other way out of the life as a rebel and no alternatives present themselves, a hardening of positions can ensue that constitute escalation.

Secondly, internal spoiling is a form of an extremity shift. Group pressures, group think, leadership challenges and leadership militancy can cause the rebel group to adopt increasingly more extreme positions. This can be independent of outside influence.

Thirdly, within the wider social movement, if present, there are instances where the signalling of dissidence or, alternatively, continued commitment, the fighting over spoils of conflict or simple chain-ganging are forms of spoiling activity. Spoiling is a form of strategic behaviour to serve the interests of some faction of the rebel group or movement.

Fourthly, also within the wider social movement from which the rebel group can derive, elimination of the more moderate voice can occur. This is called outbidding and signifies another form of extremity shift, constituting escalation. Outbidding is also a type of behaviour that is engaged in as a form of wilful strategic endeavour to advance particular interests of part(s) of rebel groups. These routes are largely endogenous processes to the rebel group and its accompanying social movement, if present.

There are also exogenous actions that can give rise to an extremity shift. We have found, in particular, the divide and rule approach linked to polarisation. Divide and rule activities, playing against each other in the different parts of a rebel movement, usually for the political benefit of the state, can signal escalation. The state tends to operate based on the belief that it can weaken the rebel group as a precursor to defeating it. Little thought or consideration seems to be given to the effect of complicating any form of resolution when more parties and their interests need to eventually be accommodated or addressed. We propose that when a divide and rule approach is applied by the state, this can trigger an extremity shift within the rebel group, which constitutes escalation.

Targeted killing and attempting to take out the leadership of rebel groups have been activities adversaries have engaged in to undermine the effectiveness of rebel groups. The record is very mixed, and recent scholarship has pointed out that the role the leadership had played previously, as well as the longevity of the organisation, can explain the diverging effects on the rebel groups. In general, when the leadership is removed, positions tend to harden and more extreme leaders are likely to take over.

Another form of exogenous action is third-party intervention, which can also contribute to an extremity shift. The intervention in the shape of group support, the provision of legitimacy and justification not only facilitates rebel groups but also emboldens them, when they feel assured of material and immaterial backing. This can lead to a shift in extremity.

The extremity shift is distinct from the atrocity shift and the saliency shift. The atrocity shift relies on a choice to cross an ethical boundary by killing civilians. The saliency shift is based on the raising of conflict salience for all involved and is directly related to interaction. The extremity shift focuses primarily on the group and can be caused by endogenous and exogenous factors.

We propose here that a shift in individual and group extremity constitutes escalation. The examples we have looked at in more detail were the Punjab crisis and the cases of the Rote Armee Fraktion and the Brigate Rosse. This is the first of our hypothesis, which needs to be investigated further in order to assess its wider viability and tenability as a form of escalation: conflict escalation occurs taking the shape of a shift in extremity caused by situational entrapment, group pressures, spoiling behaviour, outbidding, divide and rule practices, targeted killing or third-party intervention focused on the rebel group itself. This hypothesis could be further substantiated by investigating specific individual and group behaviours.

THE SALIENCY SHIFT

A saliency shift occurs when the significance or the weight attached to the issue(s) of contention is raised. We have identified several circumstances in which this phenomenon occurs. Firstly, a saliency shift can occur when the political opportunity structure changes and the weight attached to the issue or perceived issues at stake increases. Secondly, this shift can also result from the state's countermeasures via provocation, the use of overwhelming force, negotiation or concession. Thirdly, a saliency shift occurs when organisational survival is at stake. Fourthly, conflict saliency can also be reinforced via third-party or outside intervention.

The Changing of the Opportunity Structure

This study started out with an overview of a generally regarded prerequisite for political violence, which is a conducive political opportunity structure. Two main structures were identified and discussed for their conflict-generating potential: patrimonial structures and rational legalistic structures, representing the two dominant and ideal-type polities. The routes to violence diverged based, among others, on the roles of state capacity, political entrepreneurs, ideology and grievance frames. Rather than presenting a linear model of mobilisation and the engagement in violence, the examples showed that significant mobilisation occurred after violence broke out and individuals were confronted with it in their neighbourhoods or streets. The examples we looked at were Argentina in the 1970s and Sierra Leone in the 1990s.

To explain escalation, we found that when the political opportunity structure closes, the saliency of the perceived political issues receives an impetus and the enabling link to violence is made. This finding is commensurate with existing insights in the literature about contentious politics. This route to escalation is largely exogenous to the rebel group but dictated upon it by an environment or context, in which it has only moderate shaping power due to the presence of the state opponent and developments among the general public. Moreover, the case of Sierra Leone has indicated that the opportunity structure and social mobilisation mattered little in comparison to the mobilising potential of the use of violence itself.

Escalation in this case can be seen as a rational choice but largely bound by circumstances and path dependencies. These are created by previous commitment to specific political claims, the need to display resolve and credibility and also possibly out of a need for cognitive consistency. This hypothesis would find further reinforcement by looking at cases, in both regime types of patrimonial and rational legalistic systems, where closure of the opportunity structure took place and issue salience remained unaffected or was reduced. Furthermore, investigation is warranted to see to what extent open opportunity structures facilitate de-escalation, as discussed in Chapter 9.

Countermeasures: Provocation, Overwhelming Force, Negotiation and Concession

Chapter 4 sketched four courses of action open when responding to violence. In particular, half-hearted or incomplete re-establishment of the monopoly of force can form a crucial initial contributor to escalation. There is a risk that when more violence becomes necessary to remedy the shortcomings of earlier efforts, it can work in favour of the rebels. The rebel group can benefit when the police or army acts in a heavy-handed fashion. When as a consequence of this approach, the rebel group can capitalise on mistakes by the state, it can wean away support and build its own legitimacy. A second course of action consisted of outright forceful repression. The state envisions that quick action would nip the violence in the bud, in the hope of re-establishing the monopoly of force. Thirdly, the state can focus its efforts to contain violence by offering negotiations and concessions. It is believed that by addressing underlying grievances, these can be resolved and the grounds for the use of force removed. In some cases, this has worked, in other cases it has been interpreted as a sign of weakness and formed an excuse to demand more and continue or step-up violence. The fourth course of action, not responding at all to armed challenges, has not been substantially investigated but would constitute an interesting avenue for future research. It is clear that the non-response option is not connected in a linear fashion to de-escalation, as there are cases of non-response which were followed by more or heavier violence.

Rebel groups, based on prescriptions of revolutionary war thinkers, would actively seek to trigger provocation and overwhelming force responses to benefit from the state overreacting. Similarly, negotiations and concessions can be used by rebel groups to recuperate or regroup to buy time for a new round of fighting rather than seeking conflict resolution. The offer of concessions can be a sign to ask for more or cause a rift between hardliners and moderates, prompting the former to more violence.

These courses of action can all lead to a shift in saliency of the perceived issues at stake, which forms an important expression of conflict escalation. We conclude that important escalatory potential can be found in the response of the state towards the expression of opposition. The examples that were brought forward in the discussion of these causal mechanisms earlier were Northern Ireland and the Philippines, where vocal opposition was a trigger for use of force by the government, which reinforced issue saliency and formed a substantial escalation of the conflicts.

Organisational Survival

Endurance and expansion are natural tendencies for any type of organisation. When survival is jeopardised, any organised group will logically use the means at its disposal to ward off the threat and safeguard its continued existence. The exogenous threat to the survival of the rebel group as organisation could be seen as an extreme form of raising the saliency by putting on the line the future of the organisation. The process can be expected to be rational and deliberate and will most likely be reciprocated. It is presumed here that the rebel group is not weakened severely and still possesses the capacity to defend and resist.

Third-Party Intervention

A diverse set of motivations can cause intervention in an ongoing civil war. The most important interveners remain outside states. Offering material support, sanctuary or political and military guidance have all been found to provide an advantage for the rebel group during the course of war. A saliency shift can materialise when third parties engage in actions that reinforce or raise the saliency of the conflict issues the rebels have embraced. These actions can come in the shape of public statements, speeches and public visits and photo opportunities, which can bestow legitimacy to the rebels and their claimed issues. Saliency can also be raised via recognition in the shape of being a recipient of material and immaterial aid.

The saliency of the perceived issues at stake rises in a context where there is commitment, previous investment and political resolve, which all gain in significance when the interaction turns violent. Escalation is subject here to the circumstances and might not be entirely deliberate. The number of alternative courses of action is reduced by the choices the state has made. For the rebel group it is therefore rational but not entirely voluntary to raise the issue saliency. The saliency shift is largely caused by exogenous factors. Our hypothesis is: escalation emerges resulting from the raising of the salience of the issues of contention caused by changes in the opportunity structure, countermeasures enacted by the state, the imperative of organisational survival or third-party intervention. This hypothesis of a shift in saliency constituting escalation should be the subject of further testing to assess its validity and tenability.

THE ATROCITY SHIFT

Escalation via the targeting of civilians, or indiscriminate killing, is the main suggestion in the existing literature for the occurrence of rebel conflict escalation. The indiscriminate killing of civilians, caused by the mechanism of contested control, via the specific resource base of the rebels, their ideology or the absence of potential rebel targets, causes a significant aggravation of conflict. This study finds confirmation for the existence of the atrocity shift. The atrocity shift entails an increase in both political will and capability in the shape of means and methods to transgress the ethical boundary. We find evidence in our case material that there is indeed augmented political will to hurt the opponent and both a qualitative and quantitative increase in means necessary to engage in this shift. Even though existing means and methods in the shape of bomb attacks are the most common instrument used, they increase substantially in quantity, and the quality of using them against civilians make them stand out.

We find, however, that the conceptualisation of the atrocity shift in the existing literature might be too narrow. We propose here that the atrocity shift constitutes more than the limited conceptualisation of indiscriminate targeting of civilians but includes the scaling of boundaries by ways of broader transgressions. Firstly, the rebel group is far from the only actor transcending ethical and moral boundaries. While we have seen several cases of rebel groups indiscriminately targeting civilians, the state engages in this behaviour as well, often in the shape of violent policing. This idea obviously reflects the conflict studies literature more broadly. Moreover, retaliating after an attack by the state or the rebel group has not been singularly related to an aggravation of conflict in the literature. Still, retaliation in itself has produced higher levels of violence and often more extreme levels of violence. There is often the strong political desirability of doing something after violent attack, that is the countermeasure imperative. Furthermore, the actions of third-party intervention, as brought forward in a study about intervention, has also triggered more extreme violence. Secondly, we find that the atrocity shift is not followed by a consistently higher level of violence or a maintenance of the level of indiscrimination. This shift is therefore not linear but appears in episodes or spurts. We will shortly discuss this notable aspect of escalation in more detail.

The discussion in Chapter 9 has also pointed to important limitations to this form of escalation. Rebel violence operates under importantly self-imposed material or capability restraints, based on choice rather than material circumstances. In particular, the latter had been argued to form the most important brake on escalation. Wilful limitations, such as political and strategic calculations and acceptance by claimed constituents, do play a significant role in curbing the drive to limitless escalation. The hypothesis we can formulate here is: escalation takes place based on a shift in atrocity caused by indiscriminate killing, retaliation or third-party intervention. This proposition of a shift in atrocity as constituting escalation deserves to be further substantiated, tested and possibly refined in order to assess its viability and tenability to explain rebel violence.

SUBSTITUTION

Not only the overall response of the state but also the effects of the state's measures, such as the use of force or the adoption of dialogue, can give rise to escalation in the form of substitution. Substitution, also called the waterbed effect or risk transfer, occurs as a result of countermeasures and forms a displacement of violent activities towards other targets, tactics, territory or time frames. Rebels are very adaptive organisations, at least more so than their state opponent. Substitution, as a form of escalation, is therefore a common occurrence in rebel conflict.

Rebels can substitute targets and have done so repeatedly in the past. Metal detectors, fortification and surveillance are some of the measures instituted as countermeasures, which have caused the rebel group to opt for different targets. Tactical substitution has occurred after the institution of protection measures, security increases and weapon development, which caused a downturn in kidnapping, hostage-taking and airplane highjacking over the years. It did lead to increased severity of individual attacks, the popularity of suicide attacks and the use of IEDs. Geographical substitution is a third form of escalation that is closely associated with rebel violence. When one theatre of operations has been closed or more difficult to access, rebels can adapt their geographical focus, widening or shifting the theatre of operations and causing conflict spillover. Especially rebels who need to defend a territorial base, either in the countryside or in the city, display a potential weakness by being visible, which could be latched on by the state and pose a target for counter-action. Substitution in time, postponing attacks or campaigns until a later more convenient or appropriate time is a difficult form to fully substantiate. This does occur and is linked to investment in time and duration, which can also aid again in the raising of the saliency of the issues at stake. We looked at the examples of Nicaragua and Sri Lanka to assess the adaptability of the rebel group in these respects.

The substitution phenomenon is really the story of unintended consequences or 'blowback' (Johnson 2000). There might be short-term rationality involved in devising and implementing measures, but consequences are either not taken into account, could not be foreseen or imagined or were taken for granted because something needed to be done. This short-termism can be seen in both the behaviour of the state and the rebel group. For the latter, who might easily shift focus, the link to, or rationality of, bringing goals closer is difficult to observe. Widening the geographical scope or changing targets are not always logically and linearly linked to a political logic or political gain.

Substitution as a form of escalation is caused by exogenous factors, which are beyond the full control of the rebel group. They do augment the investments made in the struggle and are signs of entrenchment, resolve and commitment. We hypothesise that escalation occurs by ways of substitution caused by countermeasures against the rebel group. The causal chain of countermeasures, substitution and escalation can and should be tested to assess its further validity.

DE-ESCALATION

This study has also uncovered some de-escalatory mechanisms. It is important to stress again, firstly, that de-escalation is an under-investigated and under-theorised topic compared to escalation and more research is necessary. Secondly, de-escalation is not necessarily the same as conflict termination. Escalation itself can be a route to termination, as the case of Sri Lanka, for instance, has demonstrated. Thirdly, the routes to de-escalation, perhaps even more so than for escalation, are not always under the direct control of the actors involved and cannot be manipulated at will. The de-escalatory mechanisms that this study has brought forward are the de-legitimation shift and the inability shift. They come in the shape of self-de-legitimation and norm convergence and a loss of foreign sanctuary and support and defection, respectively. Table 10.2 provides the overview of the findings which will be discussed in more detail next.

TABLE 10.2 *Dimensions of De-Escalation*

Dimensions of de-escalation	Causes	Escalation
Actors	Loss of sanctuary	**Inability shift**
Instruments	Defection	
Targets		
Tactics		
Time		
Territory		
Issues of contention	Self-de-legitimation	**De-legitimation shift**
	Norm-convergence	

THE DE-LEGITIMATION SHIFT

Self-De-Legitimation

Self–de-legitimation is a causal pathway that is witnessed when a rebel group undertakes an action that imperils the group's often carefully crafted legitimacy claims. As we have seen in the cases of Italy, Canada and Colombia, the loss of legitimacy was due to strategic mistakes, almost entirely of the making of the rebels themselves. A wrong choice of target, killing an individual in the name of independence or Marxist world revolution, compromised the group's claims to legitimately represent these agendas. In the cases of Northern Ireland, there was a loss of support at several points in the struggle but it never reached a critical level undermining the functioning of the rebel group. In the case of Argentina, the state achieved a major victory when its paramilitary attacks on the insurgent organisation pushed the Montoneros to engage in a cycle of violence. This shift in strategy was induced by the state's countermeasures but it was still up to the rebel leadership to follow suit. In the case of the Colombian M-19, the group managed to regain popular support and a measure of legitimacy by joining in with widespread demands from among the population for an end to violence. They used this to pressure the government for a place at the negotiating table. For the state actively seeking de-escalation, the opportunities for doing so appear, in fact, to be limited or at times beyond their control. The self-inflicted loss of legitimacy costs the rebel group political capital and is subsequently followed by a loss in popular support and a weakening in the ability to recruit. It ends up making the rebel group less credible and ultimately less capable to continue the campaign.

The de-legitimation shift is not the same as the escalation trap even though the phenomena may partially overlap. The escalation trap is based on the idea that the continual increase of force, and in particular the use of indiscriminate killing, reaches a point beyond which it is no longer useful to attain ends. This is when the rebel group will start losing relevance. Self-de-legitimation is brought about by strategic mistakes of the group's own making, which revolve around controversial choices of targets or operations not going to plan. These are not necessarily related to indiscriminate violence or atrocity but are linked to incorrect assessments of the impact of the choice of target, miscalculating the political opportunity structure or unexpected repercussions. These processes of self-de-legitimation are often beyond the rational and deliberate control of any of the actors involved.

In this mechanism, the rebel group loses its credibility and compromises its commitment and resolve. This self-de-legitimation is the causal mechanism that ties together most closely the trinity of politics, military and people, as it starts from a moment of decision to select a target or employ force that ends up backfiring. Falsifying it would require evidence or examples where a significant loss of legitimacy of the rebels did not lead to de-escalation.

Norm Convergence

This proposition links a change in the norms and frames of references of the belligerents to a drop in the significance of the conflict. When two actors engage in violent exchange, there are few common norms and expectations binding them together. The incompatibility of interest has turned violent and causes the frames of reference to diverge. While the exact process of the development of convergence remains under-investigated, it has been proposed in the literature that such a convergence or advent of common norms and expectations leads to de-escalation. Examples are Northern Ireland and the case of the IRA and M-19 in Colombia, with supporting evidence from the case of the Palestinian struggle.

This process of norm convergence might be either endogenous or exogenous to the conflict dyad, depending on the involvement of third parties or mediators. To what extent this process is rational and deliberate is at this point unclear and would form an interesting avenue for further investigation.

We formulate the following hypothesis: de-escalation occurs as a loss of group legitimacy to use violence takes place caused by self-de-legitimation, based on strategic mistakes or by norm convergence.

THE INABILITY SHIFT

Apart from a drop in political will to continue the struggle, inability to do so forms a second axis along which de-escalation emerges. A lack of weapons or fighting capacity can signify a very straightforward and visible route of de-escalation. The repressive approach in Sri Lanka and Chechnya led to a significant material degrading of the rebels, which in the end contributed to a reduced will to further resist. Apart from conventional attack to degrade the rebel ability to resist, the control of arms flows is another avenue to compromise the capability of rebel groups. As we have discussed earlier, the curbing of weapon flows into areas of conflict by ways of embargoes does not possess a very positive or convincing track record. In our cases, we have not found a clear example of a successful de-escalation via arms embargoes; this does not mean that it should be seen as absent. In the literature, the lack of enforcement and political will are suggested as holding the key to making this a more effective instrument. Still, there is little evidence that arms embargoes are directly linked to behavioural change of the target. More detailed investigation could shed more light on this issue.

Loss of Foreign Support

As has been known for many years, based in particular on the record of fighting colonial insurgencies, cutting ties and denying sanctuary can be highly effective means to downgrade the efforts of rebel groups. Rebels in most cases operate on a limited resource base. They can offset this disadvantage by soliciting support from outside sponsors. Alternatively, outside sponsors can see rebels as interesting objects of sponsorship in light of potential foreign policy gain. One of the main mechanisms to reduce rebel group capability is by tackling these foreign ties. In particular, financial resources, material aid, immaterial advice, training, sanctuary or recruits can all be targeted and according to several notable assessments to significant effect. In our vignettes there were few rebels without any foreign ties; the RUF was supported by Liberia, the LTTE found sanctuary across the Palk Straits in India, the MNLF in neighbouring Sabah and Sarawak. The Marxist-inspired underground supported the Rote Armee Fraktion and the Brigate Rosse, as did the East German Stasi and other supportive groups, such as the Palestinians.

Cutting foreign ties has been credited with the demise of the fighting capacity of rebels. Not only the loss of sanctuary but also the forfeit of foreign funding and legitimacy has been effective in reducing the power and influence of rebels. This form of de-escalation is both rational and deliberate and is exogenous to the rebel group. This particular proposition can be falsified when foreign support is substantially curbed and no downturn in violence can be observed.

Defection

Defection is a signal on the individual level that the rebel group and the issues it stands for are no longer worth fighting for. We have discussed the variety of personal incentives, material or immaterial, which play a role in the production of violence in civil wars. Pecuniary advantage, local and personal grievances, status and reward are some of the explanations offered. Rebel socialisation translates these personal motivations and routes into rebel groups, based on networks and grievances, among others, into the specific outward production of violence. Defection signals disengagement of the individual rebel; neither the group nor the cause is seen as worth the risk. Three mechanisms of defection have surfaced: a loss of social cohesion, a loss of material benefits or opportunities for defection to other groups and the state offering a better deal. Overall, ideologically motivated rebels have been found to be least likely to defect. The last hypothesis we can formulate is: de-escalation occurs based on an inability to continue the conflict caused by lacking capabilities, a loss of support or defection.

OBSERVATIONS

Based on the material presented so far, we can further substantiate the four scenarios of escalation, which were presented in Chapter 2. We can fill the quadrants with the propositions (Table 10.3).

TABLE 10.3 *Four Scenarios of Escalation*

<table>
<tr><td rowspan="2" style="writing-mode: vertical-rl">Political will</td><td>Scenario A
Political will +
Capabilities ~

– **Extremity shift**
– **Saliency shift**</td><td>Scenario D
Political will +
Capabilities +

– **Atrocity shift**</td></tr>
<tr><td>Scenario B
Political will ~
Capabilities ~

    – No escalation</td><td>Scenario C
Political will ~
Capabilities +

– **Substitution**</td></tr>
<tr><td colspan="3">Capabilities</td></tr>
</table>

Looking at the quadrants in a counterclockwise order, firstly, there is a scenario of increased political will coupled with existing capabilities, scenario A. Changes related to political will we have found in the shape of the extremity shift and the saliency shift. Extremity shifts caused by internal radicalisation, spoiling or outbidding constitute escalation. Raising the saliency via changes in the political opportunity structure, provocation, the use of overwhelming force, negotiation or concession constitutes escalation. Organisational survival as an extreme case of a saliency shift follows suit. In a second scenario, scenario B with no changes in either political will or capability, escalation is absent. A third scenario, scenario C, occurs when political will does not cross a threshold that contributes to an aggravation of conflict but new capabilities do. This occurs in cases where the issues at stake or the weight attached to them remain stable but where there is, for example, an influx of new recruits or material or a change of strategy that contributes to conflict. There were several examples of rebels switching strategies or the substitution of targets, tactics, territory and time that illustrate how this scenario can unfold. Fourthly, both increased political will and augmented capabilities form scenario D. The atrocity shift combines political will with capabilities, which has appeared in the shape of indiscriminate killing, retaliation and intervention.

The same overview can be presented based on the ideas about de-escalation (Table 10.4).

TABLE 10.4 *Four Scenarios of De-Escalation*

Political will	Scenario A Political will – Capabilities ~ – **De-legitimation shift**	Scenario D Political will – Capabilities – – Defeat
	Scenario B Political will ~ Capabilities ~ – No escalation	Scenario C Political will ~ Capabilities – – **Inability shift**
Capabilities		

Scenario A, a change in political will but no decrease in capabilities forms a de-legitimation shift, which can be caused, as we have seen earlier, by processes of self–de-legitimation or norm convergence. When the legitimacy of the group is called into question, de-escalation can result. When groups lose legitimacy, as a consequence their ability to recruit will be affected and this will lead eventually to a change in capabilities. When there is a convergence of frames of reference between the belligerents and the use of violence is no longer necessary or justified, de-escalation ensues. Scenario B with no changes in either will or capability will not exhibit anything significant to understand de-escalation. Scenario C with no changes in political will but a reduction in capabilities forms the inability shift, causally linked to a loss of material and immaterial means to continue, loss of sanctuary, defection and fighting capability. Scenario D with a loss of both political will and capability would signal the road to defeat.

The propositions we have identified are non-exclusive and compatible, that is linkages exist between the different propositions. A salience shift can be linked, for example, to substitution or a shift in targets or tactics. We have seen with the Montoneros in Argentina that the closing of the opportunity structure raised the saliency of the issues and caused a narrowing of the targeting towards the representatives of the regime rather than the propaganda by deed activities that marked the violence before. Another example formed the Rote Armee Fraktion, which shifted from firebombing to killing after the government declared them a threat to state security and the group moved underground. The Chechen rebels changed their ideological agenda, based on outside influences, and commensurate with the jihadi agenda, the tactics and targeting changed, witness the Dubrovka and Beslan attacks. Several groups changed their strategies from terrorism to insurgency or vice versa, from rural to urban terrain or vice versa and their tactics and operational style changed accordingly, for example the MNLF, the Sandinistas, the Tamil Tigers and the Colombian M-19.

Several mechanisms are the result of deliberate activity, such as spoiling, outbidding, divide and rule, targeted killing, retaliation, countermeasures and third-party support. However, a significant number of the causal links are the result of inadvertent, if not accidental, processes. A closing opportunity structure, group pressures and situational entrapment do not seem to be under any individual's specific control. Those factors causing de-escalation such as self–de-legitimation and norm convergence, as well as a loss of sanctuary and defection, do not seem to be particularly wilful from the perspective of the rebel group but are more likely inadvertent or accidental. Many of these processes, but in particular the saliency shift and the extremity shift, seem to be strongly path-dependent.

Overall, this study has brought forward that, in order to understand escalation and de-escalation, political will and capabilities form useful parameters to think through these phenomena. We find that in armed conflict involving states and rebels, several thresholds can be crossed, not so much related to an ethical transgression as the existing literature stresses, although this does play out. Rather, escalation materialises when on a group level issues that matter most to the rebel group receive an impetus. These impetuses can result from the external circumstances in which they operate, that is the political opportunity structure, the wider social movement, the countermeasures or foreign support. But just as important are the impetuses that come from internal processes that are largely beyond control or influence, that is individual entrapment or group think. Moreover, escalation in the shape of substitution is triggered largely by countermeasures with a very short shelf life; because of the high degree of adaptability, the effects are often quickly negated. The de-escalation thresholds appear, in contrast, more inadvertent and beyond control compared to those constituting escalation. At the same time, the opportunities for manipulation appear, in the cases we looked at, underutilised. We will address these further next.

PROBLEMS AND CHALLENGES

There are a series of problems and challenges related to these findings. Firstly, the propositions on escalation and de-escalation await further testing. Hypotheses by their very nature require further weighing and assessment of their tenability both in an empirical and theoretical sense. Are there cases of escalation in which none of the proposed thresholds are crossed? Are there cases in which the thresholds have been crossed which did not amount to a further aggravation of conflict? These are key questions, which we have to leave for our peers and for future generations to consider. In case the propositions are falsified, what alternative explanations for the phenomena of escalation and de-escalation present themselves?

Secondly, some of the propositions based on the existing literature or the available material could not be fully tested or substantiated because of a lack of information. Rebel groups are notoriously difficult to investigate, not only because of the context in which they operate, conflict, disorder and insecurity, but also because it is difficult, once access has been attained, to track the required information (Kruck and Schneiker 2017). It has been particularly difficult, in some senses even impossible, to find evidence from among rebel groups about unwitting sensitivities or evidence of a lack of understanding the opponent. Future field work might very well uncover relevant material on these aspects of rebel group behaviour.

Thirdly, and perhaps the largest challenge for practice is that most, if not all, of our thresholds can only be ascertained with hindsight. It is not only frustrating that increases in issue saliency or extremity shifts occur without much notice or even awareness by the individuals involved at the time. It is also a signal that the idea of controlling escalation is largely illusionary.

In a more general sense, this study has concentrated on trying to increase our understanding of the phenomena of escalation and de-escalation. In the analysis, the dynamic, relational and interactive aspects of political violence have received less attention compared to specific factors that explain the development of (de-)escalation (McAdam et al. 2001; Della Porta 2013). Moreover, it has favoured the perspective of the rebel group over the state and has, therefore, an inherent imbalance. This has been justified by the fact that our knowledge about the behaviour of rebel groups is in need of further study. The black box of the actors has only partially been pried open. While a challenge, they would also form an invitation for further study. We see the relevance of this exercise of unpacking (de-)escalation primarily in creating a larger sensitivity for these issues. Later we will discuss in more detail the relevance for policy.

THEORISING ON ESCALATION

In the introduction of this study, several characteristics of escalation and de-escalation were presented, based on the existing literature. (De-)escalation, it was argued, revolve around the crossing of thresholds, based on rationality and wilfulness, on linearity, reciprocity and a tacit understanding between the protagonists. In this present study, we find only limited confirmation for most of these supposed core features.

Rationality

To what extent is escalation a rational process? To what extent is it a deliberate and conscious choice to escalate? As the Cold War scholars surmised, in particular Herman Kahn, escalation is rational and deliberate (Schelling 1980, 4, 16, passim; Kahn 2012, 220). Accidental or inadvertent escalation went beyond the scope of their conceptualisation: 'The point of escalation is that it is undertaken for a conscious, politically coercive purpose and not for something that happens through an involuntary momentum of events' (Smith and Jones 2015, 151). Some of the cases discussed earlier displayed a certain measure of deliberate escalation, a conscious decision. In the case of spoiling and outbidding, the rebel group decides to eliminate the moderate opposition in order to present itself as the sole and legitimate representative of the perceived cause. It is a deliberate act to target opposing individuals and factions and to cause the dismemberment of the rebel group.

However, these seem to represent a minority of the cases. Rationality as displayed in most of the cases is dominated by very short-term considerations. Most often escalation is inadvertent or accidental. Both the state and the rebel group often display a glaring lack of strategic vision. In one assessment, the state approach has been described as deriving mainly from 'desperation' (Morgan et al. 2008, 118–119). This does not seem to be uncommon. Other suggestions have been indiscipline, institutional culture and lack of information to explain the state response (Lyall 2009, 331).

This study underlines these impressions, without being able to fully and systematically confirm them so far (Silwal 2017). The choice for a particular approach is often based on unrealistic expectations of the utility of force (Smith 2006) or displays a lack of imagination for alternative courses of action. Therefore, the deliberate nature of escalation and in particular escalatory behaviour needs to be called into question. There are many examples of escalation as a result of a lack of imagination or thinking ahead. The state often opts for short-term escalation without considering longer term consequences but also rebels exhibit this tendency, see the problem of substitution. Consequently, escalation is largely subject to path dependency, rather than rational and deliberate calculation, weighing costs and benefits and taking into account the longer term.

Escalation results more often from a short-term reactionary measure or simply from that what happens: In the case of Northern Ireland, for example, as Smith and Jones have noted, 'those escalation measures that did occur were invariably employed primarily in reaction to a perceived increasing of the military pressure by the IRA (rather than proactively introduced to crush the threat)' (Smith and Jones 2015, 168). We see this also in the case of Argentina and the Montoneros, where the social fabric of society was severely affected. The Argentine state had a clear vision for a homogenous society. There was no place for revolutionary opposition and other undermining ideas. The destructive effects of these choices that are still relevant today witness the trials against suspected collaborators of the dictatorial regime. The Rote Armee Fraktion had many preconceived ideas about the German state, which they saw confirmed time and again in their interactions. The wilful nature of the escalation manifested itself in the decisions taken, for the short to very short term. In the cases of the Philippines and India, there are even strong indications that the choice to escalate was importantly informed by the personal electoral benefit

Ferdinand Marcos and Indira Gandhi hoped to derive from appearing to be on top of the perceived threat by instituting stringent measures.

Contrary to the Cold War explanations, we find that escalation is more often than not something that happens rather than a product of rational calculation. Escalation is driven by the circumstances rather than a consciously deliberate act. Circumstances might drive the interaction in a certain direction because of frames of reference and preference. Escalation is a strongly path-dependent phenomenon.

Linearity and Reciprocity

In many cases, processes developed their own dynamic, based on the escalatory mechanisms identified earlier, which were far from linearly conceived of, anticipated or controllable as much of the traditional escalation literature claims. Furthermore, escalation did not develop in a hierarchical fashion with each consecutive step being higher on a perceived ladder or rungs towards increasing severity of conflict. Rather, in most examples we have looked at, violence waxed and waned and was not subject to a linear and hierarchical step up in thresholds.

Escalation was not only largely inadvertent, it was in many cases also completely unwitting and accidental, where the state or the rebel group found itself in a situation where escalation materialised without it being the product of any conscious decision or premeditation. This finding reflects the earlier Cold War critiques of the conceptualisation of escalation as a ladder or an escalator (Wohlstetter and Wohlstetter 1965). Aggravation of conflict does not occur in a gradual process with incremental severity. Rather, it occurs in fits and starts. We see some cases driven by a logic of consequences beyond anyone's immediate control, or as a result of completely unforeseen events. In particular, the case of the IRA in the early 1970s is revealing, where the events of Bloody Sunday had an effect beyond the full control of any of the actors involved.

Reciprocity is based on the premise that for escalation to materialise there is some sort of tacit bargaining taking place. Between the protagonists there is a tacit understanding about the incompatibility of interests and the realms within which it has to be resolved. Earlier, we have found that the bounds of the realm are often not clear and transgressed inadvertently without signalling. Tacit understanding between protagonists of the development of the process is absent. Reciprocity or tit-for-tat responses do occur but there are too many deviations on the ideal-type linearity and reciprocal model of escalation to consider it a constitutive feature. This goes against the idea offered in the Cold War literature on nuclear escalation that tacit bargaining defines conflict.

Escalation Dominance

Escalation dominance was a central preoccupation during the period of the Cold War for many of the escalation scholars. It was deemed of crucial importance in the superpower rivalry to always and under any circumstances command more capabilities than the opponent to go up the escalation ladder and either force your opponent to follow suit or force him or her to give up. More recently, Smith and Jones have argued that the state in its confrontations always possesses escalation dominance (Smith and Jones 2015, 173). This means that the state is always able to raise the level of capability in order to bear down its strength on its opponent: 'Sufficiently determined, it [the state] has the capacity to re-contain any conflict with a lesser actor to a level of its choosing' (Smith and Jones 2015, 173). The state, of course, hopes that it can push the rebel group towards the escalation trap or force it to defend territorial strongholds and hasten the severing of its links with the supportive environment and compromise its legitimacy. The shortcoming in this argument is, first, that the state is not always willing or able to exert this escalation dominance.[1] The divergence in salience of issues at stake compromises the drive to exert escalation dominance. There might be a divergence in commitment between the state and the rebels, in particular in cases of crisis management or intervention in ongoing armed conflict. Secondly, the rebel group might not be sensitive to this kind of pressure on its capabilities and the conflict saliency is reinforced by this kind of state action. Finally, as we have noted, many of the escalation processes are beyond deliberate control, which makes the claims on state escalation dominance questionable.

The opposite has also been argued. It is not the state with its superior *capacity* that possesses escalation dominance but rather the rebels' superior *will* that dominates. As quoted in the Chapter 1, Christopher Daase has argued that the escalation dominance lies with the rebel group: 'the escalation dominance lies with the insurgent since the state will be the first to quit the "competition of outrage"' (Daase 2007, 194). This argument echoes the atrocity shift, with at its core the willingness to transgress ethical boundaries. However, this is a similarly debatable claim in light

---

[1] To some extent, this argument also relies on an ideal type image of a strong and capable state, that is Western democracies, which is inherently problematic.

of our discussion about the self-imposed restraints and limitations of rebels. The violence they perpetrate has to serve the purpose of not exceeding that what is acceptable to its constituents to further the aims. As the case material has demonstrated, when the rebels cross this boundary, they lose the legitimacy and support necessary to be successful and fall into the escalation trap.

The possession of escalation dominance has a completely different meaning and significance in state-rebel confrontations, compared to the existing theorising on interstate escalation dominance. Escalation dominance holds little significance if we reason through the logics, we have found so far. Firstly, we have seen in this study that the mere possession and employment of capabilities is a large source of problems. From the perspective of the state, with the application of force, for example, it can trigger the substitution mechanism. The rebel group becomes a multi-headed Hydra, which can nullify any further effectiveness of state countermeasures. Furthermore, as just noted, the use of more capabilities runs the risk of raising the commitment and cohesion of the rebel group and the salience of the perceived issues at stake. Finally, the state runs the risk of alienating its own constituency and losing the legitimacy it requires to operate and survive.

Secondly, when the state or the rebel group is able and willing to continually escalate, they run the risk of compromising the aims they have set. In the escalation trap, the terrorist overshoots the utility of force by losing their support base. The liberated zone drive of the insurgent demands expansion and consolidation in order to substantiate claims to power, otherwise the rebel group runs the risk of compromising its legitimacy. On the part of the state, ever-increasing escalation has limited utility in light of the fact that the political will of the opponent is of paramount importance. Force can be effective to change the equation in light of further armed resistance. It is less likely to directly change the political will of the opponent. The tipping point as to where the rebel group will stop defiance and start to exhibit compliance behaviour is still poorly understood, if it exists at all (Mandel 2015; Pampinella 2015; Ucko 2015). In this context, the issue of actor legitimacy surfaces again as of overriding importance (Josua and Edel 2015; Mandel 2015).

Escalation dominance is of limited utility in understanding state-rebel conflict. The emphasis on using the capabilities to create a military *fait accompli* that will deliver the political will of the opponent, as Clausewitz postulated, is misplaced. Such escalation dominance would require ample resources to replenish capabilities. However, for the rebel group, the capabilities are used to directly influence the political will of the state opponent rather than the latter's capabilities. Possessing escalation dominance, in its traditional understanding of superiority in capability, is thus of less significance. Rather, escalation dominance understood as sustaining political will to continue the confrontation is key in state-rebel confrontations. Constraints in the utility of force and the risk of alienating support bases further curb the relevance of the escalation dominance concept.

Culminating Points

Once a struggle is underway, the rebel group might reach a point whereby escalation becomes inevitable. At the same time, the aggravation of conflict becomes detrimental to the chance of fulfilling the rebel agenda. It does not seem to hold universally true that rebels are inept at gauging the restraints of their campaigns, witness the discussion about the self-imposed limitations and the phenomenon of rebels apologising for mistakes. In each campaign there is a culminating point beyond which the application of more force has reduced utility. Rebels have been accused of possessing little acumen to recognise the culminating point of their campaign, for example the escalation trap and the diminishing return mechanisms. It would be interesting for future research endeavours to focus on the analysis of these culminating points to better understand how they are brought about and how they are interpreted by the rebels. Possible explanations for the continuation of violence are the paramount importance attached to political will, the paradoxes of victory and defeat in state-rebel struggles and the absence of a way out of violence, which we will further address shortly.

THEORISING ON DE-ESCALATION

Similar to escalation, de-escalation has been traditionally understood as a rational, linear and a largely reciprocal phenomenon. Again, similar to escalation, this is not a tenable perspective for de-escalation either. De-escalation is not a step down on an imaginary ladder. In contrast to the existing scholarship, which has claimed that accidental or inadvertent de-escalation is non-existent (Morgan et al. 2008, 34), we find that the opposite is true. De-escalation can be the product of deliberate action in the shape of cutting foreign sanctuary but is also produced by intangible and inadvertent processes of self-de-legitimation and norm convergence.

If outside states aim to promote de-escalation, the focus on capabilities seems more productive than a preoccupation with political will. This is also in contrast to the existing literature, which displays a heavy emphasis on the role of international mediation and intervention to bring down the level of violence, with controversy surrounding its claimed effectiveness.

In the course of a conflict between a state and a rebel group, there is generally an inverse relationship between the actors seeking de-escalation and termination of violence (Bapat 2005). At the start, the rebel group has little capability, power and legitimacy and runs the risk of being annihilated. It can often appreciate the benefits of achieving its aims through other than violent channels. The state for its part, because of the power disparity, trusts it will quickly gain the upper hand and can therefore be less amenable to negotiations and concessions. However, after the rebel group has survived the initial phase of violent interaction, its confidence grows, issues gain in salience, investments increase and it becomes less inclined to negotiate and display compliance behaviour. The stronger the rebel group becomes, the less inclined it will be, for example, to observe international humanitarian law (Jo 2015, 219). The state often undergoes an opposite development. The longer it participates in the violent exchanges, the more interested it tends to become in talking and compromise. Earlier we have found that de-escalation arrives when an actor loses legitimacy or the will or capacity to continue further opposition and resistance is diminished. While escalation is importantly informed by political will, de-escalation via capabilities appears most striking in the case material this study has brought forward. Overall, much more attention is warranted for the topic of de-escalation.

ENDING REBEL VIOLENCE

Ultimately, there are several different pathways out of violence. Violence can abate when the goals of the group have been reached (Cronin 2009). As has been pointed out in several statistical analyses, this is not a very common occurrence for rebels (Arreguín-Toft 2005; Abrahms 2006, 2011; Chenoweth and Stephan 2011). Still, there are examples of rebels successfully attaining their stated goals. As we have seen earlier, in Nicaragua, the regime was overthrown and a rebel group, and a rebel government, succeeded it. Success can also materialise when the political opportunity structure opens up, either by force or through concessions and the rebel group can realise some of its stated goals, such as a measure of autonomy or political access. Earlier we have looked at the example of the Irish Republican Army, which saw at least some of its major issues addressed in the Good Friday agreement.

Termination can occur when the rebel group is militarily defeated. Similar to outright success, this is not a very common phenomenon either. Defeat can result when the leadership is killed, when the group is success-fully repressed, when the support for the group declines among the popu-lation (Cronin 2009), when state sponsorship is withdrawn (Connable and Libicki 2010, 62–65) or when the group implodes internally (Cronin 2009).

Overwhelming force is a route that many states have adopted in the past, often in the hope of crushing the rebel group with a defeating blow. Several explanations have been offered for the belief in the effectiveness of severe repression as a route to escalation and subsequent defeat. The success of the state in fully repressing rebel violence has been attributed to a conventional strategy used against territorial strongholds of the groups. Furthermore, the level of violence: some authors have suggested that if enough violence is used, rebels can be repressed (Merom 2003). Others have pointed to a possible curvilinear phenomenon in which at first repressive violence is counterproductive but at a certain level it attains a pacifying effect (Eastin and Gade 2016). Another important factor seems to be the link between the rebel group and a wider social movement. When this is absent and the rebels lack support and legitimacy, repression can work. However, the puzzle here is that in both the cases –the Chechens and the Tamils – there was a substantial support base for the Chechen and Tamil movements and both possessed a measure of legitimacy (Connable and Libicki 2010, 31). At the same time, there was very little legitimacy or support for the Russian and Sri Lankan state activities but still the repres-sion managed to achieve the state goal of subduing nationalist resistance. Finally, the organisational cohesion has been linked to the success of repression. The stronger the group, the less likely repression is to lead to the demise of the rebels (Matesan 2018). However, overall, overwhelming force has a very mixed record and has, importantly, been linked to escal-ation via the salience shift.

The issues of legitimacy and popular support have been awarded great importance in the analyses of defeat (Ross and Gurr 1989; Crenshaw 1991). We have seen defeat earlier for the Montoneros, the RUF, the LTTE and the FQL. Apart from the Montoneros and the FQL, which saw some of the issues they raised translated in political measures in democratic Argentina and Canada, respectively, the underlying issues the RUF and the LTTE tried to address in the shape of economic and social disparities in their respective societies were not resolved in either case. In the case of implosion, the state can manage to raise the price for continued engagement to such a level that the group disintegrates. We have seen this in the Brigate Rosse and the Rote Armee Fraktion. Alternatively, a successor generation can fail to develop or internal disagreements can lead to a weakening of the group.

In the debate about stalemates and negotiation, there has been a lot of attention for third-party intervention. Rebels, who have been active for a long time, are supposedly more susceptible to outside pressures to de-escalate rather than opt for a self-chosen path to wind down violence (Becker 2015, 9–10). The role of intermediaries in the final phases of conflict can be of great importance to facilitate conflict termination (Walter 2002).

However, enlisting the help of intermediaries is not unequivocally linked to de-escalation. Even though many studies have concluded that the activities by, among others, the United Nations are largely responsible for the overall declining number of armed conflicts in the contemporary world (Fortna 2004; Human Security Report Project 2008), others have found that it is not so much unbiased intervention but rather biased intermediaries that are successful at mediating and resolving conflict (Kydd 2003). It is problematic that the results these intermediaries generally work towards, negotiation and compromise, produce highly unstable and unsustainable peace and recurrent conflict (Licklider 1995; Toft 2010). Others have found that the recurrences of violence reach not only higher levels of violence but are often also confrontations between former allies (Licklider 1995; Atlas and Licklider 1999; Boyle 2009, 2014), which points again to the problem of spoilers.

For both victory and defeat, Clausewitz's warning that results in war are rarely final rings very true. In Sri Lanka, we saw four rounds of violence after previous rounds had the deceiving appearance of resolution. Similarly, in Chechnya, there were two phases in the civil war. A direct link existed between the first round and the way it was terminated and the second round. Not only are there problems with the resurgence of violence based on the manner in which armed conflict (temporarily) terminates (Licklider 1995; Human Security Centre 2007). There are also, importantly, diverging perceptions as to what constitutes victory and defeat.

The Paradox of Victory and Defeat

Winning and losing in an armed conflict involving rebels is not always perceived in a similar fashion as in interstate conflict (Johnson and Tierney

2006; Angstrom and Duyvesteyn 2007, 241; Simpson 2012). An often-heard claim in the study of insurgency is that winning is simply not losing, based on an observation by Henry Kissinger during the Vietnam War (Kissinger 1969). This idea is revealing of how the nature of victory and defeat is regarded.

A first important distinction is one between military and political defeat. Rebels can be militarily defeated but still be politically victorious. A second distinction is between types of incompatibilities and their links to success. Conflict can revolve around incompatibilities of interests and incompatibilities of values. Interests can be subject to compromise (Sullivan 2007; Sullivan and Koch 2009). Values are by definition very difficult, if not impossible, to compromise on in light of individual and group psychological consequences. Examples of conflicts that appeared from the outset to revolve around incompatible values were the struggles of the Rote Armee Fraktion, the Brigate Rosse but also the Montoneros. Where the initial conflict focused more on gaining a piece of the political pie were the cases of the MNLF in the Philippines, the LTTE, and the Punjab crisis. When incompatible interests are at stake, assessments have pointed out that a measure of success for the rebel group is attainable. In decolonisation or nationalist struggles, success is seen as more common (Wilkinson 1987, 460; Sederberg 1990, 277; Hoffman 1998; Laqueur 2001; Cronin 2009). The non-zero-sum terms of many of these confrontations allowed for subsequent compromise and solutions compatible with rebel aims, for example independence, secession or autonomy. In confrontations involving the use of force to change the behaviour as an expression of values of an actor, violence tends to be less effective (Sullivan 2007; Sullivan and Koch 2009).

Most conflicts, however, will in fact involve both interests and values or over the course of time become a mix of the two. It is likely that in conflicts where a salience shift occurs that involves an incompatibility of values, the actors are manoeuvring themselves into a cul-de-sac. The conflict reaches higher levels of intensity but the chances of agreement of compromise become more remote. As we have seen, the salience shift is one of the most significant escalatory mechanisms we have found in this study.

Winning and losing can be highly paradoxical phenomena in state-rebel confrontations. Firstly, the model of interstate war where strategic actions are linked in a direct manner to operations and tactics does not apply in many of these cases. It is therefore problematic to apply the yardstick of optimally aligning of ends, ways and means as the core of the strategic enterprise to rebels in a similar manner. For rebels using insurgency and terrorist strategies, a direct and causal link can exist between the tactics employed and the strategic level ends (Gray 2018). In other words, the cumulative effect of the means employed can yield political ends for which the war was engaged in (Wylie 2014). Means or tactics can form a main conduit for winning a war, more so than in conventional war fighting strategies. How tactics can have a decisive effect is revealed by a telling example from the Vietnam War. In an exchange between Colonel Harry Summers and a North Vietnamese colonel named Tu in Hanoi in 1975, Summers recounted telling Tu, 'You know, you never defeated us on the battlefield', to which Tu replied, 'That may be so. But it is also irrelevant' (Zabecki n.d.). This illustrates how wearing down the political will of the opponent over the course of time can be linked to attaining strategic-level goals of the realisation of political aims.

A second paradox of victory and defeat is that for rebel groups, in particular, even a strategic defeat can signify victory. There are several notable examples where the rebel group was defeated, or all but defeated, on the battlefield and still managed to attain its stated goals. Again, we see here a direct link between the political will of the state opponent that is under attack on the battlefield but also confronted in the public domain where legitimacy and support are at stake. A prime example is the FLN in Algeria, which was defeated both in the countryside and in the Casbah in Algiers but which won a resounding victory with independence granted in 1962. In this case, the legitimacy turned into a key factor, in particular in French metropolitan politics (Horne 2002). Capacity to resist might be completely negated and political will can triumph. Algeria is not the only example. Also, in Vietnam by 1972 and Kenya by 1959, the counter-insurgent forces had gained the upper hand but ended up losing the conflict (Connable and Libicki 2010, 20).

A third paradox of victory and defeat is that in some cases rebels can be defeated, both politically and militarily, without dealing with any under-lying grievances or addressing political claims. This apparently seems to sever the important link between the use of force as a political instrument and the attainment of political goals. Defeat in interstate war tends to come with declarations and clarification of the terms of the peace, for example German reparations after the First World War, and denazifica-tion after the Second World War. As we have seen in the case of Sri Lanka, no such developments were visible. This study is thus, finally, also a further invitation to think through the meaning of victory and defeat for rebel groups.

POLICY RELEVANCE

The first and overriding impression of the debate and propositions regarding escalation and de-escalation is that modesty is warranted. Despite ideals and ambitions, shaping the environment in which the actors operate is extremely difficult. We come across, time and again, unintended consequences and blowback as a result of what seemed to be a good short-term response or attractive immediate solution. In particular, this focus on the short term has been notable, echoing discussions during the Cold War about escalation: 'The history of this [the Cuban missile] crisis should be an important corrective for the loose assumption that the only time available for decision in the nuclear age is 15 minutes – a magic number supposed to represent the time from radar intercept to impact of an ICBM following a least energy path' (Wohlstetter and Wohlstetter 1965, 24). Careful contemplation can potentially avert calamitous results.

Furthermore, a winning recipe does not exist, even though the strategies that the rebels tend to adopt display inherent weaknesses. Decision-makers would be wise to consider these, and when developing responses or options exploit weaknesses and vulnerabilities. Moreover, the circumstances and the context matter a great deal. The environment in which the conflict is fought out, the audiences, both near and far, and the presentation and perceptions can exert a large influence on the course of conflict.

Several policy consequences can be derived from the material presented in this study. Firstly, we have argued that the role of the state should not be accepted uncritically, since the state shapes its own opposition. It creates, in a large measure, the shape and form of this violent opposition. Using targeted killing, retaliation, intervention, divide and rule and measures to fragment rebels, in many cases the state has created more problems than it solved. Based on the insights, an urgent rethinking of the consequences of actions is necessary.

Secondly, as shown in Table 10.3 with the scenarios of escalation, the political will stood out as carrying large weight in the quadrants where we see the dominant dynamics. When the aim is to avoid escalation, actors might do well considering the following: avoid raising the political resolve or salience of issues that the opponent holds dear. This forms a significant, if not a dominant, route to initial escalation, which might be to some extent controllable. If de-escalation is the immediate concern, policymakers would be well advised to focus on rebel group capabilities. Cutting off resources and life lines can be very effective routes to curb the ability of rebels to fight. This applies specifically, however, to larger groups using an insurgency strategy rather than terrorists.

Thirdly, exploit the weaknesses and dilemmas of the rebel group. We concluded that rebels are strategic actors who adopt an approach based on consideration of restraints and opportunities in their environment. The choice for a particular strategy is informed by a degree of like-minded or parallel response by the state, by foreign sponsorship and the issues at stake. We have noted instances of collaboration; there is even substantial evidence of alliance formation and even in environments with scarce resources, rebels use tried and tested tactical scripts. When rebels coordinate and collaborate, they intrinsically display strategic behaviour. Repertoires of activities are copied and shared among rebels. A shared objective, a delimited geographical space and a set of tactical actions form the prerequisites for this phenomenon to take shape. With the rebel group being limited in its tactical repertoire but all pervasive, the state will find itself in the uncomfortable position of needing to be everywhere at the same time to deal with the threat, dispersing rather than concentrating. This provides an advantage to the rebels.

The two strategies of terrorism and insurgency discussed and debated in this study have both inherent strong points and several notable weaknesses. Terrorism excels in surprise and adaptability, and displays a high degree of substitution. The terrorists can hit easily there where it hurts most. A major weakness, we note in this study, is the careful balancing between the violence that is supported by the rebel's constituents and that what is necessary in the logic of the strategy itself. This is the escalation trap. For terrorists, the quest for recognition and display of presence, coupled with the diminishing returns of each attack, drive an action imperative. This is the particular weak point in this approach, since committing atrocities runs the risk of compromising the necessary support for it to be successful. Furthermore, the link with the population is weaker compared to the insurgency strategy, and when the rebel group is successful in attracting supporters but fails to organise them, a transition becomes very difficult. Finally, the link between specific attacks and the strategic goal is often distant. The self-explanatory nature of attacks for control or punishment the insurgents often carry out is not always present in terrorist targeting. The insurgent strategy is strong in creating cumulative pressure on the government, in creating support bases and offering alternative social contracts in different shapes and guises. For insurgents, the territoriality, organisational structure and visibility and measure of social contract and embeddedness in communities create vulnerabilities. The risk of detection is far larger and the presence and visibility form targets for state countermeasures.

Fourthly, some of the causal mechanisms focused on internal group processes. This would require a careful rethinking of the premises of countermeasures. The idea that a group socialisation process occurs provides some interesting food for thought. If socialisation is at the core of the rebel group, this would require an approach that tackles identity, status and an individual's perspective on the world (also Tilly 2004). Furthermore, if it is the role of leadership and political entrepreneurs in rebel organisations that are of paramount importance, this would warrant further research into key leader engagement, transformation of patrimonial politics and networks (Kitzen 2012). Targeting key leaders can rob the rebels of potential interlocutors for negotiations and of talents to carry the organisation out of violence and into mainstream politics and society. Finally, if indeed it is individual disposition and social solidarity that holds rebel groups together (Abrahms 2008), political or ideological alternatives might be less effective in comparison to personal ways out of a life in the underground.

Legitimacy or the perception of legitimacy forms a central battleground for the actors in state-rebel struggles. Are the political claims and the use of violent means to bring these about seen as legitimate by the population the actors claim to represent? Can the actor provide viable alternatives to the claims of its opponent? What is the rebel narrative and why does it appeal to certain groups? The challenge is to create or recreate a political order that is seen as legitimate. The careful balancing act between what is necessary and what is acceptable is what the rebels are struggling with. The control of territory and the offer of a modicum of social contract make the insurgent visible and vulnerable. The continual need to signal relevance and the risk of alienating audiences makes the terrorists strategy vulnerable. When legitimacy of the actor is lost, it is difficult, if not impossible, to regain. Especially, the intangible aspects of the conflict dynamics in the shape of legitimacy and common norms and expectations appear to be worthwhile avenues to take seriously and pursue further.

A RESEARCH AGENDA

This study has, as any scientific enterprise, inherent limitations. Still, by looking at the available material relevant to increase our understanding of escalation and de-escalation, we have aimed to advance our knowledge. As Mearsheimer and Walt, criticising the hypothesis-based approach so dominant in the field of international relations, have argued: 'A single article that advances a new theory or makes sense of a body of disparate findings will be more valuable than dozens of empirical studies with short shelf-lives' (Mearsheimer and Walt 2013, 448). Taking this to heart, we have made an attempt in this concluding chapter to make some sense of a large collection of findings and added the formulation of some theoretical premises. While rebels need to be justifiably seen as strategic actors, calibrating ends, ways and means, the process of escalation and de-escalation is to a degree beyond the rational and deliberate control of any actor in armed conflict. Controlling escalation appears even harder in dyads involving rebels, compared to the Cold War superpower rivalry, which initially inspired the debate about escalation. Escalation between the state and a rebel group develops differently compared to state versus state escalation. The format of the testable proposition adopted in this study is an invitation to other scholars to advance our understanding further.

This study shows some other limitations; as noted, the role of the state has been highlighted less compared to the rebel group, due to the fact that we know to date very little about the perspective of the latter. Still, if the state were put centre stage, a different emphasis might possibly emerge. If a different dyad were adopted, apart from the state-rebel one, different causalities might surface. We do not think this is very likely in light of the Cold War contributions that were incorporated in the research framework. Still, with the rise of inter-rebel group conflict, alternative routes and causality of (de-)escalation can still be imagined.

While a negative statistical correlation has been found between violence and the attaining of rebel strategic ends (Chenoweth and Stephan 2011), our findings have shown that, in effect, violent rebel campaigns do possess a strategic logic. Escalation and de-escalation form natural components of this strategic logic, even though it is oftentimes beyond rational and deliberate control. This formed the central puzzle of this book: How and when do escalation or de-escalation occur? What mechanisms could be uncovered that would lend themselves to intervention or manipulation and what would prevent the aggravation of conflict or speed up its amelioration?

War is a true chameleon – changing drivers are responsible for a continuation of violence. War, as Clausewitz wrote 200 years ago, is an activity suspended between the factors of passion, reason and chance: the passions of the population, the reason and reasons of the decision-makers and the chance under which the military forces have to operate. Trying to dig deeper into the dynamics of the chameleon-like nature of war, we have tried to demonstrate what these changes are that cause war to adapt its characteristics to its context and circumstance.

Wars have an interactive nature, and the anticipation of, and response to, a calculating opponent is one of the hardest parts of preparing for violent engagement. As this study has shown again, it would not hurt to think more strategically (Duyvesteyn 2013; Duyvesteyn and Michaels 2016). While we cannot predict the future, we can certainly prepare for it better.

References

Abdullah, Ibrahim and Patrick Muana. 1998. 'The Revolutionary United Front of Sierra Leone: A Revolt of the Lumpenproletariat'. In: Christopher Clapham, ed., *African Guerrillas*, Oxford: James Currey, 172–193.

Abrahms, Max, Nicholas Beauchamp, and Joseph Mroszczyk. 2017. 'What Terrorist Leaders Want: A Content Analysis of Terrorist Propaganda Videos'. *Studies in Conflict & Terrorism* 40 (11): 899–916.

Abrahms, Max and Jochen Mierau. 2015. 'Leadership Matters: The Effects of Targeted Killings on Militant Group Tactics'. *Terrorism and Political Violence* 25 (9): 1–22.

Abrahms, Max and Philip BK Potter. 2015. 'Explaining Terrorism: Leadership Deficits and Militant Group Tactics'. *International Organization* 69 (2): 311–342.

Abrahms, Max. 2018. *Rules for Rebels: The Science of Victory in Militant History*. New York: Oxford University Press.

2011. 'Does Terrorism Really Work? Evolution in the Conventional Wisdom since 9/11'. *Defence and Peace Economics* 22 (6): 583–594.

2008. 'What Terrorists Really Want'. *International Security* 32 (4): 78–105.

2006. 'Why Terrorism Does Not Work'. *International Security* 31 (2): 42–78.

Akcinaroglu, Seden. 2012. 'Rebel Interdependencies and Civil War Outcomes'. *Journal of Conflict Resolution* 56 (5): 879–903.

Akers, Ronald L. and Adam Silverman. 2015. 'Toward a Social Learning Model of Violence and Terrorism'. In: Margaret A. Zahn, Henry H. Brownstein, and Shelly L. Jackson, eds., *Violence: From Theory to Research*, London: Routledge, 19–36.

Alexander, John. 2012. 'Decomposing an Insurgency: Reintegration in Afghanistan'. *The RUSI Journal* 157 (4): 48–54.

Alexander, Yonah. ed. 2002. *Combating Terrorism: The Strategies of Ten Countries*. Ann Arbor, MI: University of Michigan Press.

Alimi, Eitan, Lorenzi Bosi, and Chares Demetriou. 2015. *The Dynamics of Radicalization: A Relational and Comparative Perspective*. Oxford: Oxford University Press.

2012. 'Relational Dynamics and Processes of Radicalization: A Comparative Framework'. *Mobilization* 17 (1): 7–26.

Alimi, Eitan. 2011. 'Relational Dynamics in Factional Adoption of Terrorist Tactics: A Comparative Perspective'. *Theory and Society* 40: 95–118.

Allison, Graham T. and Philip Zelikow. 1999. *Essence of Decision: Explaining the Cuban Missile Crisis*. New York: Longman.

Allison, Graham T. 2017. *Destined for War: Can America and China Escape Thucydides Trap?*. Boston: Houghton Mifflin Harcourt.

Angstrom, Jan. and Magnus Petersson. 2019. 'Weak Party Escalation: An Underestimated Strategy for Small States?'. *Journal of Strategic Studies* 42 (2): 282–300.

Angstrom, Jan and Isabelle Duyvesteyn. eds. 2007. *Understanding Victory and Defeat in Contemporary War*. Abingdon: Routledge.

Angstrom, Jan. 2017. 'Escalation, Emulation, and the Failure of Hybrid Warfare in Afghanistan'. *Studies in Conflict & Terrorism* 40 (10): 838–856.

2008. 'Inviting the Leviathan: External Forces, War, and State-Building in Afghanistan'. *Small Wars & Insurgencies* 19 (3): 374–396.

Aning, Emmanuel Kwesi. 2010. 'Understanding the Character and Politics of the Revolutionary United Front in Sierra Leone'. In: Klejda Mulaj, ed., *Violent Non-State Actors in World Politics*, London: Hurst, 277–292.

Arce M., Daniel G. and Todd Sandler. 2005. 'Counterterrorism: A Game-Theoretic Analysis'. *Journal of Conflict Resolution* 49 (2): 183–200.

Arendt, Hannah. 1970. *On Violence*. San Diego, CA: Harcourt Brace Javanovich.

Argo, Nicole. 2009. 'Why Fight?: Examining Self-Interested versus Communally Oriented Motivations in Palestinian Resistance and Rebellion'. *Security Studies* 18 (4): 651–680.

Arjona, Ana, Nelson Kasfir, and Zachariah Mampilly. eds. 2015. *Rebel Governance in Civil War*. Cambridge: Cambridge University Press.

Arjona, Ana M. and Stathis N. Kalyvas. 2012. 'Recruitment into Armed Groups in Colombia: A Survey of Demobilized Fighters'. In: Yvan Guichaoua, ed., *Understanding Collective Political Violence*, London: Palgrave, 143–171.

Arjona, Ana M. 2016. *Rebelocracy: Social Order in the Colombian Civil War*. Cambridge: Cambridge University Press.

Arquilla, John. 2007. 'The End of War as We Knew It? Insurgency, Counterinsurgency and Lessons from the Forgotten History of Early Terror Networks'. *Third World Quarterly* 28 (2): 369–386.

Arreguín-Toft, Ivan. 2012. 'Contemporary Asymmetric Conflict Theory in Historical Perspective'. *Terrorism and Political Violence* 24 (4): 635–657.

2005. *How the Weak Win Wars: A Theory of Asymmetric Conflict*. Cambridge: Cambridge University Press.

2001. 'How the Weak Win Wars: A Theory of Asymmetric Conflict'. *International Security* 26 (1): 93–128.

Art, Robert J. and Louise Richardson. eds. 2007. *Democracy and Counterterrorism: Lessons from the Past*. Washington, DC: United States Institute of Peace.

Asal, Victor, Paul Gill, R. Karl Rethemeyer, and John Horgan. 2015. 'Killing Range: Explaining Lethal Variance within a Terrorist Organization'. *Journal of Conflict Resolution* 59 (3): 401–427.

Asal, Victor, Mitchell Brown, and Angela Dalton. 2012. 'Why Split? Organizational Splits among Ethnopolitical Organizations in the Middle East'. *Journal of Conflict Resolution* 56 (1): 94–117.

Asal, Victor and R. Karl Rethemeyer. 2008. 'The Nature of the Beast: Organizational Structures and the Lethality of Terrorist Attacks'. *Journal of Politics* 70 (2): 437–449.

Atlas, Pierre M. and Roy Licklider. 1999. 'Conflict among Former Allies after Civil War Settlement: Sudan, Zimbabwe, Chad, and Lebanon'. *Journal of Peace Research* 36 (1): 35–54.

Atran, Scott. 2006. 'The Moral Logic and Growth of Suicide Terrorism'. *Washington Quarterly* 29 (2): 127–147.

Aust, Stefan. 2008. *The Baader-Meinhof Complex*. New York: Random House.

Azam, Jean Paul. 2001. 'The Redistributive State and Conflicts in Africa'. *Journal of Peace Research* 38 (4): 429–444.

Bach, Daniel C. 2013. 'Patrimonialism and Neopatrimonialism: Comparative Receptions and Transcriptions'. In: Daniel C. Bach and Mamoudou Gazibo, eds., *Neopatrimonialism in Africa and Beyond*, London: Routledge, 37–57.

Bakke, Kristin M., Kathleen Gallagher Cunningham, and Lee J. M. Seymour. 2012. 'A Plague of Initials: Fragmentation, Cohesion, and Infighting in Civil Wars'. *Perspectives on Politics* 10 (2): 265–283.

Bakonyi, Jutta and Berit Bliesemann de Guevara. 2009. 'The Mosaic of Violence – An Introduction'. *Civil Wars* 11 (4): 397–413.

Bapat, Navin A. 2005. 'Insurgency and the Opening of Peace Processes'. *Journal of Peace Research* 42 (6): 699–717.

Barakat, Sultan and Steven A. Zyck. 2010. 'Afghanistan's Insurgency and the Viability of a Political Settlement'. *Studies in Conflict & Terrorism* 33 (3): 193–210.

Barker, Rodney. 2001. *Legitimating Identities: The Self-Presentations of Rulers and Subjects*. Cambridge: Cambridge University Press.

 1990. *Political Legitimacy and the State*. Oxford: Clarendon.

Barros, Carlos Pestana. 2003. 'An Intervention Analysis of Terrorism: The Spanish ETA Case'. *Defence and Peace Economics* 14 (6): 401–412.

Bassford, Christopher. 2007. 'The Primacy of Policy and the "Trinity" in Clausewitz's Mature Thought'. In: Hew Strachan and Andreas Herberg-Rothe, eds., *Clausewitz in the Twenty-First Century*, Oxford: Oxford University Press, 74–90.

Bastug, Mehmet F. and Ahmet Guler. 2018. 'The Influence of Leadership on the Strategies and Tactics of Islamic State and Its Predecessors'. *Journal of Policing, Intelligence and Counter Terrorism* 13 (1): 38–59.

Becker, Michael. 2015. 'Why Violence Abates: Imposed and Elective Declines in Terrorist Attacks'. *Terrorism and Political Violence* 29 (2): 1–21.

Beckett, Ian F. W. 2005. 'The Future of Insurgency'. *Small Wars & Insurgencies* 16 (1): 22–36.

Beetham, David. 1991. *The Legitimation of Power*. Basingstoke: Macmillan.

Beevor, Eleanor. 2017. 'Coercive Radicalization: Charismatic Authority and the Internal Strategies of ISIS and the Lord's Resistance Army'. *Studies in Conflict & Terrorism* 40 (6): 496–521.

Benard, Stephen. 2012. 'Cohesion from Conflict: Does Intergroup Conflict Motivate Intragroup Norm Enforcement and Support for Centralized Leadership?'. *Social Psychology Quarterly* 75 (2): 107–30.

Bennett, Huw. 2009. '"A Very Salutary Effect": The Counter-Terror Strategy in the Early Malayan Emergency, June 1948 to December 1949'. *Journal of Strategic Studies* 32 (3): 415–444.

2007. 'The Mau Mau Emergency as Part of the British Army's Post – War Counter – Insurgency Experience'. *Defense & Security Analysis* 23 (2): 143–163.

Berdal, Mats R. and David M. Malone. 2000. *Greed & Grievance: Economic Agendas in Civil Wars*. Boulder: Lynne Rienner.

Berry, Nicholas O. 1987. 'Theories on the Efficacy of Terrorism'. In: Paul Wilkinson and Alasdair M. Stewart, eds., *Contemporary Research on Terrorism*, Aberdeen: Aberdeen University Press, 293–306.

Betts, Richard K. 1994. 'The Delusion of Impartial Intervention'. *Foreign Affairs* 73 (6): 20–33.

Bhatia, Michael Vinay and Mark Sedra. 2008. *Afghanistan, Arms and Conflict: Post-9//11 Security and Insurgency*. London: Routledge.

Biggs, Michael. 2007. 'The Logic of Violence in Civil War'. *American Journal of Sociology* 113 (2): 558–560.

Black, Michelle. 2019. 'Explaining Insurgency Progression in Iraq 2003–2011'. *Dynamics of Asymmetric Conflict* 12 (3): 257–281.

Blakeley, Ruth. 2007. 'Bringing the State Back into Terrorism Studies'. *European Political Science* 6 (3): 228–235.

Blomberg, S. Brock, Gregory D. Hess, and Akila Weerapana. 2004. 'Economic Conditions and Terrorism'. *European Journal of Political Economy* 20 (2): 463–478.

Bloom, Mia. 2007. *Dying to Kill: The Allure of Suicide Terror*. New York: Columbia University Press.

2004. 'Palestinian Suicide Bombing: Public Support, Market Share, and Outbidding'. *Political Science Quarterly* 119 (1): 61–88.

2003. 'Ethnic Conflict, State Terror and Suicide Bombing in Sri Lanka'. *Civil Wars* 6 (1): 54–84.

Bosi, Lorenzo, Chares Demetriou, and Stefan Malthaner. eds. 2014. *Dynamics of Political Violence : A Process-Oriented Perspective on Radicalization and the Escalation of Political Conflict*. London: Ashgate.

Boudon, Lawrence. 2001. 'Colombia's M-19 Democratic Alliance: A Case Study in New-Party Self-Destruction'. *Latin American Perspectives* 28 (1): 73–92.

Boyle, Michael J. 2014. *Violence after War: Explaining Instability in Post-Conflict States*. Baltimore: Johns Hopkins University Press.

2009. 'Explaining Strategic Violence after Wars'. *Studies in Conflict & Terrorism* 32 (3): 209–236.

Brophy-Baermann, Bryan and John A. C. Conybeare. 1994. 'Retaliating against Terrorism: Rational Expectations and the Optimality of Rules versus Discretion'. *American Journal of Political Science* 38 (1): 196–210.

Brown, Michael E. 1993. *Ethnic Conflict and International Security*. Princeton, NJ: Princeton University Press.

Brum, Pablo. 2014. 'Revisiting Urban Guerrillas: Armed Propaganda and the Insurgency of Uruguay's MLN-Tupamaros, 1969–70'. *Studies in Conflict & Terrorism* 37 (5): 387–404.

Brzoska, Michael. 2008. 'Measuring the Effectiveness of Arms Embargoes'. *Peace Economics, Peace Science and Public Policy* 14 (2): 1–34.

Bueno de Mesquita, Ethan and Eric S. Dickson. 2007. 'The Propaganda of the Deed: Terrorism, Counterterrorism and Mobilization'. *American Journal of Political Science* 51 (2): 364–381.

Bueno de Mesquita, Ethan B. 2005. 'Conciliation, Counterterrorism, and Patterns of Terrorist Violence'. *International Organization* 59 (1): 145–176.

Bultmann, Daniel. 2018. 'The Social Structure of Armed Groups: Reproduction and Change During and After Conflict'. *Small Wars and Insurgencies* 29 (4): 607–628.

Burch, Michael and Leslie Ochreiter. 2020. 'The Emergence of Splinter Factions in Intrastate Conflict'. *Dynamics of Asymmetric Conflict* 13 (1): 47–66.

Burgoon, Brian. 2006. 'On Welfare and Terror: Social Welfare Policies and Political – Economic Roots of Terrorism'. *Journal of Conflict Resolution* 50 (2): 176–203.

Busher, Joel, Donald Holbrook, and Graham Macklin. 2019. 'The Internal Brakes on Violent Escalation: A Typology'. *Behavioral Sciences of Terrorism and Political Aggression* 11 (1): 3–35.

Busher, Joel and Graham Macklin. 2015. 'Interpreting "Cumulative Extremism": Six Proposals for Enhancing Conceptual Clarity'. *Terrorism and Political Violence* 27 (5): 884–905.

Byman, Daniel, Peter Chalk, Bruce Hoffman, William Rosenau, and David Brannan. 2001. *Trends in Outside Support for Insurgent Movements*. Santa Monica: Rand Corporation.

Byman, Daniel. 2016. '"Death Solves all Problems": The Authoritarian Model of Counterinsurgency'. *Journal of Strategic Studies* 39 (1): 62–93.

2013. 'Outside Support for Insurgent Movements'. *Studies in Conflict and Terrorism* 36 (12): 981–1004.

2006. 'Do Targeted Killings Work?'. *Foreign Affairs* 85 (2): 95–111.

Carlson, Lisa J. 1995. 'A Theory of Escalation and International Conflict'. *Journal of Conflict Resolution* 39 (3): 511–534.

Carr, Andrew. 2018. 'It's About Time: Strategy and Temporal Phenomena'. *Journal of Strategic Studies* Published on-line 15 October 2018. www.tandfonline.com/doi/abs/10.1080/01402390.2018.1529569.

Carrigan, Ana. 1993. *The Palace of Justice: A Colombian Tragedy*. New York: Four Walls Eight Windows.

Carter, Alexander James. 2017. 'Cumulative Extremism: Escalation of Movement–countermovement Dynamics in Northern Ireland between 1967 and 1972'. *Behavioral Sciences of Terrorism and Political Aggression* 9 (1): 37–51.

Carter, David B. 2016. 'Provocation and the Strategy of Terrorist and Guerrilla Attacks'. *International Organization* 70 (1): 133–173.

Carvin, Stephanie. 2012. 'The Trouble with Targeted Killing'. *Security Studies* 21 (3): 529–555.

Cauley, Jon and Eric Iksoon Im. 1988. 'Intervention Policy Analysis of Skyjackings and Other Terrorist Incidents'. *American Economic Review* 78 (2): 27–31.

Chabal, Patrick and Jean-Pascal Daloz. 1999. *Africa Works: Disorder as Political Instrument*. Oxford: James Currey.

Charters, David A. 1997. 'The Amateur Revolutionaries: A Reassessment of the FLQ'. *Terrorism and Political Violence* 9 (1): 133–169.

1994. *The Deadly Sin of Terrorism: Its Effects on Democracy and Civil Liberty in Six Countries*. Westport: Greenwood Press.

Chase, Alston. 2003. *Harvard and the Unabomber: The Education of an American Terrorist*. New York: Norton.

Chenoweth, Erica and Maria J. Stephan. 2011. *Why Civil Resistance Works: The Strategic Logic of Nonviolent Conflict*. New York: Columbia University Press.

Chenoweth, Erica, Nicholas Miller, Elizabeth McClellan, Hillel Frisch, Paul Staniland, and Max Abrahms. 2009. 'What Makes Terrorists Tick'. *International Security* 33 (4): 180–202.

Chenoweth, Erica. 2013. 'Terrorism and Democracy'. *American Review of Political Science* 16: 355–378.

Chima, Jugdep S. 2002. 'Back to the Future in 2002?: A Model of Sikh Separatism in Punjab'. *Studies in Conflict & Terrorism* 25 (1): 19–39.

Christia, Fotini. 2012. *Alliance Formation in Civil Wars*. Cambridge: Cambridge University Press.

Chris Mason, M. 2016. 'Is Nation-Building a Myth? Nation-Building Is an Oxymoron'. *Parameters* 46 (1): 67–79.

Cimbala, Stephen J. 2012. *Clausewitz and Escalation: Classical Perspective on Nuclear Strategy*. London: Routledge.

Clancy, James and Chuck Crossett. 2007. 'Measuring Effectiveness in Irregular Warfare'. *Parameters* 37 (2): 88–100.

Clapham, Christopher. 2003. 'Terrorism in Africa: Problems of Definition, History and Development'. *South African Journal of International Affairs* 10 (2): 13–28.

Clarke, Colin P. 2015. *Terrorism, Inc.: The Financing of Terrorism, Insurgency, and Irregular Warfare: The Financing of Terrorism, Insurgency, and Irregular Warfare*. Santa Barbara: ABC-CLIO.

Clarke, Richard A. and Robert Knake. 2010. *Cyber War: The Next Threat to National Security and What to Do about It*. New York: Ecco.

Clauset, Aaron, Lindsay Heger, Maxwell Young, and Kristian S. Gleditsch. 2010. 'The Strategic Calculus of Terrorism: Substitution and Competition in the Israel—Palestine Conflict'. *Cooperation and Conflict* 45 (1): 6–33.

Clauset, Aaron, Maxwell Young, and Kristian Skrede Gleditsch. 2007. 'On the Frequency of Severe Terrorist Events'. *Journal of Conflict Resolution* 51 (1): 58–87.

Clausewitz, Carl von. 1993. *On War* [Vom Kriege]. Michael Howard and Peter Paret. eds. transl. New York: Everyman's Library.

Clément, Dominique. 2008. 'The October Crisis of 1970: Human Rights Abuses Under the War Measures Act'. *Journal of Canadian Studies* 42 (2): 160–186.

Clifford, Bob. 2005. *The Marketing of Rebellion: Insurgents, Media, and International Activism*. Cambridge: Cambridge University Press.

Cohen-Almagor, Raphael. 2000. 'The Terrorists' Best Ally: The Quebec Media Coverage of the FLQ Crisis in October 1970'. *Canadian Journal of Communication* 25 (2): 1–31.

Colby, Elbridge and Jonathan Solomon. 2015. 'Facing Russia: Conventional Defence and Deterrence in Europe'. *Survival* 57 (6): 21–50.

Collier, Paul, Lani Elliot, Håvard Hegre, Anke Hoeffler, Marta Reynal-Querol, and Nicholas Sambanis. 2003. *Breaking the Conflict Trap: Civil War and Development Policy*. A World Bank Policy Research Report. Washington: The World Bank.

Collier, Paul and Anke Hoeffler. 2004. *Greed and Grievance in Civil War*: Oxford: Oxford University Press.

Collier, Paul and Nicholas Sambanis. 2005. *Understanding Civil War: Evidence and Analysis*. Washington DC: World Bank Publications.

Condra, Luke N. and Jacob N. Shapiro. 2012. 'Who Takes the Blame? The Strategic Effects of Collateral Damage'. *American Journal of Political Science* 56 (1): 167–187.

Connable, Ben and Martin C. Libicki. 2010. *How Insurgencies End*. Santa Monica: Rand Corporation.

Connolly, Kate. 2016. 'Former Red Army Faction Members Linked to Botched Robbery'. *The Guardian*, 19 January. www.theguardian.com/world/2016/jan/19/former-red-army-faction-members-linked-to-botched-robbery.

Coogan, Tim P. 2002. *The Troubles: Ireland's Ordeal, 1966–1996, and the Search for Peace*. London: Palgrave MacMillan.

Coser, Lewis A. 1956. *The Functions of Social Conflict*. New York: Free Press.

Crelinsten, Ronald D. and Alex P. Schmid. 1993. 'Western Responses to Terrorism: A Twenty-Five Year Balance Sheet'. In: Alex P. Schmid and Ronald D. Crelinsten, eds., *Western Responses to Terrorism*, London: Frank Cass, 307–340.

Crelinsten, Ronald D. 2002. 'Analysing Terrorism and Counter – Terrorism: A Communication Model'. *Terrorism and Political Violence* 14 (2): 77–122.

2001. 'The Internal Dynamics of the FLQ During the October Crisis of 1970'. In: David C. Rapoport, ed., *Inside Terrorist Organizations*, London: Frank Cass, 59–89.

1987. 'Terrorism as Political Communication: The Relationship between the Controller and the Controlled'. In: Paul Wilkinson and Alasdair M. Stewart, eds., *Contemporary Research on Terrorism*, Aberdeen: Aberdeen University Press, 3–23.

Crenshaw, Martha. 2001. 'Counterterrorism Policy and the Political Process'. *Studies in Conflict & Terrorism* 24 (5): 329–337.

2000. 'Democracy, Commitment Problems and Managing Ethnic Violence: The Case of India and Sri Lanka'. *Terrorism and Political Violence* 12 (3/4): 134–159.

1999. *How Terrorism Ends*. Washington, DC: United States Institute of Peace.

1995. *Terrorism in Context*. University Park, PA: Pennsylvania State University Press.

1991. 'How Terrorism Declines'. *Terrorism and Political Violence* 3 (1): 69–87.

1990. 'The Logic of Terrorism: Terrorist Behaviour as a Product of Strategic Choice'. In: Walter Reich, ed., *Origins of Terrorism: Psychologies, Ideologies, Theologies, States of Mind*, Cambridge: Cambridge University Press, 7–24.

1987. 'Theories of Terrorism: Instrumental and Organizational Approaches'. *Journal of Strategic Studies* 10 (4): 13–31.

1985. 'An Organizational Approach to the Analysis of Political Terrorism'. *Orbis* 29 (3): 465–489.

ed. 1983b. *Terrorism, Legitimacy and Power: The Consequences of Political Violence*. Middletown, Connecticut: Wesleyan University Press.

1983a. 'Introduction: Reflection on the Effects of Terrorism'. In: Martha Crenshaw, ed., *Terrorism, Legitimacy and Power: The Consequences of Political Violence*, Middletown, Connecticut: Wesleyan University Press, 1–37.

1981. 'The Causes of Terrorism'. *Comparative Politics* 13 (4): 379–399.

Cronin, Audrey Kurth. 2019. *Power to the People: How Open Technological Innovation is Arming Tomorrow's Terrorists*. Oxford: Oxford University Press.

2015. 'ISIS Is Not a Terrorist Group: Why Counterterrorism Won't Stop the Latest Jihadist Threat'. *Foreign Affairs* 94 (2): 87–98.

2009. *How Terrorism Ends: Understanding the Decline and Demise of Terrorist Campaigns*. Princeton: Princeton University Press.

2006. 'How Al-Qaida Ends: The Decline and Demise of Terrorist Groups'. *International Security* 31 (1): 7–48.

Cunningham, Kathleen Gallagher. 2013. 'Actor Fragmentation and Civil War Bargaining: How Internal Divisions Generate Civil Conflict'. *American Journal of Political Science* 57 (3): 659–672.

Cunningham, David, Kristian S. Gleditsch and I. Salehyan. 2009. 'It Takes Two: A Dyadic Analysis of Civil War Duration and Outcome'. *Journal of Conflict Resolution* 53 (4): 570–597.

Daase, Christopher. 2007. 'Clausewitz and Small Wars'. In: Hew Strachan and Andreas Herberg-Rothe, eds., *Clausewitz in the Twenty-First Century*, Oxford: Oxford University Press, 182–195.

Dahl, Robert. 1965. *Modern Political Analysis*. Englewood Cliffs: Prentice – Hall.

Davenport, Christian, David Armstrong and Mark Lichbach. 2008. 'From Mountains to Movements: Dissent, Repression and Escalation to Civil War'. Paper presented at the International Studies Association Conference, San Diego.

De la Calle, Luis and Ignacio Sánchez-Cuenca. 2015. 'How Armed Groups Fight: Territorial Control and Violent Tactics'. *Studies in Conflict & Terrorism* 38 (10): 795–813.

    2012. 'Rebels without a Territory: An Analysis of Nonterritorial Conflicts in the World, 1970–1997'. *Journal of Conflict Resolution* 56 (4): 580–603.

Debray, Régis. 1973. *Strategy for Revolution.* Harmondsworth: Pelican Books.

Della Porta, Donatella. 2018. 'Radicalization: A Relational Perspective'. *Annual Review of Political Science* 21: 461–474.

    2014. 'Competitive Escalation During Protest Cycles: Comparing Left-Wing and Religious Conflicts'. In: Lorenzo Bosi, Chares Demetriou, and Stefan Malthaner, eds., *Dynamics of Political Violence: A Process-Oriented Perspective on Radicalization and the Escalation of Political Conflict,* London: Ashgate, 93–114.

    2013. *Clandestine Political Violence.* Cambridge: Cambridge University Press.

    1995b. *Social Movements, Political Violence, and the State: A Comparative Analysis of Italy and Germany.* Cambridge: Cambridge University Press.

    1995a. 'Left-Wing Terrorism in Italy'. In: Martha Crenshaw, ed., *Terrorism in Context,* University Park, PA: Pennsylvania State University Press, 105–159.

    1992. 'Introduction: On Individual Motivations in Underground Political Organisations'. In: Donatella Della Porta, ed., *International Social Movement Research; Social Movements and Violence; Participation in Underground Organisations, Volume 4,* Greenwich: JAI Press, 3–28.

    1988. 'Recruitment Processes in Clandestine Political Organizations: Italian Left-Wing Terrorism'. *International Social Movement Research* 1: 155–169.

DeRouen, Karl R. Jr. and Jacob Bercovitch. 2008. 'Enduring Internal Rivalries: A New Framework for the Study of Civil War'. *Journal of Peace Research* 45 (1): 55–74.

Deutsch, Morton. 1973. *The Resolution of Conflict: Constructive and Destructive Processes.* New Haven: Yale University Press.

Dhillon, Kirpal. 1990. 'Extremism and Terrorism in Punjab'. In: S. G. Tiwari, ed., *Terrorism in India,* New Delhi: South Asian, 199–215.

Dickson, Brice. 2009. 'Counter-Insurgency and Human Rights in Northern Ireland'. *Journal of Strategic Studies* 32 (3): 475–493.

Dissanayaka, T. D. S. A. 1998. *War and Peace in Sri Lanka,* Volume II. Colombo, Sri Lanka: Swastika.

Dixon, Matthew. 2020. 'Militants in Retreat: How Terrorists Behave When They Are in Retreat'. *Studies in Conflict and Terrorism* Published on-line 7 July 2020. www.tandfonline.com/doi/abs/10.1080/1057610X .2020.1751460.

Donohue, Laura K. 2008. *The Cost of Counterterrorism: Power, Politics, and Liberty.* New York: Cambridge University Press.

Drake, Charles J. M. 1998. 'The Role of Ideology in Terrorists' Target Selection'. *Terrorism and Political Violence* 10 (2): 53–85.

Dudouet, Véronique. 2012. 'Intra-Party Dynamics and the Political Transformation of Non-State Armed Groups'. *International Journal of Conflict and Violence* 6 (1): 96–108.

Dugan, Laura and Erica Chenoweth. 2012. 'Moving beyond Deterrence the Effectiveness of Raising the Expected Utility of Abstaining from Terrorism in Israel'. *American Sociological Review* 77 (4): 597–624.

Dunham, Matthew E. 2002. 'Eliminating the Domestic Terrorist Threat in the United States: A Case Study on the Eradication of the Red Brigades'. *Dickinson Law Review* 107 (1): 151–178.

Duyvesteyn, Isabelle and Wolfgang Minatti. 2020. 'Concepts of Legitimacy; Congruence and Divergence in the Afghan Conflict'. *Civil Wars* 22(1): 1–25.

Duyvesteyn, Isabelle and Jeffrey H. Michaels. 2016. 'Revitalizing Strategic Studies in an Age of Perpetual Conflict'. *Orbis* 60 (1): 22–35.

Duyvesteyn, Isabelle and Leena Malkki. 2012. 'The Fallacy of the New Terrorism Thesis'. In: Richard Jackson and Samuel Justin Sinclair, eds., *Contemporary Debates on Terrorism*, London: Routledge, 35–42.

Duyvesteyn, Isabelle and Bart Schuurman. 2011. 'The Paradoxes of Negotiating with Terrorist and Insurgent Organisations'. *Journal of Imperial and Commonwealth History* 39 (4): 677–692.

Duyvesteyn, Isabelle and William Murphy. 2010. 'Interventie in Staatsvormingsprocessen: Dictatuur versus Democratie?' *Internationale Spectator*: 220–224.

Duyvesteyn, Isabelle. ed. 2018. *Rebels and Legitimacy: Processes and Practices*. London; Routledge.

2017. 'Rebels & Legitimacy: An Introduction'. *Small Wars and Insurgencies* 28 (4–5): 669–685.

2014. 'The Determinants of the Continuation of Civil War'. In: Edward Newman and Karl R. DeRouen Jr., eds., *Routledge Handbook of Civil Wars*, London: Routledge, 224–235.

2013. *Strategic Illiteracy: The Art of Strategic Thinking in Modern Military Operations*. Inaugural Lecture. Leiden: Leiden University. https://openaccess.leidenuniv.nl/handle/1887/20944.

2012. 'The Escalation and De-Escalation of Irregular War: Setting Out the Problem'. *Journal of Strategic Studies* 35 (5): 601–611.

2009. 'The Effectiveness of Intervention Instruments in Armed Conflict; Conflict Resolution Is the Only Solution?'. In: Gelijn Molier and Eva Nieuwenhuys, eds., *Peace, Security and Development in an Era of Globalization: A Multidisciplinary Approach to the Process of Peace Building after Armed Conflict*, Leiden: Martinus Nijhoff, 99–128.

2008. 'Great Expectations: The Use of Armed Force to Combat Terrorism'. *Small Wars & Insurgencies* 19 (3): 328–351.

2005. *Clausewitz and African War: Politics and Strategy in Liberia and Somalia*. London: Frank Cass.

2004. 'How New Is the New Terrorism?'. *Studies in Conflict & Terrorism* 27 (5): 439–454.

Eastin, Joshua and Emily Kalah Gade. 2016. 'Beheading the Hydra: Counterinsurgent Violence and Insurgent Attacks in Iraq'. *Terrorism and Political Violence* 30 (3): 384–407.

Echevarria, Antulio J. 1996. 'War, Politics, and RMA-the Legacy of Clausewitz'. *Joint Force Quarterly* 10 (Winter): 76–80.

Egnell, Robert. 2010. 'Winning "Hearts and Minds"? A Critical Analysis of Counter-Insurgency Operations in Afghanistan'. *Civil Wars* 12 (3): 282–303.

Enders, Walter and Todd Sandler. 2005. 'After 9/11: Is It All Different Now?'. *Journal of Conflict Resolution* 49 (2): 259–277.

2000. 'Is Transnational Terrorism Becoming More Threatening?: A Time-Series Investigation'. *Journal of Conflict Resolution* 44 (3): 307–332.

Enders, Walter, Todd Sandler, and Joe Cauley. 1990. 'UN Conventions, Technology and Retaliation in the Fight against Terrorism: An Econometric Evaluation'. *Terrorism and Political Violence* 2 (1): 84–105.

Enders, Walter. 2004. 'What Do We Know about the Substitution Effect in Transnational Terrorism?'. In: Andrew Silke, ed., *Research on Terrorism: Trends, Achievements & Failures*, London: Frank Cass, 119–137.

Engene, Jan Oskar. 2007. 'Five Decades of Terrorism in Europe: The TWEED Dataset'. *Journal of Peace Research* 44 (1): 109–121.

English, Richard. 2005. *Armed Struggle: The History of the IRA*. Oxford: Oxford University Press.

Eppright, Charles T. 1997. '"Counterterrorism" and Conventional Military Force: The Relationship between Political Effect and Utility'. *Studies in Conflict & Terrorism* 20 (4): 333–344.

Erickson, Jennifer. 2013. 'Stopping the Legal Flow of Weapons: Compliance with Arms Embargoes 1981–2004'. *Journal of Peace Research* 50 (20): 159–174.

Etzioni, Amitai. 2007. *Security First: For a Muscular, Moral Foreign Policy*. New Haven: Yale University Press.

Eubank, William L. and Leonard B. Weinberg. 2001. 'Terrorism and Democracy: Perpetrators and Victims'. *Terrorism and Political Violence* 13 (1): 155–164.

1994. 'Does Democracy Encourage Terrorism?'. *Terrorism and Political Violence* 6 (4): 417–435.

Evans, Michael. 2003. 'From Kadesh to Kandahar: Military Theory and the Future of War'. *Naval War College Review* 56 (3): 132–149.

Evelegh, Robin. 1978. *Peace Keeping in a Democratic Society: The Lessons of Northern Ireland*. Toronto: University of Toronto Press.

Ezrow, Natasha and Erica Frantz. 2013. 'Revisiting the Concept of the Failed State: Bringing the State Back In'. *Third World Quarterly* 34 (8): 1323–1338.

Fanon, Frantz. 2004. *The Wretched of the Earth*. New York: Grove Press.

Farrell, Theo. 2020. 'Military Adaptation and Organisational Convergence in War: Insurgents and International Forces in Afghanistan'. *Journal of Strategic Studies* Published on-line 25 May 2020. www.tandfonline.com/doi/abs/10.1080/01402390.2020.1768371.

Fearon, James D. and David D. Laitin. 2003. 'Ethnicity, Insurgency, and Civil War'. *American Political Science Review* 97 (1): 75–90.

Fearon, James D. 1998. 'Commitment Problems and the Spread of Ethnic Conflict'. In: David A. Lake and Donald S. Rothchild, eds., *The International Spread of Ethnic Conflict: Fear, Diffusion and Escalation*, Princeton, NJ: Princeton University Press, 107–126.

1995. 'Rationalist Explanations for War'. *International Organization* 49 (3): 379–414.

1994. 'Domestic Political Audiences and the Escalation of International Disputes'. *American Political Science Review* 88 (3): 577–592.

Findley, Michael G. and Joseph K. Young. 2012. 'More Combatant Groups, More Terror?: Empirical Tests of an Outbidding Logic'. *Terrorism and Political Violence* 24 (5): 706–721.

Finnemore, Martha and Kathryn Sikkink. 1998. 'International Norm Dynamics and Political Change'. *International Organization* 52 (4): 887–917.

Fjelde, Hanne and Desirée Nilsson. 2012. 'Rebels against Rebels: Explaining Violence between Rebel Groups'. *Journal of Conflict Resolution* 56 (4): 604–628.

Ford, Franklin L. 1985. *Political Murder: From Tyrannicide to Terrorism*. Cambridge: Harvard University Press.

Fortna, Virginia Page. 2015. 'Do Terrorists Win? Rebels' Use of Terrorism and Civil War Outcomes'. *International Organization* 69 (3): 519–556.

2004. 'Does Peacekeeping Keep Peace? International Intervention and the Duration of Peace after Civil War'. *International Studies Quarterly* 48 (2): 269–292.

Fournier, Louis. 1984. *F.L.Q.: The Anatomy of an Underground Movement* [F.L.Q.: histoire d'un mouvement clandestin]. Edward Baxter. Transl. Toronto: NC Press.

Freedman, Lawrence. 2013. *Strategy: A History*. Oxford: Oxford University Press.

2006. *The Transformation of Strategic Affairs*. Abingdon: Routledge.

2004. *Deterrence*. Cambridge: Polity.

Freeman, Michael. 2014. 'A Theory of Terrorist Leadership (and Its Consequences for Leadership Targeting)'. *Terrorism and Political Violence* 26 (4): 666–687.

Frey, Bruno S. 2004. *Dealing with Terrorism: Stick or Carrot?*. London: Edward Elgar.

Freytag, Andreas, Jens J. Krueger, Daniel Meierrieks, and Friedrich Schneider. 2011. 'The Origins of Terrorism: Cross-Country Estimates of the Socio-Economic Determinants of Terrorism'. *European Journal of Political Economy* 27 (1): S5-S16.

Fromkin, David. 1975. 'The Strategy of Terrorism'. *Foreign Affairs* 53 (4): 683–698.

Fruchart, D., P. Holtom, S. T. Wezeman, D. Strandow, and P. Wallensteen. 2007. *United Nations Arms Embargoes: Their Impact on Arms Flows and Target Behaviour*. Stockholm: Stockholm International Peace Research Institute.

Fujii, Lee Ann. 2013. 'The Puzzle of Extra-Lethal Violence'. *Perspectives on Politics* 11 (2): 410–426.

Fumerton, Mario and Isabelle Duyvesteyn. 2009. 'Insurgency and Terrorism-What's the Difference?'. In: Caroline Holmqvist-Jonsater and Christopher Coker, eds., *The Character of War in the Early 21st Century*, London: Routledge, 27–41.

Furlong, Paul. 1981. 'Political Terrorism in Italy: Responses, Reactions and Immobilism'. In: Juliet Lodge, ed., *Terrorism: A Challenge to the State*, Oxford: Martin Robertson, 57–91.

Gaibulloev, Khrusav and Todd Sandler. 2009. 'Hostage Taking: Determinants of Terrorist Logistical and Negotiation Success'. *Journal of Peace Research* 46 (6): 739–756.

Ganor, Boaz. 2005. *The Counter-Terrorism Puzzle: A Guide for Decision Makers*. New Brunswick: Transaction.

Gartenstein-Ross, Daveed, Jason Fritz, Bridget Moreng, and Nathaniel Barr. 2015. *Islamic State versus Al-Qaeda; Strategic Dimensions of a Patricidal Conflict*. Washington DC: New America. Available at: https://static .newamerica.org/attachments/12103-islamic-state-vs-al-qaeda/ISISvAQ_ Final.e68fdd22a90e49c4af1d4cd0dc9e3651.pdf.

Gates, Scott. 2002. 'Recruitment and Allegiance: The Microfoundations of Rebellion'. *Journal of Conflict Resolution* 46 (1): 111–130.

Gent, Stephen E. 2008. 'Going in When It Counts: Military Intervention and the Outcome of Civil Conflicts'. *International Studies Quarterly* 52 (4): 713–735.

George, Alexander L. and William E. Simons. 1994. *The Limits of Coercive Diplomacy*. Boulder: Westview Press.

Gill, K. P. S. 1999. 'Endgame in Punjab: 1988–1993'. *Faultlines* 1. Available at: www.satp.org/satporgtp/publication/faultlines/volume1/Fault1-kpstext.htm.

Goodwin, Jeff and James M. Jasper. 2009. *The Social Movements Reader: Cases and Concepts*. Oxford: Wiley Blackwell.

Goodwin, Jeff and Theda Skocpol. 1989. 'Explaining Revolutions in the Third World'. *Politics and Society* 17 (4): 489–509.

Goodwin, Jeff. 2006. 'A Theory of Categorical Terrorism'. *Social Forces* 84 (4): 2027–2046.

Gow, James and Milena Michalski. 2007. *War, Image and Legitimacy: Viewing Contemporary Conflict*. London: Routledge.

Grauer, Ryan and Dominic Tierney. 2017. 'The Arsenal of Insurrection: Explaining Rising Support for Rebels'. *Security Studies* 27 (2): 263–295.

Gray, Colin. 2018. *Theory of Strategy*. Oxford: Oxford University Press.

Gross, Michael L. 2003. 'Fighting by Other Means in the Mideast: A Critical Analysis of Israel's Assassination Policy'. *Political Studies* 52 (2): 350–368.

Guelke, Adrian. 1995. *The Age of Terrorism and the International Political System*. London: Tauris.

Gurr, Ted Robert. 2006. 'Economic Factors'. In: Louise Richardson, ed., *The Roots of Terrorism*, New York: Routledge, 85–101.

1970. *Why Men Rebel*. Princeton: Princeton University Press.

Hack, Karl. 2009. 'The Malayan Emergency as Counter-Insurgency Paradigm'. *Journal of Strategic Studies* 32 (3): 383–414.

Haer, Roos, Lilli Banholzer, and Verena Ertl. 2011. 'Create Compliance and Cohesion: How Rebel Organizations Manage to Survive'. *Small Wars & Insurgencies* 22 (3): 415–434.

Hafez, Mohammed M. 2020. 'Fratricidal Rebels: Ideological Extremity and Warring Factionalism in Civil Wars'. *Terrorism and Political Violence* 32 (3): 604–629.

Hamilton, Lawrence C. and James D. Hamilton. 1983. 'Dynamics of Terrorism'. *International Studies Quarterly* 27 (1): 39–54.

Hammes, Thomas X. 2012. 'The Future of Counterinsurgency'. *Orbis* 56 (4): 565–587.

Hanle, Donald J. 1989. 'Counter-Terrorism: Conclusions and Countermeasures'. In: Donald J. Hanle, ed., *Terrorism: The Newest Face of Warfare*, Washington, DC: Pergamon – Brassey's, 198–230.

Harkavy, Robert E. 1998. 'Triangular or Indirect Deterrence/Compellence: Something New in Deterrence Theory?'. *Comparative Strategy* 17 (1): 63–81.

Harmon, Christopher C. 2008. *Terrorism Today*. London: Routledge.

Hassner, Ron E. 2011. 'Sacred Time and Conflict Initiation'. *Security Studies* 20 (4): 491–520.

Heck, Axel. 2017. 'Images, Visions and Narrative Identity Formation of ISIS'. *Global Discourse* 7 (2–3): 244–259.

Hedström, Peter and Richard Swedberg. 1998. *Social Mechanisms: An Analytical Approach to Social Theory*. Cambridge: Cambridge University Press.

Heiberg, Marianne, Brendan O'Leary, and John Tirman. eds. 2007. *Terror, Insurgency, and the State: Ending Protracted Conflicts*. Philadelphia: University of Pennsylvania Press.

Helman, Gerald B. and Steven R. Ratner. 1992. 'Saving Failed States'. *Foreign Policy* 89 (Winter): 3–20.

Hepworth, Daniel P. 2014. 'Terrorist Retaliation? An Analysis of Terrorist Attacks Following the Targeted Killing of Top-Tier Al Qaeda Leadership'. *Journal of Policing, Intelligence and Counterterrorism* 9 (1): 1–18.

Herbst, Jeffrey. 2000. *States and Power in Africa: Comparative Lessons in Authority and Control*. Princeton: Princeton University Press.

Herreros, Francisco and Henar Criado. 2009. 'Pre-Emptive or Arbitrary: Two Forms of Lethal Violence in a Civil War'. *Journal of Conflict Resolution* 53 (3): 419–445.

Herreros, Francisco. 2006. '"The Full Weight of the State": The Logic of Random State-Sanctioned Violence'. *Journal of Peace Research* 43 (6): 671–689.

Heuser, Beatrice. 2011. *Reading Clausewitz*. London: Random House.

Hewitt, Christopher. 1984. *The Effectiveness of Anti-Terrorist Policies*. Lanham: University Press of America.

Hironaka, Ann. 2005. *Never Ending Wars*. Cambridge: Harvard University Press.

Hoffman, Bruce and Jennifer Morrison-Taw. 2000. 'A Strategic Framework for Countering Terrorism'. In: Fernando Reinares, ed., *European Democracies Against Terrorism: Governmental Policies and Intergovernmental Cooperation*, Aldershot: Ashgate/Dartmouth, 3–30.

1992. *A Strategic Framework for Countering Terrorism and Insurgency*. Santa Monica: Rand Corporation.

Hoffman, Bruce. 2014. 'Low-Tech Terrorism'. *National Interest* 130 (March–April): 61–71.

1998. *Inside Terrorism*. New York: Columbia University Press.

Hofmann, David C. and Lorne L. Dawson. 2014. 'The Neglected Role of Charismatic Authority in the Study of Terrorist Groups and Radicalization'. *Studies in Conflict & Terrorism* 37 (4): 348–368.

Hoffman, Frank G. 2009. 'Hybrid Warfare and Challenges'. *Joint Forces Quarterly* 52 (1): 34–48.

Holsti, Kalevi J. 1996. *The State, War, and the State of War*. Cambridge: Cambridge University Press.

Holsti, Ole R. 1972. *Crisis, Escalation, War*. Montreal: McGill-Queen's Press.

Holtermann, Helge. 2019. 'Blinding the Elephant: Combat, Information and Rebel Violence'. *Terrorism and Political Violence* Published on-line 19 July 2019. www.tandfonline.com/doi/abs/10.1080/09546553.2019.1630383.

Horgan, John. 2005. *The Psychology of Terrorism*. London: Frank Cass.

Horne, Alistair. 2002. *A Savage War of Peace: Algeria, 1954–1962*. New York: History Book Club.

Horowitz, Donald L. 1985. *Ethnic Groups in Conflict*. Berkeley: University of California Press.

Hoyt, Timothy D. 2004. 'Military Force'. In: Audrey Kurth Cronin and James M. Ludes, eds., *Attacking Terrorism: Elements of a Grand Strategy*, Washington, DC: Georgetown University Press, 162–185.

Hultquist, Philip. 2015. 'Is Collective Repression an Effective Counterinsurgency Technique? Unpacking the Cyclical Relationship between Repression and Civil Conflict'. *Conflict Management and Peace Science* 34 (5): 507–525.

Human Security Centre. 2007. *Human Security Report 2005*. Vancouver: Human Security Report Project.

Human Security Report Project. 2008. *Human Security Brief 2007*. Vancouver: Human Security Report Project.

Humphreys, Macartan and Jeremy M. Weinstein. 2008. 'Who Fights? The Determinants of Participation in Civil War'. *American Journal of Political Science* 52 (2): 436–455.

Hussain, Syed Rifaat. 2010. 'The Liberation Tigers of Tamil Eelam (LTTE): Failed Quest for a "Homeland"'. In: Klejda Mulaj, ed., *Violent Non-State Actors in World Politics*, London: Hurst, 381–412.

Idler, Annette and James Forest. 2015. 'Behavioral Patterns Among (Violent) Non-State Actors: A Study of Complementary Governance'. *Stability: International Journal of Security and Development* 4 (1): 1–19.

International Crisis Group. 2013. *Syria's Metastasising Conflicts*. Brussels: International Crisis Group.

Jäckle, Sebastian and Marcel Baumann. 2017. '"New Terrorism" = Higher Brutality? An Empirical Test of the "Brutalization Thesis"'. *Terrorism and Political Violence* 29 (5): 875–901.

Jackson, Richard. 2007. 'The Core Commitments of Critical Terrorism Studies'. *European Political Science* 6 (3): 244–251.

Janis, Irving Lester. 1972. *Victims of Groupthink: A Psychological Study of Foreign-Policy Decisions and Fiascoes*. Boston: Houghton Mifflin.

Jardine, Eric and Simon Palamar. 2014. 'Numerous, Capable, and Well-Funded Rebels: Insurgent Military Effectiveness and Deadly Attacks in Afghanistan'. *Terrorism and Political Violence* 27 (4): 628–656.

_eafeer

Jardine, Eric. 2014. 'The Insurgent's Dilemma: A Theory of Mobilization and Conflict Outcome'. PhD manuscript, Carleton University Ottawa, Canada. https://curve.carleton.ca/4043e1a5-90ab-4835-bafe-96274c75ce2a.

2012. 'The Tacit Evolution of Coordination and Strategic Outcomes in Highly Fragmented Insurgencies: Evidence from the Soviet War in Afghanistan'. *Journal of Strategic Studies* 35 (4): 541–572.

2009. 'Why Time Works against a Counterinsurgency'. *Journal of Military and Strategic Studies* 11 (4): 1–34.

Jenkins, Brian Michael. 2014. 'The Deadliness of Terrorist Attacks'. In: Gary LaFree, Laura Dugan, and Erin Miller, eds., *Putting Terrorism in Context: Lessons from the Global Terrorism Database*, London: Routledge, 125–145.

1985b. *International Terrorism: The Other World War*. Santa Monica: Rand Corporation.

1985a. *The Likelihood of Nuclear Terrorism*. Santa Monica: Rand Corporation.

1975. 'International Terrorism: A New Mode of Conflict'. In: David Carlton and Carlo Schaerf, eds., *International Terrorism and World Security*, London: Croom Helm, 13–49.

Jensen, Richard Bach. 2004. 'Daggers, Rifles and Dynamite: Anarchist Terrorism in Nineteenth Century Europe'. *Terrorism and Political Violence* 16 (1): 116–153.

Jentzsch, Corinna. 2014. *Militias and the Dynamics of Civil War*. New Haven: Yale University Press.

Jervis, Robert. 1968. 'Hypotheses on Misperception'. *World Politics* 20 (3): 454–479.

Jetter, Michael. 2019. 'More Bang for the Buck: Media Coverage of Suicide Attacks'. *Terrorism and Political Violence* 31 (4): 779–799.

Jo, Hyeran. 2015. *Compliant Rebels: Rebel Groups and International Law in World Politics*. Cambridge: Cambridge University Press.

Johnson, Dominic and Dominic Tierney. 2006. *Failing to Win: Perceptions of Victory and Defeat in International Politics*. Cambridge: Harvard University Press.

Johnson, Chalmers. 2000. *Blowback: The Costs and Consequences of American Empire*. London: Macmillan.

Johnston, Patrick B. 2012. 'Does Decapitation Work? Assessing the Effectiveness of Leadership Targeting in Counterinsurgency Campaigns'. *International Security* 36 (4): 47–79.

2009. 'The Effectiveness of Leadership Decapitation in Counterinsurgency'. Doctoral Dissertation, Center for International Security and Cooperation, Stanford University. http://citeseerx.ist.psu.edu/viewdoc/download?doi=10.1.1.460.4957&rep=rep1&type=pdf.

Jones, Sam. 2018. '"We Are Truly Sorry": ETA Apologises for Four Decades of Deadly Violence'. *The Guardian*, 20 April. www.theguardian.com/world/2018/apr/20/eta-apologises-basque-separatists-deadly-violence.

Jordan, Jenna. 2009. 'When Heads Roll: Assessing the Effectiveness of Leadership Decapitation'. *Security Studies* 18 (4): 719–755.

Joshi, Manoj. 1996. 'On the Razor's Edge: The Liberation Tigers of Tamil Eelam'. *Studies in Conflict & Terrorism* 19 (1): 19–42.

Josua, Maria and Mirjam Edel. 2015. 'To Repress or Not to Repress: Regime Survival Strategies in the Arab Spring'. *Terrorism and Political Violence* 27 (2): 289–309.

Kahn, Herman. 2012. *On Escalation: Metaphors and Scenarios*. New Brunswick: Transaction.

Kaldor, Mary. 2001. *New and Old Wars: Organized Violence in a Global Era*. Cambridge: Polity.

Kalpakian, Jack. 2003. 'Terrorism and Guerrilla Warfare Theory and Practice: Al-Qaeda and Sudan's SPLA'. *South African Journal of International Affairs* 10 (2): 41–61.

Kalyvas, Stathis. 2018. 'Jihadi Rebels in Civil War'. *Daedalus* 147 (1): 36–47.

    2011. 'The Changing Character of Civil Wars 1800–2009'. In: Hew Strachan and Sibylle Scheipers, eds., *The Changing Character of War*, Oxford: Oxford University Press, 202–219.

    2006. *The Logic of Violence in Civil War*. New York: Cambridge University Press.

    2004b. 'The Urban Bias in Research on Civil Wars'. *Security Studies* 13 (3): 160–190.

    2004a. 'The Paradox of Terrorism in Civil War'. *Journal of Ethics* 8: 97–138.

    2003. 'The Ontology of "Political Violence": Action and Identity in Civil Wars'. *Perspectives on Politics* 1 (3): 475–494.

    1999. 'Wanton and Senseless? The Logic of Massacres in Algeria'. *Rationality and Society* 11 (3): 243–285.

Kaplan, Robert. 1994. 'The Coming Anarchy: How Scarcity, Crime, Overpopulation, Tribalism and Disease Are Rapidly Destroying the Social Fabric of Our Planet'. *Atlantic Monthly* 2 (2): 44–79.

Kaplan, Jeffrey. 1997. 'Leaderless Resistance'. *Terrorism and Political Violence* 9 (3): 80–95.

Katagiri, Noriyuki. 2014. *Adapting to Win: How Insurgents Fight and Defeat Foreign States in War*. Philadelphia: University of Pennsylvania Press.

    2013. 'Suicidal Armies: Why do Rebels Fight Like an Army and Keep Losing?'. *Comparative Strategy* 32 (4): 354–377.

Kattelman, Kyle T. 2020. 'Assessing Success of the Global War on Terror: Terrorist Attack Frequency and the Backlash Effect'. *Dynamics of Asymmetric Conflict* 13 (1): 67–86.

Kaufman, Stuart J. 1996. 'Spiraling to Ethnic War: Elites, Masses, and Moscow in Moldova's Civil War'. *International Security* 21 (2): 108–138.

Kaufmann, Chaim. 1996a. 'Intervention in Ethnic and Ideological Civil Wars: Why One Can Be Done and the Other Can't'. *Security Studies* 6 (1): 62–101.

    1996b. 'Possible and Impossible Solutions to Ethnic Civil Wars'. *International Security* 20 (4): 136–175.

Kearns, Erin, Allison Betus, and Anthony Lemieux. 2018. 'Why Do Some Terrorist Attacks Receive More Media Attention than Others?'. *Justice Quarterly*. Available at http://dx.doi.org/10.2139/ssrn.2928138.

Keegan, John. 2011. *The Face of Battle: A Study of Agincourt, Waterloo and the Somme*. London: Random House.

1993. *A History of Warfare*. New York: Knopf.

Keen, David. 2012. *Useful Enemies: When Waging War Is More Important than Winning Them*. New Haven: Yale University Press.

2005. *Conflict and Collusion in Sierra Leone*. Oxford: James Currey.

1998. *The Economic Functions of Violence in Civil Wars*. Oxford: Oxford University Press.

Kegley, Charles W. Jr. 1990. *International Terrorism: Characteristics, Causes, Controls*. New York: St. Martin's.

Kennedy-Pipe, Caroline. 1997. *The Origins of the Present Troubles in Northern Ireland*. New York: Longman.

Kettle, Louise and Andrew Mumford. 2017. 'Terrorist Learning: A New Analytical Framework'. *Studies in Conflict & Terrorism* 40 (7): 523–538.

Khalil, James. 2013. 'Know Your Enemy: On the Futility of Distinguishing between Terrorists and Insurgents'. *Studies in Conflict & Terrorism* 36 (5): 419–430.

Kilcullen, David. 2013. *Out of the Mountains: The Coming Age of the Urban Guerrilla*. Oxford: Oxford University Press.

2009. *The Accidental Guerrilla: Fighting Small Wars in the Midst of a Big One*. New York: Oxford University Press.

2006. 'Counter-Insurgency *Redux*'. *Survival* 48 (4): 111–130.

2005. 'Countering Global Insurgency'. *The Journal of Strategic Studies* 28 (4): 597–617.

Kissinger, Henry A. 1969. 'The Viet Nam Negotiations'. *Foreign Affairs* 47 (2): 211–234.

Kitzen, Martijn. 2012. 'Close Encounters of the Tribal Kind: The Implementation of Co-Option as a Tool for De-Escalation of Conflict – The Case of the Netherlands in Afghanistan's Uruzgan Province'. *Journal of Strategic Studies* 35 (5): 713–734.

Knopf, Jeffrey W. 2010. 'The Fourth Wave in Deterrence Research'. *Contemporary Security Policy* 31 (1): 1–33.

Kocher, Matthew Adam, Thomas B. Pepinsky, and Stathis N. Kalyvas. 2011. 'Aerial Bombing and Counterinsurgency in the Vietnam War'. *American Journal of Political Science* 55 (2): 201–218.

Koehler-Derrick, Gabriel and Daniel James Milton. 2017. 'Choose Your Weapon: The Impact of Strategic Considerations and Resource Constraints on Terrorist Group Weapon Selection'. *Terrorism and Political Violence* 31 (5): 909–928.

Krause, Peter. 2014. 'The Structure of Success: How the Internal Distribution of Power Drives Armed Group Behavior and National Movement Effectiveness'. *International Security* 38 (3): 72–116.

2013. 'The Political Effectiveness of Non-State Violence: A Two-Level Framework to Transform a Deceptive Debate'. *Security Studies* 22 (2): 259–294.

Kreutz, Joakim. 2010. 'How and When Armed Conflicts End: Introducing the UCDP Conflict Termination Dataset'. *Journal of Peace Research* 47 (2): 243–250.

Kriger, Norma J. 1992. *Zimbabwe's Guerrilla War: Peasant Voices*. Cambridge: Cambridge University Press.

Kruck, Andreas and Andrea Schneiker. 2017. *Researching Non-State Actors in International Security: Theory and Practice*. London: Routledge.

Krueger, Alan B. and Jitka Malečková. 2003. 'Education, Poverty and Terrorism: Is There a Causal Connection?'. *Journal of Economic Perspectives* 17 (4): 119–144.

Kruijt, Dirk. 2008. *Guerrillas: War and Peace in Central America*. London: Zed Books.

Kuperman, Alan J. and Timothy Crawford. 2014. *Gambling on Humanitarian Intervention*. London: Routledge.

Kuperman, Alan J. 2008. 'The Moral Hazard of Humanitarian Intervention: Lessons from the Balkans'. *International Studies Quarterly* 52 (1): 49–80.

Kydd, Andrew H. and Barbara F. Walter. 2006. 'The Strategies of Terrorism'. *International Security* 31 (1): 49–80.

Kydd, Andrew. 2003. 'Which Side Are You On? Bias, Credibility, and Mediation'. *American Journal of Political Science* 47 (4): 597–611.

Ladbury, Sarah. 2009. *Testing Hypotheses on Radicalisation in Afghanistan: Why Do Men Join the Taliban and Hizb-i Islami?: How Much Do Local Communities Support Them?*. London: Independent Report for the Department of International Development.

Lake, David. 2010. 'Building Legitimate States after Civil War'. In: Caroline Hartzell and Matthew Hoddie, eds., *Strengthening Peace in Post-Civil War States: Transforming Spoilers into Stakeholders*, Chicago: Chicago University Press, 29–51.

Laqueur, Walter. 2003. *No End to War: Terrorism in the Twenty-First Century*. New York: Continuum.

2001. *A History of Terrorism*. New Brunswick: Transaction.

1998. *Guerrilla Warfare: A Historical & Critical Study*. New Brunswick: Transaction.

Lasswell, Harold Dwight. 1950. *Politics: Who Gets What, When, How*. New York: P. Smith.

Latham, Michael E. 2010. 'The Cold War in the Third World 1963–1965'. In: Melvyn P. Leffler and Odd Arne Westad, eds., *The Cambridge History of the Cold War; Crisis and Detente*, Volume II. New York: Cambridge University Press, 258–280.

LeBlanc, Jörg. 2013. 'The Urban Environment and Its Influences on Insurgent Campaigns'. *Terrorism and Political Violence* 25 (5): 798–819.

2012. *Political Violence in Latin America: A Cross-Case Comparison of the Urban Insurgency Campaigns of Montoneros, M-19, and FSLN in a Historical Perspective*. Cambridge: Cambridge Scholars Publishing.

Leonhard, Robert R. 1994. *Fighting by Minutes: Time and the Art of War*. New York: Praeger.

Levitt, Matthew. 2014. 'Terrorist Financing and the Islamic State'. *The Washington Institute for Near East Policy, Washington.*

2013. *Hezbollah: The Global Footprint of Lebanon's Party of God.* Washington, DC: Georgetown University Press.

Levy, Jack S. 2012. 'Coercive Threats, Audience Costs, and Case Studies'. *Security Studies* 21 (3): 383–390.

Lewis, David. 2012. 'Counterinsurgency in Sri Lanka: A Successful Model?'. In: Paul B. Rich and Isabelle Duyvesteyn, eds., *The Routledge Handbook of Insurgency and Counterinsurgency*, London: Routledge, 312–323.

Li, Quan. 2005. 'Does Democracy Promote or Reduce Transnational Terrorist Incidents?'. *Journal of Conflict Resolution* 49 (2): 278–297.

Lichbach, Mark Irving. 1987. 'Deterrence or Escalation? The Puzzle of Aggregate Studies of Repression and Dissent'. *Journal of Conflict Resolution* 31 (2): 266–297.

Licklider, Roy. 1995. 'The Consequences of Negotiated Settlements in Civil Wars, 1945–1993'. *American Political Science Review* 89 (3): 681–690.

Liff, Adam P. 2012. 'Cyberwar: A New "Absolute Weapon"? The Proliferation of Cyberwarfare Capabilities and Interstate War'. *Journal of Strategic Studies* 35 (3): 401–428.

Lockyer, A. 2011. 'Foreign Intervention and Warfare in Civil Wars: The Effect of Exogenous Resources on the Course and Nature of the Angolan and Afghan Conflicts'. *Review of International Studies* 37 (5): 2337–2364.

Luft, Gal. 2003. 'The Logic of Israel's Targeted Killing'. *Middle East Quarterly* 10 (1): 3–13.

Lum, Cynthia, Leslie W. Kennedy, and Alison J. Sherley. 2006. 'Are Counter-Terrorism Strategies Effective? The Results of the Campbell Systematic Review on Counter-Terrorism Evaluation Research'. *Journal of Experimental Criminology* 2 (4): 489–516.

Luttwak, Edward N. 2007. 'Dead End: Counterinsurgency Warfare as Military Malpractice'. *Harper's Magazine* 1881 (2): 33–42.

2001. *Strategy: The Logic of War and Peace.* New York: Belknap Press.

Lutz, James M. and Brenda J. Lutz. 2004. *Global Terrorism.* London: Routledge.

Lyall, Jason. 2015. 'Process Tracing, Causal Inference and Civil War'. In: Andrew Bennett and Jeffrey T. Checkel, eds., *Process Tracing: From Metaphor to Analytic Tool*, Cambridge: Cambridge University Press, 186–208.

2010. 'Are Coethnics More Effective Counterinsurgents? Evidence from the Second Chechen War'. *American Political Science Review* 104 (1): 1–20.

2009. 'Does Indiscriminate Violence Incite Insurgent Attacks?: Evidence from Chechnya'. *Journal of Conflict Resolution* 53 (3): 331–362.

Lynd, Paul W. 1996. 'The Disappearance of FLQ Terrorism and the Cycle of Social Protest in Quebec 1963–1976'. Master of Sociology thesis, University of Windsor. Available at: https://scholar.uwindsor.ca/etd/3849/.

Mack, Andrew. 1975. 'Why Big Nations Lose Small Wars: The Politics of Asymmetric Conflict'. *World Politics* 27 (2): 175–200.

Mackinlay, John. 2009. *The Insurgent Archipelago.* London: Hurst.

Mahoney, Charles W. 2018. 'End of the Cycle: Assessing ETA's Strategies of Terrorism'. *Small Wars and Insurgencies* 29 (5–6): 916–940.

2017. 'Splinters and Schisms: Rebel Group Fragmentation and the Durability of Insurgencies'. *Terrorism and Political Violence* 32 (2): 345–364.

Mahood, Samantha and Halim Rane. 2017. 'Islamist Narratives in ISIS Recruitment Propaganda'. *Journal of International Communication* 23 (1): 15–35.

Maloney, Sean M. 2000. 'A "Mere Rustle of Leaves": Canadian Strategy and the 1970 FLQ Crisis'. *Canadian Military Journal* 1 (2): 71–84.

Malthaner, Stefan. 2015. 'Violence, Legitimacy, and Control: The Microdynamics of Support Relationships between Militant Groups and Their Social Environment'. *Civil Wars* 17 (4): 425–445.

Malvesti, Michele L. 2003. 'Explaining the United States' Decision to Strike Back at Terrorists'. In: Russell D. Howard and Reid L. Sawyer, eds., *Terrorism and Counterterrorism*, New York: MacGraw Hill, 404–425.

Mamdani, Mahmood. 2014. *When Victims Become Killers: Colonialism, Nativism, and the Genocide in Rwanda*. Princeton: Princeton University Press.

Mampilly, Zachariah Cherian. 2011. *Rebel Rulers: Insurgent Governance and Civilian Life during War*. New York: Cornell University Press.

Mandala, Marissa. 2017. 'Assassination as a Terrorist Tactic: A Global Analysis'. *Dynamics of Asymmetric Conflict* 10 (1): 14–39.

Mandel, Robert. 2015. *Coercing Compliance: State-Initiated Brute Force in Today's World*. Stanford: Stanford University Press.

Mansfield, Edward D. and Jack L. Snyder. 2005. *Electing to Fight: Why Emerging Democracies Go to War*. Cambridge: MIT Press.

1995. 'Democratization and the Danger of War'. *International Security* 20 (1): 5–38.

Manwaring, Max G. 2001. *Internal Wars: Rethinking Problem and Response*. Studies in Asymmetry. Carlisle Barracks, PA: U.S. Army War College Strategic Studies Institute.

Marighella, Carlos. 1974. 'Minimanual of the Urban Guerrilla'. In: James Kohl and John Litt, eds., *Urban Guerrilla Warfare in Latin America*, London: MIT Press, 81–135.

Marks, Thomas A. 2004. 'Ideology of Insurgency: New Ethnic Focus or Old Cold War Distortions?'. *Small Wars & Insurgencies* 15 (1): 107–128.

Marsden, Sarah V. 2016. 'A Social Movement Theory Typology of Militant Organisations: Contextualising Terrorism'. *Terrorism and Political Violence* 28 (4): 750–773.

Marten, Kimberly Zisk. 2004. *Enforcing the Peace: Learning from the Imperial Past*. New York: Columbia University Press.

Matesan, Ioana Emy and Ronit Berger. 2017. 'Blunders and Blame: How Armed Non-State Actors React to Their Mistakes'. *Studies in Conflict & Terrorism* 40 (5): 376–398.

Matesan, Ioana Emy. 2018. 'Organizational Dynamics, Public Condemnation and the Impetus to Disengage from Violence'. *Terrorism and Political Violence* 32 (5): 949–969.

McAdam, Douglas, Sidney Tarrow, and Charles Tilly. 2001. *Dynamics of Contention*. New York: Cambridge University Press.

McCauley, Clark, Mary Segal, and Clyde Hendrick. 1987. 'Social Psychology of Terrorist Groups'. *Review of Personality and Social Psychology* 9: 231–256.

McCormick, Gordon H. 2003. 'Terrorist Decision Making'. *Annual Review of Political Science* 6 (1): 473–507.

McCuen, John J. 1966. *The Art of Counter-Revolutionary War: The Strategy of Counter-Insurgency*. Harrisburg: Stackpole Books.

McKenna, Thomas M. 1998. *Muslim Rulers and Rebels: Everyday Politics and Armed Separatism in the Southern Philippines*. Berkeley: University of California Press.

McLauchlin, Theodore and Wendy Pearlman. 2012. 'Out-Group Conflict, In-Group Unity? Exploring the Effect of Repression on Intramovement Cooperation'. *Journal of Conflict Resolution* 56 (1): 41–66.

McLauchlin, Theodore. 2014. 'Desertion, Terrain, and Control of the Home Front in Civil Wars'. *Journal of Conflict Resolution* 58 (8): 1419–1444.

Mearsheimer, John J. and Stephen M. Walt. 2013. 'Leaving Theory Behind: Why Simplistic Hypothesis Testing Is Bad for International Relations'. *European Journal of International Relations* 19 (3): 427–457.

Merkl, Peter. 1995. 'West German Left – Wing Terrorism'. In: Martha Crenshaw, ed., *Terrorism in Context*, University Park: Pennsylvania State University Press, 160–210.

Merlo, Germana Tappero and Sergio Marchisio. 2006. 'Italy'. In: Yonah Alexander, ed., *Counterterrorism Strategies: Successes and Failures of Six Nations*, Washington, DC: Potomac, 99–126.

Merom, Gil. 2003. *How Democracies Lose Small Wars: State, Society, and the Failures of France in Algeria, Israel in Lebanon, and the United States in Vietnam*. Cambridge: Cambridge University Press.

Metelits, Claire. 2009. *Inside Insurgency: Violence, Civilians, and Revolutionary Group Behavior*. New York: New York University Press.

Miakinkov, Eugene. 2011. 'The Agency of Force in Asymmetrical Warfare and Counterinsurgency: The Case of Chechnya'. *Journal of Strategic Studies* 34 (5): 647–680.

Michael, George. 2012. *Lone Wolf Terror and the Rise of Leaderless Resistance*. Nashville: Vanderbilt University Press.

Midlarsky, Manus I., Martha Crenshaw, and Fumihiko Yoshida. 1980. 'Why Violence Spreads: The Contagion of International Terrorism'. *International Studies Quarterly* 24 (2): 262–298.

Miller, Gregory D. 2013. 'Terrorist Decision Making and the Deterrence Problem'. *Studies in Conflict & Terrorism* 36 (2): 132–151.

Miller, Martin A. 1995. 'The Intellectual Origins of Modern Terrorism in Europe'. In: Martha Crenshaw, ed., *Terrorism in Context*, University Park: Pennsylvania State University Press, 27–62.

Millett, Richard L. 2002. *Colombia's Conflicts: The Spillover Effects of a Wider War*. Carlisle Barracks, PA: U.S. Army War College Strategic Studies Institute.

Mitton, Kieran. 2015. *Rebels in a Rotten State: Understanding Atrocity in the Sierra Leone Civil War*. London: Hurst.

    2012. 'Irrational Actors and the Process of Brutalisation: Understanding Atrocity in the Sierra Leonean Conflict (1991–2002)'. *Civil Wars* 14 (1): 104–122.

Moghadam, Assaf and Michel Wyss. 2020. 'The Political Power of Proxies: Why Non-State Actors Use Local Surrogates'. *International Security* 44 (4): 119–157.

Moghadam, Assaf. 2008. *The Globalization of Martyrdom: Al Qaeda, Salafi Jihad and the Diffusion of Suicide Attacks*. Baltimore: John Hopkins University Press.

Moloney, Ed. 2007. *A Secret History of the IRA*. London: Penguin.

Morgan, Forrest E., Karl P. Mueller, Evan S. Medeiros, Kevin L. Pollpeter, and Roger Cliff. 2008. *Dangerous Thresholds: Managing Escalation in the 21st Century*. Santa Monica: Rand Corporation.

Morral, Andrew R. and Brian A. Jackson. 2014. *Understanding the Role of Deterrence in Counterterrorism Security*. Santa Monica: Rand Corporation.

Mueller, John E. 2005. 'Six Rather Unusual Propositions about Terrorism'. *Terrorism and Political Violence* 17 (4): 487–505.

    2004. *The Remnants of War*. New York: Cornell University Press.

Murphy, William P. 2003. 'Military Patrimonialism and Child Soldier Clientalism in the Liberian and Sierra Leonean Civil Wars'. *African Studies Review* 46 (2): 61–87.

Neumann, Peter R. and M. L. R. Smith. 2007. *The Strategy of Terrorism: How it Works, and Why it Fails*. New York: Routledge.

    2005. 'Strategic Terrorism: The Framework and Its Fallacies'. *Journal of Strategic Studies* 28 (4): 571–595.

Neumann, Peter R. 2003. *Britain's Long War: British Strategy in the Northern Ireland Conflict, 1969–98*. London: Palgrave Macmillan.

Nevin, John A. 2003. 'Retaliating against Terrorists'. *Behavior and Social Issues* 12 (2): 109–128.

Newman, Edward and Karl DeRouen Jr. 2014. *The Routledge Handbook of Civil Wars*. London: Routledge.

Nilsson, Marco. 2018. 'The Logic of Suicide Terrorism: Does Regime Type Affect the Choice of Targets?'. *Behavioral Sciences of Terrorism and Political Aggression* 10 (2): 176–185.

Norris, Pippa, Montague Kern, and Marion Just. 2003. *Framing Terrorism: The News Media, the Government and the Public*. New York: Routledge.

Nye, Joseph S. Jr. 2010. 'Cyber Power'. *On-Line Paper, Harvard Kennedy School, Belfer Center* May: 1–23. Available at: https://apps.dtic.mil/dtic/tr/fulltext/u2/a522626.pdf.

    1990. 'Soft Power'. *Foreign Policy* 80: 153–171.

Obayashi, Kazuhiro. 2014. 'Information, Rebel Organization and Civil War Escalation: The Case of the Liberation Tigers of Tamil Eelam'. *International Area Studies Review* 17 (1): 21–40.

Oberschall, Anthony. 1993. *Social Movements, Ideologies, Interests and Identities*. New Brunswick: Transaction.

O'Kane, Eamonn. 2006. 'When Can Conflicts Be Resolved? A Critique of Ripeness'. *Civil Wars* 8 (3–4): 268–284.

Olson Lounsbery, Marie. 2016. 'Foreign Military Intervention, Power Dynamics, and Rebel Group Cohesion'. *Journal of Global Security Studies* 1 (2): 127–141.

Olson, Mancur. 1994. *The Logic of Collective Action: Public Goods and the Theory of Groups*. Cambridge: Harvard University Press.

Oppenheim, Ben, Abbey Steele, Juan F. Vargas, and Michael Weintraub. 2015. 'True Believers, Deserters, and Traitors: Who Leaves Insurgent Groups and Why'. *Journal of Conflict Resolution* 59 (5): 794–823.

Palfy, Arpad. 2003. 'Weapon System Selection and Mass-Casualty Outcomes*'. *Terrorism and Political Violence* 15 (2): 81–95.

Pampinella, Stephen. 2015. 'The Effectiveness of Coercive and Persuasive Counterinsurgency Practices since 1945'. *Civil Wars* 17 (4): 503–526.

Pape, Robert A. 2005. *Dying to Win: The Strategic Logic of Suicide Terrorism*. New York: Random House.

Paquette, Laure. 1991. 'Strategy and Time in Clausewitz's *On War* and Sun Tzu's *The Art of War*'. *Comparative Strategy* 10 (1): 37–51.

Parker, Tom and Nick Sitter. 2015. 'The Four Horsemen of Terrorism: It's Not Waves, it's Strains'. *Terrorism and Political Violence* 28 (2): 1–20.

Parker, Tom. 2007. 'Fighting an Antaean Enemy: How Democratic States Unintentionally Sustain the Terrorist Movements They Oppose'. *Terrorism and Political Violence* 19 (2): 155–179.

Parkinson, Sarah Elizabeth. 2013. 'Organizing Rebellion: Rethinking High-Risk Mobilization and Social Networks in War'. *American Political Science Review* 107 (3): 418–432.

Pasco, Christophe and French Navy. 2008. 'The Influence of "Time" on Counter-Insurgency'. *Defence Studies* 8 (1): 49–77.

Paul, Christopher. 2010. 'As a Fish Swims in the Sea: Relationships between Factors Contributing to Support for Terrorist or Insurgent Groups'. *Studies in Conflict & Terrorism* 33 (6): 488–510.

Payne, Kenneth. 2011. "Building the Base: Al Qaeda's Focoist Strategy." *Studies in Conflict & Terrorism* 34 (2): 124–143.

Pearlman, Wendy and Kathleen Gallagher Cunningham. 2012. 'Nonstate Actors, Fragmentation, and Conflict Processes'. *Journal of Conflict Resolution* 56 (1): 3–15.

Pearlman, Wendy. 2013. 'Emotions and the Microfoundations of the Arab Uprisings'. *Perspectives on Politics* 11 (2): 387–409.

2012. 'Precluding Nonviolence, Propelling Violence: The Effect of Internal Fragmentation on Movement Protest'. *Studies in Comparative International Development* 47 (1): 23–46.

Pechenkina, Anna O. and Jakana L. Thomas. 2020. 'Battle Stalemates and Rebel Negotiation Attempts in Civil Wars'. *Security Studies* 29 (1): 64–91.

Pedahzur, Amy. 2009. *The Israeli Secret Services and the Struggle against Terrorism*. New York: Columbia University Press.

Peters, Krijn and Paul Richards. 1998. '"Why We Fight": Voices of Youth Combatants in Sierra Leone'. *Africa* 68 (2): 183–210.

Peters, Ralph. 2004. 'In Praise of Attrition'. *Parameters* 34 (2): 24–32.

Petersen, Roger D. 2011. *Western Intervention in the Balkans: The Strategic Use of Emotion in Conflict*. Cambridge: Cambridge University Press.

Petraeus, David H. and James F. Amos. 2006. *FM 3–24: Counterinsurgency*. Washington: U.S. Army.

Pettigrew, Joyce. 1995. *The Sikhs of the Punjab: Unheard Voices of State and Guerilla Violence*. London: Zed Books.

Phillips, Vaughan. 2017. 'The Islamic State's Strategy: Bureaucratizing the Apocalypse through Strategic Communications'. *Studies in Conflict and Terrorism* 40 (9): 731–757.

Piazza, James A. and Scott Piazza. 2020. 'Crime Pays: Terrorist Group Engagement in Crime and Survival'. *Terrorism and Political Violence* 32 (4): 701–723.

Piazza, James. 2017. 'Repression and Terrorism: A Cross-National Empirical Analysis of Types of Repression and Domestic Terrorism'. *Terrorism and Political Violence* 29 (1): 102–118.

Pierskalla, Jan H. 2010. 'Protest, Deterrence, and Escalation: The Strategic Calculus of Government Repression'. *Journal of Conflict Resolution* 54 (1): 1–29.

Pion-Berlin, David. 1989. *The Ideology of State Terror: Economic Doctrine and Political Repression in Argentina and Peru*. Boulder: Lynne Rienner.

Pisano, Vittorfranco S. 1980. *The Red Brigades: A Challenge to Italian Democracy*. London: The Institute for the Study of Conflict.

Pitcher, Anne, Mary H. Moran, and Michael Johnston. 2009. 'Rethinking Patrimonialism and Neopatrimonialism in Africa'. *African Studies Review* 52 (1): 125–156.

Posen, Barry S. 1993. 'The Security Dilemma and Ethnic Conflict'. *Survival* 35 (1): 27–47.

Post, Jerrold M. 1990. 'Terrorist Psycho-Logic: Terrorist Behaviour as a Product of Psychological Forces'. In: Walter Reich, ed., *Origins of Terrorism: Psychologies, Ideologies, Theologies, States of Mind*, Cambridge: Cambridge University Press, 25–40.

Powell, Robert. 2002. 'Bargaining Theory and International Conflict'. *Annual Review of Political Science* 5 (1): 1–30.

Price, Brian C. 2019. *Targeting Top Terrorists: Understanding Leadership Removal in Counterterrorism Strategy*. New York: Colombia University Press.

  2012. 'Targeting Top Terrorists: How Leadership Decapitation Contributes to Counterterrorism'. *International Security* 36 (4): 9–46.

Pruitt, Dean G., Jeffrey Rubin, and Sung Hee Kim. 2004. *Social Conflict: Escalation, Stalemate, and Settlement*. New York: McGraw-Hill.

Pruitt, Dean G. and Jeffrey Z. Rubin. 1986. *Social Conflict: Escalation, Stalemate, and Settlement*. New York: Random House.

Pruitt, Dean G. 2006. 'Negotiation with Terrorists'. *International Negotiation* 11 (2): 371–394.

Prunckun, Henry W. Jr. and Philip B. Mohr. 1997. 'Military Deterrence of International Terrorism: An Evaluation of Operation El Dorado Canyon'. *Studies in Conflict & Terrorism* 20 (3): 267–280.

Prunier, Gerard. 2009. *From Genocide to Continental War: The 'Congolese' Conflict and the Crisis of Contemporary Africa*. London: Hurst.

Rapoport, David C. 2001b. 'The Fourth Wave: September 11 in the History of Terrorism'. *Current History* 100 (650): 419–424.

2001a. 'The Four Waves of Modern Terrorism'. *Current History* 100: 419–24.

1984. 'Fear and Trembling: Terrorism in Three Religious Traditions'. *American Political Science Review* 78 (3): 658–677.

Rattray, Gregory J. 2001. *Strategic Warfare in Cyberspace*. Cambridge: MIT Press.

Re, Matteo. 2017. '"The Red Brigades" Communiqués: An Analysis of the Terrorist Group's Propaganda'. *Terrorism and Political Violence* 32 (2): 275–292.

Record, Jeffrey. 2007. *Beating Goliath: Why Insurgencies Win*. Washington, DC: Potomac Books.

Reed, Alastair. 2013. 'Understanding Conflict Dynamics: A Comparative Analysis of Ethno-Separatist Conflicts in India and the Philippines'. PhD manuscript, Utrecht University, the Netherlands.

Regan, Patrick M. and Aysegul Aydin. 2006. 'Diplomacy and Other Forms of Intervention in Civil Wars'. *Journal of Conflict Resolution* 50 (5): 736–756.

Reiter, D. 2003. 'Exploring the Bargaining Model of War'. *Perspectives on Politics* 1 (1): 27–43.

Reno, William. 2000. 'Shadow States and the Political Economy of Civil Wars'. In: M. Berdal and D. Malone, eds., *Greed and Grievance in Civil Wars*, Boulder: Lynne Rienner, 43–68.

1998. *Warlord Politics and African States*. Boulder: Lynne Rienner.

Rich, Paul B. and Isabelle Duyvesteyn. eds. 2012. *The Routledge Handbook of Insurgency and Counterinsurgency*. London: Routledge.

Rich, Paul B. 2018. 'Are Mao Zedong and Maoist Thought Irrelevant in the Understanding of Insurgencies?'. *Small Wars & Insurgencies* 29 (5–6): 1065–78.

2016. 'How Revolutionary Are Jihadist Insurgencies? The Case of ISIL'. *Small Wars & Insurgencies* 27 (5): 777–99.

Richards, Joanne. 2018. 'Troop Retention in Civil Wars: Desertion, Denunciation, and Military Organization in the Democratic Republic of Congo'. *Journal of Global Security Studies* 3 (1): 38–55.

Richards, Paul. 1996. *Fighting for the Rain Forest: War, Youth and Resources in Sierra Leone*. Oxford: James Currey.

Richardson, Louise. ed. 2006. *The Roots of Terrorism*. New York: Routledge.

Roberts, Adam. 2005. 'The "War on Terror" in Historical Perspective'. *Survival* 47 (2): 101–130.

Rosendorff, B. Peter and Todd Sandler. 2005. 'The Political Economy of Transnational Terrorism'. *Journal of Conflict Resolution* 49 (2): 171–182.

2004. 'Too Much of a Good Thing?: The Proactive Response Dilemma'. *Journal of Conflict Resolution* 48 (5): 657–671.

Ross, Jeffrey Ian and Ted Robert Gurr. 1989. 'Why Terrorism Subsides: A Comparative Study of Canada and the United States'. *Comparative Politics* 21 (4): 405–426.

Ross, Jeffrey Ian. 1995. 'The Rise and Fall of Québecois Separatist Terrorism: A Qualitative Application of Factors from Two Models'. *Studies in Conflict & Terrorism* 18 (4): 285–298.

Rothstein, Bo. 2009. 'Creating Political Legitimacy Electoral Democracy versus Quality of Government'. *American Behavioral Scientist* 53 (3): 311–330.

Ruhe, Constantin. 2015. 'Anticipating Mediated Talks: Predicting the Timing of Mediation with Disaggregated Conflict Dynamics'. *Journal of Peace Research* 52 (2): 243–257.

Sageman, Marc. 2011. *Leaderless Jihad: Terror Networks in the Twenty-First Century*. Philadelphia: University of Pennsylvania Press.

   2004. *Understanding Terror Networks*. Philadelphia: University of Pennsylvania Press.

Salehyan, Idean, David Siroky, and Reed M. Wood. 2014. 'External Rebel Sponsorship and Civilian Abuse: A Principal-Agent Analysis of Wartime Atrocities'. *International Organization* 68 (3): 633–661.

Salehyan, Idean. 2007. 'Transnational Rebels: Neighboring States as Sanctuary for Rebel Groups'. *World Politics* 59 (2): 217–242.

Sambanis, Nicholas. 2001. 'Do Ethnic and Nonethnic Civil Wars Have the Same Causes?: A Theoretical and Empirical Inquiry (Part 1)'. *Journal of Conflict Resolution* 45 (3): 259–282.

San Akca, Belgin. 2009. 'Supporting Non-State Armed Groups: A Resort to Illegality?'. *Journal of Strategic Studies* 32 (4): 589–613.

Sandler, Todd, John T. Tschirhart and Jon Cauley. 1983. 'A Theoretical Analysis of Transnational Terrorism'. *American Political Science Review* 77 (1): 36–53.

Sanín, Francisco Gutiérrez and Antonio Giustozzi. 2010. 'Networks and Armies: Structuring Rebellion in Colombia and Afghanistan'. *Studies in Conflict & Terrorism* 33 (9): 836–853.

Sanín, Francisco Gutiérrez and Elisabeth Jean Wood. 2014. 'Ideology in Civil War Instrumental Adoption and Beyond'. *Journal of Peace Research* 51 (2): 213–226.

Sawyer, Katherine, Kathleen Gallagher Cunningham, and William Reed. 2017. 'The Role of External Support in Civil War Termination'. *Journal of Conflict Resolution* 61 (6): 1174–1202.

Schelling, Thomas C. 2008. *Arms and Influence*. New Haven: Yale University Press.

   1980. *The Strategy of Conflict*. Cambridge: Harvard University Press.

Schlichte, Klaus and Ulrich Schneckener. 2015. 'Armed Groups and the Politics of Legitimacy'. *Civil Wars* 17 (4): 409–424.

Schlichte, Klaus. 2009. *In the Shadow of Violence: The Politics of Armed Groups*. Frankfurt: Campus Verlag.

Schmitt, Olivier. 2020. 'Wartime Paradigms and the Future of Western Military Power'. *International Affairs* 96 (2): 401–418.

Schneckener, Ulrich. 2017. 'Militias and the Politics of Legitimacy'. *Small Wars & Insurgencies* 28 (4–5): 799–816.

Schneider, Mark and Paul Teske. 1992. 'Toward a Theory of the Political Entrepreneur: Evidence from Local Government'. *American Political Science Review* 86 (3): 737–747.

Schultz, Kenneth A. 2012. 'Why We Needed Audience Costs and What We Need Now'. *Security Studies* 21 (3): 369–375.

Schuurman, Bart. 2013. 'Defeated by Popular Demand: Public Support and Counterterrorism in Three Western Democracies, 1963–1998'. *Studies in Conflict & Terrorism* 36 (2): 152–175.

  2010. 'Clausewitz and the "New Wars" Scholars'. *Parameters* 40 (1): 89–100.

Sederberg, Peter C. 1990. 'Responses to Dissident Terrorism: From Myth to Maturity'. In: Charles W. Kegley Jr., ed., *International Terrorism: Characteristics, Causes, Controls*, New York: St. Martin's, 262–280.

Seifert, Katherine R. and Clark McCauley. 2014. 'Suicide Bombers in Iraq, 2003–2010: Disaggregating Targets Can Reveal Insurgent Motives and Priorities'. *Terrorism and Political Violence* 26 (5): 803–820.

Seymour, Lee JM. 2014. 'Why Factions Switch Sides in Civil Wars: Rivalry, Patronage, and Realignment in Sudan'. *International Security* 39 (2): 92–131.

Silke, Andrew. 2008. 'Holy Warriors: Exploring the Psychological Processes of Jihadi Radicalization'. *European Journal of Criminology* 5 (1): 99–123.

  2005. 'Fire of Iolaus: The Role of State Countermeasures in Causing Terrorism and What Needs to Be Done'. In: Tore Bjørgo, ed., *Root Causes of Terrorism: Myths, Reality and Ways Forward*, London: Routledge, 241–255.

Silwal, Shikha. 2017. 'Myopic Government and Strategic Rebels: Exchange and Escalation of Violence'. *Civil Wars* 19 (2): 146–175.

Simpson, Emile. 2012. *War from the Ground Up: Twenty-First-Century Combat as Politics*. London: Hurst.

Siqueira, Kevin and Todd Sandler. 2006. 'Terrorists versus the Government: Strategic Interaction, Support, and Sponsorship'. *Journal of Conflict Resolution* 50 (6): 878–898.

Smith, M. L. R. and David Martin Jones. 2015. *The Political Impossibility of Modern Counterinsurgency: Strategic Problems, Puzzles and Paradoxes*. New York: Columbia University Press.

Smith, M. L. R. 2012. 'Escalation in Irregular War: Using Strategic Theory to Examine from First Principles'. *Journal of Strategic Studies* 35 (5): 613–637.

Smith, Rupert. 2006. *The Utility of Force: The Art of War in the Modern World*. London: Penguin.

Smoke, Richard. 1977. *War: Controlling Escalation*. Cambridge: Harvard University Press.

Snyder, David. 1976. 'Theoretical and Methodological Problems in the Analysis of Governmental Coercion and Collective Violence'. *Journal of Political and Military Sociology* 4 (2): 277–293.

Snyder, Glenn. 1961. *Deterrence and Defense: Toward a Theory of National Security*. Princeton: Princeton University Press.

Sohata, Dharam Singh and Sohan Singh Sohota. 1993. *The Struggle for Sikh Autonomy 1940–1992*. Punjab: Guru Nanak Study Centre.

Souleimanov, Emil. 2007. *An Endless War: The Russian-Chechen Conflict in Perspective*. Frankfurt am Main: Peter Lang.

Southern Poverty Law Center. 'Hate Groups in the United States'. Southern Poverty Law Center. Available at: www.splcenter.org/hate-map. Last accessed 20 August 2020.

Staniland, Paul. 2017. 'Whither ISIS? Insights from Insurgent Responses to Decline'. *Washington Quarterly* 40 (3): 29–43.

2014. *Networks of Rebellion: Explaining Insurgent Cohesion and Collapse.* New York: Cornell University Press.

2012c. 'States, Insurgents and Wartime Political Orders'. *Perspectives on Politics* 10 (2): 243–264.

2012b. 'Organizing Insurgency: Networks, Resources, and Rebellion in South Asia'. *International Security* 37 (1): 142–177.

2012a. 'Between a Rock and a Hard Place: Insurgent Fratricide, Ethnic Defection, and the Rise of Pro-State Paramilitaries'. *Journal of Conflict Resolution* 56 (1): 16–40.

2010. 'Cities on Fire: Social Mobilization, State Policy and Urban Insurgency'. *Comparative Political Studies* 43 (12): 1623–1649.

2006. 'Defeating Transnational Insurgencies: The Best Offense Is a Good Fence'. *Washington Quarterly* 29 (1): 21–40.

Stedman, Stephen John. 1997. 'Spoiler Problems in Peace Processes'. *International Security* 22 (2): 5–53.

Stephan, Maria J. and Erica Chenoweth. 2008. 'Why Civil Resistance Works: The Strategic Logic of Nonviolent Conflict'. *International Security* 33 (1): 7–44.

Stone, John. 2012. 'Escalation and the War on Terror'. *Journal of Strategic Studies* 35 (5): 639–661.

Strachan, Hew and Andreas Herberg-Rothe. 2007. 'Introduction'. In: Hew Strachan and Andreas Herberg-Rothe, eds., *Clausewitz in the Twenty-First Century*, Oxford: Oxford University Press, 1–13.

Sullivan, Patricia L. and Michael T. Koch. 2009. 'Military Intervention by Powerful States, 1945—2003'. *Journal of Peace Research* 46 (5): 707–718.

Sullivan, Patricia L. 2007. 'War Aim and War Outcomes: Why Powerful States Lose Limited Wars'. *Journal of Conflict Resolution* 51 (3): 496–524.

Swamy, MR Narayan. 2010. *The Tiger Vanquished: LTTE's Story.* New Delhi: Sage.

1994. *Tigers of Lanka, from Boys to Guerrillas.* Delhi: Konark.

Tamm, Henning. 2016. 'Rebel Leaders, Internal Rivals, and External Resources: How State Sponsors Affect Insurgent Cohesion'. *International Studies Quarterly* 60 (4): 599–610.

Tarrow, Sidney. 2007. 'Inside Insurgencies: Politics and Violence in an Age of Civil War'. *Perspectives on Politics* 5 (3): 587–600.

1994. *Power in Movement: Social Movements, Collective Action and Politics.* Cambridge: Cambridge University Press.

Taylor, Brian D. and Roxana Botea. 2008. '"Tilly Tally": War-Making and State-Making in the Contemporary Third World'. *International Studies Review* 10: 27–56.

Thompson, Peter G. 2014. *Armed Groups: The 21st Century Threat.* London: Rowman & Littlefield.

Thompson, Robert. 1966. *Defeating Communist Insurgency: The Lessons of Malaya and Vietnam.* New York: Praeger.

Thornhill, Chris. 2008. 'Towards a Historical Sociology of Constitutional Legitimacy'. *Theory and Society* 37 (2): 161–197.

Thornton, Rod. 2007. 'Getting It Wrong: The Crucial Mistakes Made in the Early Stages of the British Army's Deployment to Northern Ireland (August 1969 to March 1972)'. *Journal of Strategic Studies* 30 (1): 73–107.

Thruelsen, P. D. 2010. 'The Taliban in Southern Afghanistan: A Localised Insurgency with a Local Objective'. *Small Wars & Insurgencies* 21 (2): 259–276.

Tiernay, M. 2015. 'Killing Kony: Leadership Change and Civil War Termination'. *Journal of Conflict Resolution* 59 (2): 175–206.

Tilly, Charles and Sidney Tarrow. 2007. *Contentious Politics*. Boulder, CO: Paradigm Publishers.

Tilly, Charles. 2004. 'Social Boundary Mechanisms'. *Philosophy of Social Sciences* 34 (2): 211–236.

   2003. *The Politics of Collective Violence*. Cambridge: Cambridge University Press.

   1990. *Coercion, Capital and European States, 900–1900*. Cambridge: Blackwell.

   1985. 'War-Making and State-Making as Organized Crime'. In: Peter B. Evans, Dietrich Rueschemeyer, and Theda Skocpol, eds., *Bringing the State Back In*, Cambridge: Cambridge University Press, 169–191.

   1978. *From Mobilization to Revolution*. Reading: Addison-Wesley.

   1977. *Repertoires of Contention in America and Britain, 1750–1830*. Ann Arbor: University of Michigan Press.

Tishkov, Valery. 2004. *Chechnya: Life in a War-Torn Society*. Berkeley: University of California Press.

Tishler, Nicole A. 2018. 'Trends in Terrorist Weapon Adoption and the Study Thereof'. *International Studies Review* 20: 368–394.

Toft, Monica Duffy and Yuri M. Zhukov. 2015. 'Islamists and Nationalists: Rebel Motivation and Counterinsurgency in Russia's North Caucasus'. *American Political Science Review* 109 (2): 222–238.

   2012. 'Denial and Punishment in the North Caucasus Evaluating the Effectiveness of Coercive Counter-Insurgency'. *Journal of Peace Research* 49 (6): 785–800.

Toft, Monica Duffy. 2014. 'Territory and War'. *Journal of Peace Research* 51 (2): 185–198.

   2010. 'Ending Civil Wars: A Case for Rebel Victory?'. *International Security* 34 (4): 7–36.

   2006. *Peace Through Security: Making Negotiated Settlements Stick*. Cambridge: Harvard University Press.

Tonge, Jonathan, Peter Shirlow, and James McAuley. 2011. 'So Why Did the Guns Fall Silent? How Interplay, Not Stalemate, Explains the Northern Ireland Peace Process'. *Irish Political Studies* 26 (1): 1–18.

Tonge, Jonathan. 2000. 'From Sunningdale to the Good Friday Agreement: Creating Devolved Government in Northern Ireland'. *Contemporary British History* 14 (3): 39–60.

Tse-Tung, Mao and Che Guevara. 1961. *Guerrilla Warfare*. London: Cassell.

Tsintsadze-Maass, Eteri and Richard W. Maass. 2014. 'Groupthink and Terrorist Radicalization'. *Terrorism and Political Violence* 26 (5): 735–758.

Ucko, David. 2015. '"The People are Revolting": An Anatomy of Authoritarian Counterinsurgency'. *Journal of Strategic Studies* 39 (1): 29–61.

    2012. 'Whither Counter-Insurgency: The Rise and Fall of a Divisive Concept'. In: Paul B. Rich and Isabelle Duyvesteyn, eds., *The Routledge Handbook of Insurgency and Counterinsurgency*, London: Routledge, 67–79.

Uppsala Conflict Data Program. 2020. 'Uppsala University Conflict Data Program'. Uppsala Conflict Data Program. Available at: https://ucdp.uu.se/ Last accessed: 20 August 2020.

Van Creveld, Martin. 2006. *The Changing Face of War: Lessons of Combat, from the Marne to Iraq*. New York: Random House.

    1991. *The Transformation of War*. New York: Free Press.

Van Evera, Stephen. 1994. 'Hypotheses on Nationalism and War'. *International Security* 18 (4): 5–39.

Varon, Jeremy Peter. 2004. *Bringing the War Home: The Weather Underground, the Red Army Faction, and Revolutionary Violence in the Sixties and Seventies*. Oakland: University of California Press.

Veilleux-Lepage, Yannick. 2020. *How Terror Evolves: The Emergence and Spread of Terrorist Techniques*. London: Rowman and Littlefield.

Vinci, Anthony. 2008. 'Becoming the Enemy: Convergence in the American and Al Qaeda Ways of Warfare'. *Journal of Strategic Studies* 31 (1): 69–88.

Walter, Barbara F. 2015. 'Why Bad Governance Leads to Repeat Civil War'. *Journal of Conflict Resolution* 59 (7): 1242–1272.

    2002. *Committing to Peace: The Successful Settlement of Civil Wars*. Princeton: Princeton University Press.

    1997. 'The Critical Barrier to Civil War Settlement'. *International Organization* 51 (3): 335–364.

Walther, Olivier J. and Patrick Steen Pedersen. 2020. 'Rebel Fragmentation in Syria's Civil War'. *Small Wars and Insurgencies* 31 (3): 445–475.

Waltz, Kenneth N. 1979. *Theory of International Politics*. New York: Addison Wesley.

Warren, T. Camber and Kevin K. Troy. 2015. 'Explaining Violent Intra-Ethnic Conflict Group Fragmentation in the Shadow of State Power'. *Journal of Conflict Resolution* 59 (3): 484–509.

Webel, Charles and Charles Fischer. 2013. 'The Group Psychology of War and Peace'. *Peace Review* 25 (2): 177–186.

Weber, Max, Guenther Roth, and Claus Wittich. 1978. *Economy and Society: An Outline of Interpretive Sociology*. Translated by Ephraim Fischoff. Berkeley: University of California Press.

Weinberg, Leonard and William L. Eubank. 1994. 'Cultural Differences in the Behavior of Terrorists'. *Terrorism and Political Violence* 6 (1): 1–28.

    1992. 'Terrorism and Changes in Political Party Systems'. *Terrorism and Political Violence* 4 (2): 125–139.

    1990. 'Political Parties and the Formation of Terrorist Groups'. *Terrorism and Political Violence* 2 (2): 125–144.

Weinberg, Leonard B. ed. 2008. *Democratic Responses to Terrorism*. New York: Routledge.

2007. 'The Red Brigades'. In: Robert J. Art and Louise Richardson, eds., *Democracy and Counterterrorism: Lessons from the Past*, Washington, DC: United States Institute of Peace, 25–62.

1998. 'An Overview of Right-Wing Extremism in the Western World: A Study of Convergence, Linkage, and Identity'. In: J. Kaplan and T. Bjorgo, eds., *Nation and Race: The Developing Euro-American Racist Subculture*, Boston: Northeastern University Press, 3–33.

Weinstein, Jeremy M. 2007. *Inside Rebellion: The Politics of Insurgent Violence.* Cambridge: Cambridge University Press.

White, Robert W. 1989. 'From Peaceful Protest to Guerrilla War: Micromobilization of the Provisional Irish Republican Army'. *American Journal of Sociology* 94 (6): 1277–1302.

Whiteside, Craig. 2016. 'The Islamic State and the Return of Revolutionary Warfare'. *Small Wars & Insurgencies* 27 (5): 743–776.

Wickham-Crowley, Timothy P. 1991. *Exploring Revolution: Essays on Latin American Insurgency and Revolutionary Theory.* Armonk: M. E. Sharp.

Wilkinson, Paul. 2000. 'Politics, Diplomacy and Peace Processes: Pathways Out of Terrorism'. In: Max Taylor and John Horgan, eds., *The Future of Terrorism*, London: Frank Cass, 66–82.

1987. 'Pathways Out of Terrorism for Democratic Societies'. In: Paul Wilkinson and Alasdair M. Stewart, eds., *Contemporary Research on Terrorism*, Aberdeen: Aberdeen University Press, 453–465.

1986. *Terrorism and the Liberal State.* New York: New York University Press.

Wilner, Alex S. 2010. 'Targeted Killings in Afghanistan: Measuring Coercion and Deterrence in Counterterrorism and Counterinsurgency'. *Studies in Conflict & Terrorism* 33 (4): 307–329.

Wohlstetter, Albert and Roberta Wohlstetter. 1965. *Controlling the Risks in Cuba, Adelphi Paper no. 17.* London: International Institute for Strategic Studies.

Woldemariam, Michael. 2016. 'Battlefield Outcomes and Rebel Cohesion: Lessons from the Eritrean Independence War'. *Terrorism and Political Violence* 28 (1): 135–156.

Wood, Reed M. and Emily Molfino. 2016. 'Aiding Victims, Abetting Violence: The Influence of Humanitarian Aid on Violence Patterns During Civil Conflict'. *Journal of Global Security Studies* 1 (3): 186–203.

Wood, Reed M. and Jacob D. Kathman. 2015. 'Competing for the Crown: Inter-Rebel Competition and Civilian Targeting in Civil War'. *Political Research Quarterly* 68 (1): 167–179.

2014. 'Too Much of a Bad Thing? Civilian Victimization and Bargaining in Civil War'. *British Journal of Political Science* 44 (3): 685–706.

Wood, Reed M., Jacob D. Kathman, and Stephen E. Gent. 2012. 'Armed Intervention and Civilian Victimization in Intrastate Conflicts'. *Journal of Peace Research* 49 (5): 647–660.

Wood, Reed. M. 2010. 'Rebel Capability and Strategic Violence against Civilians'. *Journal of Peace Research* 47 (5): 601–614.

Wood, Elisabeth J. 2003. *Insurgent Collective Action and Civil War in El Salvador.* Cambridge: Cambridge University Press.

Wrong, Dennis. 1979. *Power: Its Forms, Bases and Uses*. New York: Transaction.

Wylie, Joseph Caldwell. 2014. *Military Strategy: A General Theory of Power Control*. Annapolis: Naval Institute Press.

Young, Tom. 1990. 'The MNR/Renamo: External and Internal Dynamics'. *African Affairs* 89 (357): 491–509.

Zabecki, David T. n.d. 'Colonel Harry G. Summers, Jr., was a Soldier, Scholar, Military Analyst, Writer, Editor and Friend'. Available at: www.clause witz.com/readings/SummersObitText.htm.

Zartman, I. William and Guy Olivier Faure. 2005. *Escalation and Negotiation in International Conflicts*. Cambridge: Cambridge University Press.

Zartman, I. William and J. Aurik. 1991. 'Power Strategies in De-Escalation'. In: Louis Kriesberg and Stuart J. Thorson, eds., *Timing the De-Escalation of International Conflicts*, New York: Syracuse University Press, 152–181.

Zartman, I. William. 1989. *Ripe for Resolution: Conflict and Intervention in Africa*. New York: Oxford University Press.

Zhukov, Yuri M. 2012. 'Counterinsurgency in a Non-Democratic State: The Russian Example'. In: Paul B. Rich and Isabelle Duyvesteyn, eds., *The Routledge Handbook of Insurgency and Counterinsurgency*, London: Routledge, 286–300.

Zirakzadeh, Cyrus Ernesto. 2002. 'From Revolutionary Dreams to Organizational Fragmentation: Disputes Over Violence within ETA and Sendero Luminoso'. *Terrorism and Political Violence* 14 (4): 66–92.

Zuber, Christina Isabel. 2013. 'Beyond Outbidding? Ethnic Party Strategies in Serbia'. *Party Politics* 19 (5): 758–777.

Zurcher, Christoph. 2007. *The Post-Soviet Wars: Rebellion, Ethnic Conflict, and Nationhood in the Caucasus*. New York: New York University Press.

Index

EROS. *See* Eelam Revolutionary
     Organisation of Students
escalation, 192
   actor image of, 39
   causal processes of, 189–191
   controlling, 221–222
   dimensions of, 39
   existing ideas about, 24
   external pressure and, 136–137
   extremity shift and, 155–156
   group extremity shifts and, 127–128
   horizontal, 38–39
   initial, 155
   measuring, 38–40
   phenomenal image of, 39
   political will and, 41
   restraints and, 175–178
   scenarios of, 204
   substitution and, 125
   targeting of civilians and, 25
   theorising on, 208
   threshold of commitment
      and, 28–30
   thresholds of, 192
   vertical, 38–39
escalation dominance, 30–31, 176–177,
      211–213
escalation ladder, 20, 31
escalation trap, 27, 91–92, 93, 108, 172,
      201–202, 211–213
   Brigate Rosse and, 129
   escape from, 93
   need to acquire territorial control and,
      158
ETA. *See* Euskadi Ta Askatasuna
ethical boundaries, 27–28
ethnicity, 8, 12, 13
Euskadi Ta Askatasuna (ETA), 13–14,
      69–70
Evera, Stephen van, 43
Executive Outcomes (EO), 60–62
exogenous processes, 156
external pressure, 136–137, 142–143, 155,
      176
extremity shift, 140, 151–152, 155–156,
      185, 191, 192–194, 206, 207–208
Ezeiza massacre, 54

factionalisation, 128, 131
failed states, 26–27, 49–50
Fanon, Franz, 68–69

FARC. *See* Revolutionary Armed Forces of
     Colombia
Fearon, James, 71
First World War, 218
FLN. *See* Front de Libération Nationale
FLQ. *See* Front de Libération de Quebec
Focoism, 5, 62–63, 98–99
force multipliers, 118
foreign influence, 89–90
foreign intervention, 26–27, 85–86, 116–117
foreign sanctuary, 191
foreign support, 185–186, 203
fragmentation, 128, 137
free rider problem, 14
Freedman, Lawrence, 89
freedom of association, 51, 52
freedom of movement, 52, 76
freedom of political organisation, 51
freedom of speech, 50–51, 52
Freetown, 58
French Revolution, 48
friction, 175–176
Front de Libération de Quebec (FLQ),
      80–81, 85, 163, 163–166, 178–179
Front de Libération Nationale (FLN), 96,
      134, 218
FSLN. *See* Sandinist National Liberation
     Front

Gaddafi, Muammar, 58–59
Gandhi, Indira, 141–142, 209–210
Gandhi, Rajiv, 102, 171
geographical conditions, 39
German Federal Criminal Office, 148
German reparations, 218
German Revolutionary Cells, 92–93
German Socialist Students Association, 148
Germany, 5, 127–128, 148–151
Ghana, 58–59
Giap (General), 77
Gill, K.P.S., 142–143
global jihad, 17, 24, 50, 163
GN. *See* National Guard
Golden Temple, 142–143
Gomez Hurtado, Alvaro, 170
Good Friday agreement, 131, 180, 214–215
goods, provision of, 94
Gorman, Tommy, 69–70
Great March, 16
greed, 8, 58
grievance, 11, 58, 63–64, 91, 194–195

Milton Keynes UK
Ingram Content Group UK Ltd.
UKHW020839110324
439289UK00018B/122